"Feldman offers an elucidating look into Lincoln's incremental thinking, neatly demonstrating how he articulated the 'before' and 'after' Constitution in the Gettysburg Address as a compromise versus a moral document, using an Old Testament/New Testament analogy that embodied equality for all promised in the Declaration of Independence. Feldman never bogs down in legalese, rendering a scholarly topic accessible for general readers. A marvelously intricate work on Lincoln's writings and thoughts, which continue to offer fodder for historians." —*Kirkus Reviews* (starred review)

"Vignettes about slavery, the negotiators of the compromises, abolitionists, the Civil War, and beyond offer context for Feldman's innovative legal analysis. In describing interactions among political groups, voting rights, diverse views of abolitionists, suspending habeas corpus, and censorship, Feldman offers insights strikingly relevant to today's politics." —John Rowen, *Booklist*

"[A] probing study . . . An astute and eye-opening look at an underexamined aspect of the quest to end slavery." —*Publishers Weekly*

"Is there really a need for yet another book on Abraham Lincoln? The answer is yes, at least with regard to Noah Feldman's stunning examination of Lincoln and 'the broken Constitution.' It truly needs to be read by anyone interested not only in our tangled and tragic constitutional history but also in the continuing problems that face us today. He conveys in lucid prose the best existing overview of the constitutional issues that Lincoln (and the country) faced with regard to slavery in general and the conduct of the 'war to preserve the union' in particular.

Whether one is a general reader or a professional academic, this is a book demanding to be read and discussed."

—Sanford Levinson, Centennial Chair at the University of Texas Law School and coauthor of *Fault Lines in the Constitution*

"With his characteristic verve, erudition, and insight, Noah Feldman explores the constitutional breakup reflected and propelled by the Civil War. That he sheds fresh light on a subject that has been discussed so extensively is deeply impressive."

—Randall L. Kennedy, Michael R. Klein Professor of Law at Harvard Law School and author of *Say It Loud!*

"It's Noah Feldman's oft-demonstrated great gift to write about complex things clearly, with an eye to what's important. There are many books about the trials of the Constitution and even more about Lincoln, but very few get both as right as this one."

—David Waldstreicher, author of *Slavery's Constitution: From Revolution to Ratification*

Julia Allison

Noah Feldman

THE BROKEN CONSTITUTION

Noah Feldman is the Felix Frankfurter Professor of Law at Harvard Law School, a columnist for *Bloomberg Opinion*, and the host of Pushkin Industries' *Deep Background* podcast. He is the author of ten previous books, including *The Three Lives of James Madison* and *Scorpions: The Battles and Triumphs of FDR's Great Supreme Court Justices.*

ALSO BY NOAH FELDMAN

After Jihad: America and the Struggle for Islamic Democracy

What We Owe Iraq: War and the Ethics of Nation Building

Divided by God: America's Church-State Problem and What We Should Do About It

The Fall and Rise of the Islamic State

Scorpions: The Battles and Triumphs of FDR's Great Supreme Court Justices

Cool War: The Future of Global Competition

The Three Lives of James Madison: Genius, Partisan, President

The Arab Winter: A Tragedy

THE BROKEN
CONSTITUTION

In pursuance of the sixth section of the act of Congress entitled "An act to suppress insurrection and to punish treason and rebellion, to seize and confiscate property of rebels, and for other purposes," Approved July 17. 1862, and which act, and the joint Resolution explanatory thereof, are herewith published, I, Abraham Lincoln, President of the United States, do hereby proclaim to, and warn all persons within the contemplation of said sixth section to cease participating in, aiding, countenancing, or abetting the existing rebellion, or any rebellion against the government of the United States, and to return to their proper allegiance to the United States, on pain of the forfeitures and seizures, as within and by said sixth section provided—

And I hereby make known that it is my purpose, upon the next meeting of Congress, to again recommend the adoption of a practical measure for tendering pecuniary aid to the free choice or rejection, of any and all States which may then be recognizing and practically sustaining the authority of the United States, and which may then voluntarily adopted, or thereafter may voluntarily adopt, gradual abolishment of slavery within such State or States— that the object is to practically restore, thenceforward to be maintained, the constitutional relation between the general government and each and all the States wherein that relation

THE BROKEN CONSTITUTION

Lincoln, Slavery, and the Refounding of America

NOAH FELDMAN

PICADOR
FARRAR, STRAUS AND GIROUX
NEW YORK

Picador
120 Broadway, New York 10271

The Library of Congress has cataloged the Farrar, Straus and Giroux
hardcover edition as follows:
Names: Feldman, Noah, 1970– author.
Title: The broken constitution : Lincoln, slavery, and the refounding of America /
Noah Feldman.
Description: First edition. | New York : Farrar, Straus and Giroux, 2021. |
Includes bibliographical references and index.
Identifiers: LCCN 2021025293 | ISBN 9780374116644 (hardcover)
Subjects: LCSH: Lincoln, Abraham, 1809–1865—Political and social views. |
United States. Constitution. | United States. President (1861–1865 : Lincoln).
Emancipation Proclamation. | Executive power—United States—History—
19th century. | Federal government—United States—History—19th century. |
Slavery—Law and legislation—United States—History—19th century. |
Slaves—Emancipation—United States. | United States—Politics and
government—1783–1865.
Classification: LCC E457 .F45 2021 | DDC 973.7092—dc23
LC record available at https://lccn.loc.gov/2021025293

Paperback ISBN: 978-1-250-85878-8

Designed by Janet Evans-Scanlon

Frontispiece: Abraham Lincoln, *Abraham Lincoln papers:
Series 1. General Correspondence. 1833 to 1916: Abraham Lincoln,
Tuesday, Preliminary Draft of Emancipation Proclamation.* 1862. From
Library of Congress, Manuscript Division, Abraham Lincoln Papers.

In memory of Lois Silver

A moral crevasse has occurred: fanaticism and ignorance, political rivalry, sectional hate, strife for sectional dominion, have accumulated into a mighty flood, and pour their turgid waters through the broken Constitution.

—Jefferson Davis,
February 13, 1850

CONTENTS

THE BROKEN
CONSTITUTION

INTRODUCTION

Poised to sign the Emancipation Proclamation, Abraham Lincoln found he could not write his name. He told the breathless witnesses—his private secretary John Nicolay, Secretary of State William Seward, and Seward's son Frederick—that the reason was not any uncertainty on his part. He had been shaking hands for three hours that day and his hand was simply tired. His "whole soul" was in the decision to emancipate, Lincoln insisted. He was pausing only to avoid a "tremulous signature" because "If my hand trembles when I sign the Proclamation, all who examine the document hereafter will say, 'He hesitated.'"[1]

This story has become part of our Lincoln hagiography. It is invariably told to emphasize that the Great Emancipator had no ambivalence about his historic act. Lincoln's reassurance of his colleagues is meant to reassure the listener of the president's certainty. He acted decisively to create a new moral order, righting the wrong of slavery and ushering in a new era that would eventually be grounded in equal rights and citizenship for all.

Yet Lincoln's explanation of why his hand was trembling and his insistence on his single-minded confidence also suggest a need to reassure himself about contradicting the considered position he had held about slavery for the entire thirty years of his public life. Until that juncture in the war, Lincoln had always said publicly and believed privately that the federal government had no constitutional power to end slavery, as troubling as that institution might have been to him. If

Congress, the lawmaking branch, lacked the authority to emancipate the slaves, then the president acting on his own certainly had no such capacity.

Lincoln's act of emancipating enslaved people held in the rebellious Confederacy marked the culmination of an extraordinary transformation in his beliefs about the meaning of the Constitution. He still purported to believe that slaves were private property, and that private property was protected by constitutional guarantee. Now, however, he had allowed himself to develop an additional belief: as commander in chief, he had the legal power to order the otherwise unconstitutional taking of the property of the citizens of states prosecuting the war of rebellion.

In his first inaugural address, Lincoln had told the public that he was prepared to acknowledge the legal legitimacy of slavery if it would hold together the union. Slavery, according to this view, was enshrined in the Constitution. Indeed, as he saw it, the preservation of slavery was the condition for the creation and maintenance of the union. Union came first; freedom for African Americans a distant second. Emancipation represented a total reversal of this hierarchy of values. No wonder Lincoln's hand trembled. By signing, he was subverting the very Constitution that was supposed to provide the reason for going to war in the first place.

In doing so, we know, Lincoln was transforming the meaning of the Civil War itself. What had begun as a war justified in the name of union now became a war to end slavery. But simultaneously, and just as important, Lincoln was also re-forming the basic character of the Constitution.

Today we conceive of the Constitution as a moral compact—a higher law that embodies an ideal form of government. Yet the original Constitution was not a moral ideal. It was a compromise that preserved slavery and, by doing so, allowed the United States to form and expand westward. By breaking the compromise to achieve emancipation, Lincoln was cleansing the Constitution of its compromised character and making it into a worthy object of veneration and moral aspiration.

Emancipation was not Lincoln's only dramatic breaking and re-making of the existing Constitution through a radical, unilateral reinterpretation of its meaning. Even before he issued the proclamation, Lincoln confronted two other decision points of epochal importance that paved the way for the culminating third.

First, almost immediately on assuming the presidency, he had to decide—alone, without Congress's help—to go to war to preserve the union. Only in retrospect does it seem obvious that force was constitutionally justified in the face of secession. James Buchanan's administration had produced a report stating bluntly that the federal government had no constitutional authority to act if states seceded. Nothing in the Constitution authorized war to save the union. The precedent of 1776, as well as Lincoln's own words and views from the 1840s, supported letting the South go. Yet according to him—and only to him—his oath of office was an "oath registered in Heaven" to preserve the union.[2] Lincoln chose war, reinterpreting the Constitution through the claim that it had been broken by the South and that his action was justified to repair the breach.

Second, Lincoln acted—again alone, without Congress—to suspend habeas corpus in the first days of the war, effectively transforming himself into a constitutional dictator. The best and most obvious reading of the Constitution gave Congress alone the power to eliminate an arrested person's basic right to a judicial hearing when deemed necessary in cases of war or rebellion. Congress was not in session when Lincoln acted; but when it met months later, in July, it refused to ratify Lincoln's actions. The president ignored the implicit rebuke and began imprisoning war opponents in the territory stretching from Washington, D.C., to New York, including a member of Congress and almost half the Maryland legislature. Lincoln tried to back away a year later, offering amnesties and releasing some political prisoners. But then he acted unilaterally again, this time suspending habeas corpus nationwide on September 24, 1862. As a result, thousands of civilians all over the Union were arrested and detained without trial, often for months or even years. Scores of newspapers critical of the war were shut down or blocked from being sent through the mail. Congress did not ratify this decision until March 1863. Over the course of the war, Lincoln's policies and orders created the most extreme suppression of free speech to occur at any time in U.S. history.

Lincoln's effectiveness as a kind of dictator who could suspend con-stitutional rights at will, based on a claim of necessity, served as a model for the process that led him to abolish slavery by executive command. The Constitution—understood as the legal framework of the union—provided Lincoln with the basis for going to war in the first place on the theory that states had no constitutional authority to secede and that as president he had the constitutional duty to stop them. Once the Constitution had been broken by secession, however, the war to re-establish it created a new constitutional situation, one in which the principles and rules embodied in the peacetime Constitution could be broken and transformed by the president in the effort to save the Con-stitution itself. The breaking of the compact justified breaking the rules the compact contained. Rupture led to rupture. And that rupture led to transformation.

THE CONTRADICTORY CONSTITUTION

The subject of this book is the extraordinary arc of reversal in Lincoln's understanding of the Constitution—and its climactic, historic effects on the Constitution and the nation itself. My aim is to paint a portrait of Lincoln as a constitutional thinker: one of the most influential in U.S. history, and the most influential of all on the subject of the Con-stitution in crisis. To this end, I tell Lincoln's story and the story of the Constitution in tandem, highlighting a range of voices, including those of African Americans and women who belong in the historical record alongside elected politicians. The vicissitudes of the Constitution, including still-relevant debates about whether the Constitution was inherently a proslavery document, can help us understand Lincoln's trajectory. In turn, Lincoln's evolution and high-stakes decisions reveal how the prewar Constitution came to be ruptured and remade.

The first part of the story follows Lincoln through his early encounters with the expanding United States and his entrance into politics. It shows that the Constitution, drafted in 1787 and ratified over the next two years, had a fundamentally different moral character from the post–Civil War Constitution. The Constitution we know today enshrines the value of human equality that almost all Americans share, even if that value has not always been implemented in practice. In contrast, the antebellum Constitution rested on a compromise that was understood from the start to be amoral or even immoral: namely, the preservation and perpetuation of slavery.

That compromise over slavery was understood by the Constitution's framers and supporters to be necessary in order to achieve the greater goal of union. Slavery was a wrong, according to most of the founders, including a good number of slaveholders like James Madison. But it was a wrong that could be tolerated to serve the greater good of union. Without guarantees to continue slavery, the Southern slaveholding states would never have agreed to the Constitution. The compromise over slavery was justified to create and preserve the union.

As the United States grew, union gradually came to be an almost mystical concept. But concretely, the union developed into a practical political arrangement that enabled the United States to expand west and south into new territory and become a continental power. Without union, there could have been no settlers colonizing new territories and making them into new states—and no vast profits in land speculation and agriculture. Without union, the United States would have been stuck as an Eastern Seaboard power, prone to the same internal struggles over land and resources as the European states, which were themselves locked in by their geography. Without union, there could be no manifest destiny.

The Constitution was simply the necessary precondition for the union—the legally binding, contractual agreement that embodied the compromise that enabled the union to be. It was not a higher law in the moral sense, as many would come to believe in later years. It was, rather, an all-encompassing basic law. To Americans who sought territorial expansion, it was necessary to achieve that goal. To those more skeptical of expansion, the Constitution was nonetheless necessary to preserve the union from collapse.

Seeing it as a structure of compromise created a profound contradiction for every single supporter of the Constitution who also believed in the wrongness of slavery. From 1789 until 1861, if you believed in the Constitution, you were believing in an agreement that contained and continued a deep moral wrong. If you were willing to fight and die for the union, you were necessarily also willing to fight for the perpetuation of slavery as a subordinate but necessary condition. A handful of abolitionists, white and Black, condemned the Constitution as evil on account of the compromise. Another handful, also including thinkers of both races, insisted that the Constitution, all evidence to the contrary, actually opposed or outlawed slavery. Those white Southerners who saw slavery as morally righteous felt no conflict: they endorsed the Constitution as protecting slaveholders' rights, while fretting that the guarantees might be breached. Almost everyone else—the mainstream of antebellum Americans—treated the constitutional compromise over slavery as legitimate despite the moral wrongfulness of the institution that the compromise protected and preserved.

Lincoln accepted this contradictory compromise. More than that: as an admirer of Henry Clay, the great compromiser, and as a member of the Whig Party, the party of sectional compromise, Lincoln was fully committed to preserving the compromise Constitution in order to preserve the union.

Of course, a constitution built on a compromise with slavery was prone to ultimate crisis—and rupture. Lincoln's early beliefs and experiences reveal how this inevitable constitutional crisis was built into the compromise itself as it developed during the 1820s, '30s, and '40s. Expansion was the reason for many opponents of slavery to accept the compromise. Yet expansion created the conditions for new conflict over whether future states would be slave or free.

People like Lincoln and his family, moving from Virginia to Kentucky to Indiana to Illinois in a single generation, brought their values and beliefs with them. The frontier was thus settled by white Americans who, depending on their interests and ideals, either wanted to bring slavery or a ban on slavery into their newly settled territories. The imperative to enable this settlement movement is a large part of the reason that the North continued to accept and reaccept the compromise on slavery.

Frontier settlement—the dynamic some academics now call settler colonialism—destabilized the very compromise that had been made to enable it. The decades-long struggle over whether new states would be slave or free became itself a proxy for the struggle over the future of slavery and the possibility of a continuing constitutional union. Lincoln's own path shows this, as he traveled from prioritizing the Constitution and union to reordering his values to place the death of slavery over the constitutional value of law.

RUPTURE

Rupture in our constitutional and national fabric remains paradoxically the untold story of the Civil War—the topic almost no one has wanted to touch in the vast historiography of the war and of Lincoln's role in it. With our constitutional fabric again under pressure, now is the right time to recast the first Constitution as an enterprise that ultimately failed, and to substitute a narrative of a repaired and transformed Constitution for the received narrative of continuity.

Civil war is the very definition of a failed constitution. The U.S. Constitution failed from 1861 to 1865. It was not temporarily suspended or continued only in the North. The Constitution broke and was broken. It did not recover. It was remade in the aftermath of the war into something new and different. The "new birth of freedom" that Lincoln named in the Gettysburg Address was to be as different from the old constitutional order as the New Testament was from the Old, to use the metaphor that Lincoln intended to invoke.[3]

It is commonplace today to speak of the U.S. Constitution as the world's oldest, continuously operating since its ratification in 1789. But this claim is patently untrue. After the Civil War, both sides had strong reasons to suppress the narrative of rupture in favor of the story of continuity. The reasons for the denial continue until today.

This book seeks to retell the story of the meaning of the Constitution in the Civil War and of Lincoln's decisive action not as the story of successful salvation, but as something more dramatic, and more extreme: the frank breaking and frank remaking of the entire order of union, rights, constitution, and liberty.

Many historians who write about the Civil War are still drawn to the perennial question of what caused the conflict. No wonder, since Lincoln's own public explanation for the war changed while it was in progress. Nearly all scholars today believe that, as Lincoln put it in his second inaugural address, slavery "was, somehow, the cause of the war."[4] Yet one school of thought, the so-called neo-revisionist, emphasizes Lincoln's conservative caution when elected in 1860, and reads secession as an overreaction by Southerners who mistakenly believed that his election posed an existential threat to slavery. The other school, often called fundamentalist, holds that the threat to slavery was real, or fundamental, and that Lincoln and other Northern unionists were committed to policies intended to end slavery.[5]

This book offers a different perspective—one informed centrally by the structure of the compromise Constitution and Lincoln's changing relation to it. The compromise Constitution, I argue, was a framework for compromise over slavery so basic to the structure of the union before the war that no one could imagine breaking it by abolishing slavery nationally and still preserving the union intact. Lincoln's hope before the war that slavery would eventually become extinct depended on a vague, indeterminate fantasy that the compromise framework could eventually evolve so that slavery would be abolished voluntarily by slave states, with compensation for slaveholders and colonization of freed slaves to Africa.[6] The neo-revisionists are correct that Lincoln himself would not have countenanced any other sort of abolition were it not for secession and the war. To do so would have broken the Constitution as he knew it.

At the same time, the compromise Constitution contained a fundamental contradiction that ensured its instability: the compromise structure enabled the union to expand, yet every expansion destabilized the compromise by raising anew the question of whether slavery itself should be extended. Southern secessionists came to see this contradiction as so devastating that it would eventually make further compromise impossible. They seceded because they sensed, correctly, that compromise over the extension of slavery had come to an end. The fundamentalists are therefore right to say that, for the seceding Southern states, the threat to slavery was indeed existential.

It took Lincoln well over a year of his presidency—a period in which secession had occurred and the war raged—to acknowledge the reality that the old constitutional compromise could never be restored. When he eventually did, the Emancipation Proclamation was the result. The rupture of the Constitution opened the door for its reconstruction on new terms—as the moral Constitution we know and revere today.

The transformation took three constitutional amendments. They abolished slavery, guaranteed equal protection of the laws for all citizens, and extended voting rights to African American men. Over the next 150 years, those amendments were by turns applied during Reconstruction; betrayed through the rise of Jim Crow segregation; and redeemed by *Brown v. Board of Education*, the civil rights movement, and the landmark laws enacted as a result of the movement's influence: the Civil Rights Act of 1964 and the Voting Rights Act of 1965. Today, more than ever, we realize that the redemption was itself incomplete. We remain, however, committed to the idea that the moral Constitution embodied in those amendments should be our beacon. Lincoln's transformed, moral version of the Constitution endures.

One

THE COMPROMISE CONSTITUTION

Abraham Lincoln's early biography epitomizes the most power-
ful energy pulsing through the new republic: the energy of expansion.
His grandfather, the Revolutionary War captain Abraham Lincoln, for
whom he was named, was born in Pennsylvania and as a young man
moved to Virginia, then the population center and political power-
house of the newly formed United States. In 1781, the War of Independence not yet over, the first Abraham Lincoln moved his family to
Jefferson County, Kentucky.

Claimed by the state of Virginia, and not yet a state of its own, Kentucky was the Western frontier. It was contested territory, still peopled
by American Indians protecting their own homes. And on that frontier,
Captain Lincoln met a fate not unknown to settlers who propose to take
land from its inhabitants: he was killed during a raid by a Native American who, according to family tradition, was himself shot on the spot by
the captain's eldest son, Mordecai. Eight-year-old Thomas Lincoln, the
captain's youngest son—Abraham's father—saw it all.

Thomas grew up in Kentucky, married Nancy Hanks, and had three
children, one of whom, also named Thomas, died shortly after birth.
He repeatedly saved money and bought property to establish a farm.
But each time, he was thwarted by the uncertain land titles that were

common in Kentucky, where there had never been a single, agreed-upon land survey that could have definitively established boundaries and ownership. Thomas Lincoln lost three farms in legal disputes, a direct consequence of the piecemeal way that the Kentucky frontier had been occupied and settled. In December 1816, when Abraham Lincoln was nine, Thomas moved the family westward into southern Indiana, to a community called Little Pigeon Creek.

The Lincolns lived in Indiana for fourteen years. They did not prosper. Two years after their arrival, Lincoln's mother, Nancy, died of milk sickness. This was a distinctly frontier settlement form of poisoning: domesticated cows would eat the white snakeroot plant that grew wild in the Ohio River Valley and then produce milk containing the fatal toxin tremetol. Thomas went back to Kentucky to court and marry Sarah Bush Johnston, bringing her and her three children to join the Lincolns in Indiana. Abraham Lincoln grew up in penury, working hard from an early age to help keep the family from financial ruin.

The solution to economic hardship in Indiana was another move west. On March 6, 1830, when Abraham Lincoln was twenty-one, his family crossed the Wabash River from Indiana into Illinois. Admitted as a state twelve years earlier, Illinois lay at the edge of the country. Only Missouri extended farther west. Working together, Lincoln, his father, and a dozen relatives cleared trees, built a log cabin, and split rails to fence in ten acres of ground.

DOWN THE MISSISSIPPI

The Lincoln family's steady generational movement from Pennsylvania to Virginia to Kentucky to Indiana to Illinois mirrored the comparably gradual progress of white settlers westward. As a young man, Lincoln took two trips down the Mississippi by flatboat to New Orleans—in 1828 and 1831. These journeys showed a different direction of expansion: south, through the territory acquired in 1803 in the Louisiana Purchase.

Lincoln's trips downriver are frequently discussed in modern biographies because they exposed Lincoln firsthand to the phenomenon of African slavery, which was common in Kentucky, where he was born, but not in Indiana or Illinois, where he grew up and lived as a young man. New Orleans, Lincoln's destination on both trips, featured the largest slave markets anywhere in North America. Our first glimpses of Lincoln's attitude toward slavery do indeed emerge in connection with the flatboat journeys.

But the boat trips also introduced Lincoln to the riverine geography that shaped the structure of the economy in states like Illinois and Missouri—and thus to the underlying logic of the compromise Constitution. The produce of those central states—and of Indiana and Kentucky—flowed down the Mississippi to New Orleans. From there it could be distributed to the South, to markets along the Eastern Seaboard all the way north, and abroad to the Caribbean and Europe. The north-to-south flow of the river gave shape to the direction of commerce, and hence to the flow of wealth. Andrew Jackson's victory over the British in New Orleans at the tail end of the War of 1812 had guaranteed American control over the port and consolidated the growth of the United States on both sides of the Mississippi by ensuring free shipping. Expansion west would not have been economically viable had it not been for the outlet to the South where the agricultural products of the frontier could be sent and sold. The maintenance of the delicate balance of states for this project of expansion had come to be the real-world function of the Constitution.

The flatboats on which Lincoln made his two journeys were themselves artifacts of the geography of expansion—and of the way rivers defined reality in the early United States. Some eighty feet long and seventeen feet wide, according to the scholar who has spent the most time reconstructing the journey, the flatboat for Lincoln's first trip was almost certainly built by hand by Lincoln and his friend Allen Gentry, whose father, James Gentry, paid for the materials and employed Lincoln at a rate of eight dollars a month. The timber would have been cut down near the spot where the boat was to be built—Rockport, Indiana, in the case of the 1828 trip. The second time, in 1831, Lincoln and his cousin John Hanks built the boat at Sangamo Town, Illinois.

A flatboat was an unusual type of vessel: purpose-built for one long trip out of materials available where the trip started. It required no specialized shipbuilding skills, because there were no specialized shipbuilders on the frontier. Instead, its construction could be accomplished by anyone who possessed the general carpentry skills of a frontier resident—like the young Lincoln.

Most notably, the flatboat had no sail or engine. It was steered by a single sixty-foot oar, or "streamer," and two side oars known as "sweeps." Strictly speaking, none of these oars propelled the boat, except over very short distances. The energy to take the eighty-foot craft a distance of 1,300 miles would come almost entirely from the current, itself a product of gravity, as the rivers flowed downhill. Of those miles, more than a thousand were traveled on the great Mississippi, the river whose course shaped the history of the United States more than any other single geographical feature.

The contents of the flatboats also told a story. On Lincoln's first trip, the aim was to bring produce to market in New Orleans. James Gentry was a farmer with a thousand acres of land, but most of the produce was not his. Gentry also owned a store and controlled a river landing on the Ohio River. The produce came from other farmers nearby, who traded what they grew for goods from Gentry's store. Cash was scarce on the frontier, and barter was the common solution. By bringing what was grown along the Ohio River to New Orleans and selling it for cash, Gentry would be injecting currency into the Indiana economy.

On Lincoln's second trip downriver, the flatboat he built was outfitted to carry livestock—mostly hogs raised in Illinois, which had to be fed and tended during the long trip. Like the produce, the hogs represented the contribution that the frontier economy made to markets in the South and beyond. Of course, produce could be grown and livestock raised closer to New Orleans. But the climate there, as in the rest of the Gulf Coast and the Deep South, made it more profitable to grow cotton, which could not be profitably grown north of the Piedmont.

The way to make money in the old Northwest Territory—the area between the Great Lakes, the Mississippi, and the Ohio River—was by clearing land, settling it, and farming it. The value of produce on the frontier depended on getting it downriver to the port of New Orleans. Before navigational improvements and canals allowed steamboats to travel from Lake Michigan to the Mississippi and then all the way to New Orleans, flatboats like Lincoln's were the crucial link along the artery that defined the economy of the Northwest.

As a product of northern Kentucky, Indiana, and Illinois, Lincoln lacked direct experience of slavery before his two trips downriver. He also lacked, then and later, direct personal relationships with African Americans. What he saw and experienced on his flatboat trips south would shape his thinking in the future, but perhaps no more—and maybe less—than the fact that he had grown up in a milieu that was almost exclusively white.

The reason slavery did not flourish in the places Lincoln lived was partly economic and partly ideological. When the original thirteen states had been British colonies, slavery was legally permitted in all of them. It gradually became clear, however, that the economics of slavery would mean great profits for slaveholders primarily in states where labor-intensive cash crops—as opposed to produce for daily consumption—could be grown on a large scale and sold on the global market. Tobacco in Virginia is the most famous example from the early years of the republic; rice in South Carolina is another from the same period.

In states without cash-crop economies, moral opposition to slavery gradually drove legislatures to outlaw the practice. It is important to emphasize the gradual nature of abolition. Many states outlawed slavery by making the future-born children of existing slaves into indentured servants, keeping their parents in an enslaved status. In New York, for example, whites held slaves for household service through the revolutionary period, and in New York City slaves may have numbered high as 20 percent of the population. In 1799, New York State passed a law mandating gradual abolition, but complete abolition did not follow until 1827.

In the states where slavery on a large scale was economically valuable, the ideology of abolition never made major inroads. That is one reason to believe that economic logic was the determinative factor in the persistence of the practice. Moral beliefs and ideology mattered, to be sure—but they were given the scope to influence real-world legislation only when economic interest permitted it.

Several of the most influential framers of the Constitution, including Southerners, accepted the immorality of slavery. James Madison is an outstanding example. A Virginian slaveholder his entire life, he simultaneously acknowledged the human impulse to freedom. Writing to his father in 1783 about a slave called Billey, Madison explained that he could not "think of punishing" Billey by selling him to the Deep South or the Caribbean "merely for coveting that liberty for which we have paid the price of so much blood, and have proclaimed so often to be the right, and worthy pursuit, of every human being."[1] Madison, that is, recognized liberty as a fundamental human right. Yet his entire livelihood, and the entire structure of his daily existence, depended on the institution of slavery—and he was unable or unwilling to resolve the contradiction. Economic reality trumped moral intuitions.

Madison and other Virginians, including Thomas Jefferson, slaveholder and lead author of the Declaration of Independence, did have a story to tell themselves about how the contradiction at the heart of their worldview might someday be resolved: they expected that slavery would gradually be abolished as it gradually ceased to be economically beneficial anywhere, including the South. Implausible as it may sound now, that belief was not entirely groundless when the Constitution was drafted in 1787 and ratified two years later. The Virginia tobacco crop was already beginning to lose its profitability in the late eighteenth century, mostly as a result of soil exhaustion. Neither Madison nor Jefferson, both proprietors of large plantations, ever made much of a profit from the agriculture they practiced with the labor of enslaved persons. Indeed, both before and after their presidencies, the two men struggled to make ends meet at their plantations, despite the fact that both took a scientific interest in land management. Both understood that the rise of manufacturing would eventually transform the U.S. economy, and that it would not favor the employment of slave labor.

An epoch-making technological innovation thwarted the framers' expectations: the invention of the cotton gin, or "engine," patented by Eli Whitney in 1794. Although mechanical separation processes had previously been developed for long-staple cotton, Whitney's machine sped up the process of separating usable fibers from useless seeds for short-staple cotton, which (unlike the long-staple variety) could be grown inland, far from the sea.[2] In a single technological stroke, the cotton gin made cotton growing into a highly profitable enterprise throughout the huge swath of the North American continent that would come to be called the Cotton Belt—profitable, that is, if the intensive labor of picking the cotton could be performed by slaves who were not paid wages for their work.

Growing cotton exhausted the soil quickly. One solution was to let the land rest by planting beans or other legumes; another was to fertilize extensively. The easier and often cheaper solution was for growers to move to lands newly taken from Native Americans, bringing enslaved people to do the labor. From South Carolina and Georgia, where almost all American cotton was grown as late as 1811, cultivation expanded westward to Alabama and Louisiana, and then to Mississippi, Arkansas, and eventually Texas.[3] By 1820, a third of U.S. cotton was grown west of Georgia; by 1860, the proportion had grown to three-quarters.[4] The upshot was that national westward expansion became a necessary condition for continuing cotton-growing profits—a land rush driven by a "military-cotton complex" that, as the historian Sven Beckert has argued, "constantly pushed the boundaries" of the United States, "seeking fresh lands to grow cotton."[5] In the middle of the nineteenth century, fully two-thirds of U.S. cotton was growing on land that had not been part of the country when the century began.[6]

Once the cotton gin changed the economics of slavery, the ideology of abolition came to have a more limited scope for its operation. In places where large-scale slavery remained economically inefficient, abolitionism had opportunities to enact its objective into law. Where cotton grew, however—or where it might grow in the future—the odds of abolition gaining many white adherents were vanishingly small.

Kentucky, where Lincoln was born, was a state divided into very different cultural and economic zones. In the Bluegrass region, climate and culture resembled those of the Southern states, and slavery flourished. Where Lincoln was born, in a log cabin at Sinking Springs Farm, on what was then the Kentucky frontier, slavery existed only on a small scale. There were few African Americans, and we have no record that the young Lincoln met or knew anyone of color in the Knob Creek Valley where he lived until the age of seven. Abolitionists found a toehold, and in 1815 and 1833 the state passed laws barring the importation of slaves. Kentucky was too connected to the South for full-on abolition. But its distinctive mixed character meant that the economic realities of slavery and the moral possibilities of abolition were profoundly intertwined.

Indiana, across the Ohio River to the northwest, where Lincoln spent the formative years from age seven to twenty-one, was part of the original Northwest Territory. According to the Northwest Ordinance, adopted by Congress in 1787, "neither slavery nor involuntary servitude" was permitted there. Despite the text of the ordinance, some settlers from the South brought slaves with them and continued to hold them in bondage. But slavery at scale was never economically viable in Indiana, where it was not profitable to grow tobacco or cotton. Abolitionists began to campaign even before Indiana's statehood, and the territorial legislature made it difficult to hold slaves. Indiana became a state in 1816, the same year the Lincolns moved to Little Pigeon Creek. The state's first constitution made slavery illegal. Lincoln does not seem to have known African Americans when he lived there, either. His neighbors were white settlers, some of whom no doubt retained proslavery sympathies associated with their Southern origins.

In the Illinois that Lincoln encountered when he crossed the Wabash, the situation was roughly similar. Illinois had also been part of the original Northwest Territory, and the Illinois Constitution of 1819 stated that slavery should not be "thereafter introduced." That amounted to a gradual abolition but did not free slaves who were already being held in the state. Although there were abolitionists in Illinois, there were also many settlers from slave states. Missouri, where slavery was lawful, was right across the river. In 1824, Illinois voters rejected a proposed constitutional convention to formalize total abolition immediately. Only in 1848 did a new state constitution make slavery illegal there. So white were Indiana and Illinois that, in the early 1850s, both would enact legal regulations intended to keep Black people out of their states entirely.[7]

As Lincoln traveled downriver in 1828 and 1831, he witnessed a geography that changed gradually—and a population that changed with the topography. Just beneath the point where the Ohio River and the Wabash joined lay a mixed community of several hundred Shawnees and free Blacks. (Its name remains unknown.) As the Ohio approached its confluence with the Tennessee River, Lincoln would have seen his first Louisiana cypress.[8]

The most dramatic point in the journey was where the Ohio met the Mississippi, and the states of Illinois, Kentucky, and Missouri touched. The currents came together dangerously, requiring the boatmen to steer furiously and avoid flipping the flatboat and losing its cargo.[9] Symbolically, the flatboat's entrance into the Mississippi marked the end of the free states of the old Northwest Territory and the beginning of slave territory. As such, the boundary reflected the reality of the Constitution, which enabled states to legalize the enslavement of human beings and protected the property rights of those humans' "owners."

Much of the territory that Lincoln passed through in what is now Tennessee and Arkansas was still unsettled by Europeans. Forests dominated both sides of the river. Memphis was a tiny village.[10] Vicksburg, Mississippi, was the first significant settlement that the flatboat would encounter. From there to New Orleans, every town had a river landing—and on every river landing were enslaved African Americans, many of them shackled and for sale. The slaves were one part of the economic entrepôt to which Lincoln was contributing the cargo carried on the flatboat. Prices for commodities rose gradually as the flatboat approached the great port city. On both trips, Lincoln and his partners held out and did not sell what they had brought until they got to where the prices would be highest.

Lincoln kept no diary of his trips, and we do not know what he thought about his first encounters with large-scale slavery. Many years later, he would say he had "always hated slavery" and that he was "naturally" against it. Friends would recall that the young Lincoln "was opposed to slavery and said he thought it a curse to the land."[11] Although there is little reason to doubt these claims, the first direct evidence of what Lincoln thought about the human consequences of the institution comes from 1841, a decade after his second trip to New Orleans, when he sent a letter to the half sister of his close friend

Joshua Speed in which he described slaves he had seen then who were being transported south by steamboat on the Ohio River. "By the way," Lincoln wrote almost offhandedly, "a fine example was presented on board the boat for contemplating the effect of condition upon human happiness." This introduction was focused not on the nature of slavery, but on the psychology of happiness, a topic of perennial interest to the melancholic Lincoln.[12] Lincoln went on to offer a remarkably precise description of enslaved people in transit:

> A gentleman had purchased twelve negroes in different parts of Kentucky and was taking them to a farm in the South. They were chained six and six together. A small iron clevis was around the left wrist of each, and this was fastened to the main chain by a shorter one at a convenient distance from, the others; so that the negroes were strung together precisely like so many fish upon a trot-line.

Lincoln understood the consequences for these enslaved humans who were being literally sold down the river:

> In this condition they were being separated forever from the scenes of their childhood, their friends, their fathers and mothers, and brothers and sisters, and many of them, from their wives and children, and going into perpetual slavery, where the lash of the master is proverbially more ruthless and unrelenting than any other where.

Remarkably, however, Lincoln was fascinated by the slaves' manner, which seemed to him not melancholy, but quite the opposite:

> [A]nd yet amid all these distressing circumstances, as we would think them, they were the most cheerful and

apparantly happy creatures on board. One, whose offence for which he had been sold was an over-fondness for his wife, played the fiddle almost continually; and the others danced, sung, cracked jokes, and played various games with cards from day to day.

From this Lincoln derived a lesson about character:

> How true it is that "God tempers the wind to the shorn lamb," or in other words, that He renders the worst of human conditions tolerable, while He permits the best, to be nothing better than tolerable.[13]

Some fifteen years after this experience, Lincoln would retell the incident with a different emphasis. "You may remember, as I well do," he wrote to Joshua Speed, "that from Louisville to the mouth of the Ohio there were, on board, ten or a dozen slaves, shackled together with irons. That sight was a continual torment to me; and I see something like it every time I touch the Ohio, or any other slave-border."[14]

By then, as the historian Eric Foner has pointed out, political circumstances had changed drastically. Lincoln's views on slavery had evolved to become more critical. Referring to the effect of the "fugitive slave clause" of the Constitution, he told Speed in the same letter, "I confess I hate to see the poor creatures hunted down, and caught, and carried back to their stripes, and unrewarded toils." Yet at the same time, Lincoln in 1855 still accepted the constitutional structures that protected slavery as necessary to preserve the union. He objected morally to the recapture of fugitive slaves, he said, "but I bite my lip and keep quiet"[15]—because silence was the price of union. In any case, regardless of the emotions they conjured, the observations that Lincoln made whenever he was on the river or in a slave state were initiated on these first trips south.

Lincoln's first encounters with African Americans were not, however, restricted to seeing them as powerless and enslaved. On his 1828
trip, he and Allen Gentry were camped by the river below Baton Rouge,
when they came under attack. Lincoln described it (using the third person) in his presidential campaign autobiography decades later:

> [O]ne night they were attacked by seven negroes with
> intent to kill and rob them. They were hurt some in the
> melee, but succeeded in driving the negroes from the boat,
> and then "cut cable" "weighed anchor" and left.[16]

Lincoln's attackers may have been slaves or runaways. In any case,
they were exercising agency of a kind. Lincoln considered the event
significant enough that he put it in his extremely brief campaign autobiography as the only fact of importance connected to his 1828 voyage.
It may perhaps have contributed to Lincoln's lifelong belief that some
necessary enmity would exist between American whites and Blacks
even if slavery were to be abolished. That view was, however, held by
many other whites both in Lincoln's generation and before. It was
the primary motivating force for the American Colonization Society,
formed in 1817 to fund the transportation of freed slaves to Africa—an
organization embraced by the Virginian slaveholder presidents James
Madison and James Monroe.

The culmination of Lincoln's flatboat trips was New Orleans
itself—by far the largest city he had ever seen, then already a cosmo-
politan mélange of French speakers, free people of color, Anglos, and
others. The city was in the midst of rapid growth. In 1830, the population approached fifty thousand. By 1840, it would double. The slave
trade was a crucial industry in New Orleans, and Lincoln saw there
the largest slave markets anywhere on the continent. He saw hundreds of large ships in the harbor, poised to bring American produce
to the North, to the Caribbean, and to Europe. He also must have

seen brothels, music halls, freak shows, and the rest of a vibrant urban life. New Orleans was a universe apart from Lincoln's frontier origins in Indiana and Illinois. But it was also closely linked to the interior, through travelers like Lincoln and the commerce in which he was engaged—and through the Constitution that made them component parts of a single national organism.

In 1889, Lincoln's friend and former law partner William Herndon published a series of recollections of Lincoln's life that he had gathered in 1865 in firsthand interviews and subsequently edited and reworked. In the book, Herndon used Lincoln's visit to New Orleans to provide a causal explanation for Lincoln's much later moral outrage at slavery. "In New Orleans," Herndon wrote, "for the first time Lincoln beheld the true horrors of human slavery . . . Against this inhumanity his sense of right and justice rebelled, and his mind and conscience were awakened." He told the story of Lincoln passing a slave auction and witnessing the sale of "a vigorous and comely mulatto girl" who "underwent a thorough examination at the hands of the bidders." These men "pinched her flesh and made her trot up and down the room like a horse." Consequently, "the whole thing was so revolting that Lincoln moved away from the scene with a deep feeling of unconquerable 'hate.'" In Herndon's account, Lincoln told his companions, "If I ever get a chance to hit that thing [i.e. slavery], I'll hit it hard."[17]

Narratively striking as the story may be—and sexualized in a way that today can only be called disturbing—it is almost certainly a fabrication, perhaps one owing to Harriet Beecher Stowe's slave auction scene in her novel *Uncle Tom's Cabin*. Herndon's source was Lincoln's cousin John Hanks, who started the 1831 flatboat trip but turned back when they reached St. Louis. Hanks was never in New Orleans with Lincoln, as Lincoln stated expressly in his 1860 campaign autobiography.[18] Allen Gentry's descendants told similar stories in the 1930s, but they are clearly derivative of Herndon's account. There is no contemporaneous evidence to suggest that Lincoln responded with revulsion to the slavery he encountered on the river and in New Orleans.

Yet the question of Lincoln's personal reaction to what he saw on his trip is less telling than what the trip demonstrates about the interconnection of free and slave states, of North and South—in short, of the structure of the union in the years before the war. The frontier North needed the South to buy produce like the wheat and hogs that Lincoln brought downriver on his trips, and it needed the port of New Orleans to ship what it grew to the world. The South in turn needed what the frontier could grow so that it could clothe and feed a populace—slave and free—devoted to producing the profitable cash crop of cotton. The two sections of the country were bound together by the river system that structured their economic relationship. The South, therefore, was inextricably linked to the American project of continental expansion. And the expansion of the United States across the continent was inconceivable and impracticable without the riverine connection to the South, and the world beyond New Orleans. The system was by no means perfectly integrated. But the parts of the system were interdependent. The logic of the union required it.

BLACK HAWK

In a time before railroads or highways, the Mississippi and the river systems that fed into it were the main infrastructure that united the different expanding parts of the country. Boatmen and pilots were the masters of transportation. The skills as a pilot that Lincoln developed would become the first professional advantages he ever enjoyed and learned to use. When he left his family and moved alone to the brand-new settlement of New Salem, Illinois, in 1831, he was joining a community that owed its existence to its placement on the Sangamon River. Lincoln got there on a flatboat—which was the only sensible way to come to New Salem.

Almost as soon as he reached New Salem, Lincoln also experienced, for the first and only time in his life, direct conflict with American Indians. He was a participant in the Black Hawk War, one of the hundreds of low-intensity small wars between Native Americans and European settlers that had started some two hundred years before on the North American continent and would not come to a final end until roughly 1890, the year of the notorious massacre of Lakota Sioux at Wounded Knee. The events symbolized another facet of the expansion enabled by the Constitution: the felt necessity of removing or pacifying the original inhabitants of the land. And the Black Hawk War encapsulated a lesson that would eventually be relevant to Lincoln's decision to go to war to block secession: the military forces mustered by the United States might be weak and ineffectual when they first took the field, but superior numbers would ultimately ensure their victory over any continental opponent.

The hostilities of the small war, such as they were, began when the U.S. Army set out to capture and punish a group of Meskwaki Indians who, after being displaced from land they had inhabited by treaty right, had been involved in an exchange of hostilities with U.S.-allied Menominees. With only limited regular army troops available, the commanding U.S. general raised a temporary militia of 2,100 Illinois volunteers. The militia was formed into a brigade of five regiments, each subdivided into companies. Because this was a civilian militia, hastily formed and hastily trained, it had no professional officers. Locally formed militias were a traditional bulwark of American republicanism—the "well-regulated militia" of the Second Amendment. Accordingly, captains of companies were elected by the members, much like local government officials.

On April 21, 1832, Lincoln rode from New Salem to nearby Richland Creek to enlist in the militia. By his own later account, there was no special patriotic motivation in his heart. Work was scarce, and the militia appointment paid. Sworn in at Bearstown, Illinois, Lincoln decided to run for company captain—and won his first foray into electoral politics, receiving some three-quarters of the votes. He had no greater qualification to lead men in battle than any other member of the militia. Running for president years later, he would say that the election was "a success which gave me more pleasure than any I have had since."[19] To be chosen as a leader by strangers was a mark of Lincoln's personal charisma.

Lincoln spent two and half months in the militia in the spring and summer of 1832. The danger was real. On May 14, a detachment of 275 essentially untrained militiamen under Major Isaiah Stillman walked into an ambush set by a small group of Sauk warriors. Most of the men panicked and fled, giving the battle the derisive name of "Stillman's Run." Twelve tried to stand and fight, and all were killed in the battle. Some reports suggest that the militiamen themselves killed the captain whom they had elected and who had led them into the trap.[20]

Lincoln did not take part in the battle, but he saw its aftermath, and it made an impression. He later was quoted by a biographer:

> I remember just how those men looked as we rode up the little hill where their camp was. The red light of the morning sun was streaming upon them as they lay head towards us on the ground. And every man had a round red spot on top of his head, about as big as a dollar where the redskins had taken his scalp. It was frightful, but it was grotesque, and the red sunlight seemed to paint everything all over. I remember one man had on buckskin breeches.[21]

The panic experienced by the militia soon spread to the rest of the settlers, who fled for the safety of Chicago. The militia pursued a force of 1,500 Meskwaki, Sauk, Potawatomi, and Kickapoo Indians—which had become known as the "British Band" and was headed by a leader named Black Hawk—but could not find them. The Illinois governor, sensing political danger, asked the senior officers of the state militia whether they wanted to end their service. The officers voted in favor of disbanding. On May 28, a little more than a month after they had enlisted, most of the militiamen from the original brigade went home.

Lincoln was one of three hundred militiamen who agreed to sign up for another twenty days. He reenlisted one more time after that, serving until July 10. By then, the governor had raised a new militia, and Lincoln's company was disbanded. In later years Lincoln would downplay the courage of his decision to reenlist, explaining that he had no better prospect of employment. Whatever his motives, Lincoln certainly must have realized that hostilities could only increase. The U.S. government was not going to allow expansion to be blocked by Black Hawk's British Band—or by any other Indian adversary.

In the end, Black Hawk's resistance was undermined by his lack of a supply chain. In July, as his numbers dwindled due to hunger, he had to retreat across the Mississippi. On July 21, at the Battle of Wisconsin Heights, Black Hawk lost almost half his warriors in a desperate—and successful—effort to hold off 750 militiamen while the women and children traveling with him crossed the river. A little more than a week later, on August 1, a steamboat armed with a cannon and christened *Warrior* found Black Hawk at the mouth of the Bad Axe River. Ignoring Black Hawk's white flag, the *Warrior* opened fire, killing 23 Indians. Black Hawk fled north. The militia chased the remaining British Band, and the next day, August 2, killed 250 of them, many women and children, as they tried to cross the river. By the end of the month, Black Hawk had surrendered to U.S. authorities. The last Native American resistance to European expansion in the old Northwest was at an end.

In a final twist, Black Hawk himself was not punished but instead lionized by Andrew Jackson's administration as a useful celebrity, paraded across the country as the very model of the noble savage whose kind was passing from the earth. The Sauk and Meskwaki suffered the usual fate of those who stood in the way of American expansion: they were moved to reservations in the West, first in Iowa and then in Kansas. The consolidation of settlement along the Mississippi continued.

Lincoln had had a tiny role in an episode that was historically symbolic without quite being significant in itself. He never adopted the persona of the Indian fighter, and in his political career thereafter he was more than willing to play the events and his role in them for a laugh. In Congress in 1848, he offered an ironic picture of his own experiences to lampoon the Democratic presidential candidate, Lewis Cass of Michigan, who was being described as a hero of the War of 1812. "By the way, Mr. Speaker, did you know I am a military hero?" Lincoln asked rhetorically. He then continued:

> Yes sir; in the days of the Black Hawk war, I fought, bled, and came away. Speaking of General Cass's career reminds me of my own. I was not at Stillman's defeat, but I was about as near it, as Cass was to Hull's surrender; and like him, I saw the place very soon afterwards . . . If he saw any live, fighting Indians, it was more than I did; but I had a good many bloody struggles with the mosquitoes; and although I never fainted from loss of blood, I can truly say I was often very hungry.[22]

Lincoln also liked to tell the humorous story of how, as company commander, he had to order his men to change formation so they could pass single-file through a fence gate: "I could not for the life of me remember the right word of command for getting my company endwise so that it could get through the gate," he reminisced. "So when we came near I shouted, 'This company is dismissed for two minutes, when it will fall in again on the other side of the gate.'"[23] This anecdote, surely fictitious, was meant to show Lincoln as a ready wit without any military experience or knowledge but with the capacity to reach the right pragmatic judgment.

The most serious, morally meaningful story of Lincoln's conduct in the Black Hawk War was told in later life by William G. Greene of New Salem, who served as a private in Lincoln's company. The event is supposed to have occurred just after Stillman's Run, when militia anger at the British Band for scalping their comrades would have been especially high. As Greene told it:

> An old Indian came to camp & delivered himself up, show-
> ing us an old paper written by Lewis Cass, stating that
> the Indian was a good & true man. Many of the men of
> the Army said, "we have come out to fight the Indians and
> by God we intend to do so." Mr. Lincoln in the goodness &
> kindness and humanity & justice of his nature stood—
> got between the Indian and the outraged men—saying—
> "Men this must not be done—he must not be shot and
> killed by us." Some of the men remarked—"The Indian is
> a damned Spy." Still Lincoln stood between the Indian &
> the vengeance of the outraged soldiers.

According to Greene, Lincoln's stand did not go unchallenged:

> Some of the men said to Mr. Lincoln—"This is cowardly on
> your part Lincoln." Lincoln remarked, "If any man thinks
> I am a coward let him test it," rising to an unusual height.
> One of the Regiment made this reply to Mr. Lincoln last
> remarks—"Lincoln—you are larger & heavier than we are."
> "This you can guard against—Choose your weapons," re-
> plied Mr. Lincoln somewhat sourly. This soon put to silence
> quickly all charges of the cowardice of Lincoln.[24]

The story of Lincoln's dramatic display of his moral scruples and firm leadership is probably too good to be true. The detail that the old Indian was carrying a testimonial from Lewis Cass certainly must have been manufactured. Not only would the letter have been more than fifteen years old, but it would be a remarkable coincidence that Cass was the same Michigan politician and minor War of 1812 general whom Lincoln disparaged in the House speech in which he mentioned his own military service.

Nevertheless, the story captures something metaphorical about the historical moment, by making the young militia captain Lincoln (anachronistically to be sure) into the protector of a "good Indian," much in the way that Andrew Jackson presented himself relative to Black Hawk. In his day, Jackson had commanded militia units of his own in a brutal massacre of Creeks, most notoriously at the Battle of Horseshoe Bend. As president, he would order and enforce the Trail of Tears, deporting thousands of Cherokee, Creek, Seminole, Chickasaw, and Choctaw people from the Southeast across the Mississippi. Yet Jackson greeted Black Hawk respectfully at the White House in order to convey the mythical message of treating the adversary with honor. By the time Lincoln's old associate Greene told his story, the Black Hawk War had been transformed from what it was, a small step in the long brutal road of territorial expansion, into a romanticized relic of honorable conflict among equals. In that narrative, Lincoln could be made to fit perfectly—because the same mythologized paradigm of honorable conflict would also eventually be imposed retroactively on the Civil War.

Concretely, it is no exaggeration to say that Lincoln's Black Hawk War experience launched him on his political career. All of twenty-three years old, he had as yet done nothing else of significance except make his two flatboat trips. His failed attempt at running a general store, his appointment as postmaster of New Salem, his self-training as a surveyor, his course of reading to become a lawyer—all lay ahead of him. Just weeks after returning to New Salem from his militia service (on foot, after his horse was stolen), Lincoln presented himself as a candidate for the state legislature. The election was held on August 6, 1832, when Black Hawk and the militia were still in the field. In New

Salem, where the men who had elected him company commander had returned home, Lincoln won 277 out of 300 votes. Nevertheless, he missed being elected countywide, finishing eighth in a race where the top four would go to the statehouse. Five others finished behind him.

Lincoln had not had time to develop a comprehensive political platform. His campaign speech, reported in the *Sangamo Journal*, focused almost exclusively on a plan to improve navigation along the Sangamon River. As proof that he knew what he was talking about, Lincoln emphasized his only credential: that he had (with others) built a flatboat and gone down the river the previous year, and that he had closely observed the conditions all along the river ever since. He was, he acknowledged, "young and unknown to many of you." He had been "born and [had] ever remained in the most humble walks of life," without "wealthy or popular relations." He was appealing, he said, to "the independent voters of this county." And he was prepared to lose. "[I]f the good people in their wisdom shall see fit to keep me in the background," he said in modestly depressive tones, "I have been too familiar with disappointments to be very much chagrined."[25]

Yet Lincoln soon would develop political beliefs. The territorial expansion embodied by his experiences was plunging the nation into conflict. Two years later, Lincoln would run for state legislature on the ticket of the Whig Party. He would be drawn to the party most devoted to resolving national conflict through the only mechanism that seemed capable of preserving the union and its capacity to expand: the mechanism of compromise.

COMPROMISE AND THE CONSTITUTION

Lincoln's defeat in his run for the Illinois state legislature after returning from the Black Hawk War would be his only defeat in a direct, popular election. In 1834, he ran again, and won. This time there was a decisive difference. Not only had Lincoln lived in New Salem for two years, he had affiliated himself with a brand-new national political party known as the Whigs. That affiliation, which would last the full twenty years of the party's existence, is crucial for understanding Lincoln's relationship to the Constitution in the crisis of 1861.

The Whig Party, which arose in the spring of 1834, was to a great degree the accomplishment of one man: Senator Henry Clay, a towering figure in antebellum American life and the most important U.S. politician never to have attained the presidency. Clay was born in Virginia in 1777 and made his career in neighboring Kentucky. A political prodigy, he entered the House of Representatives in 1810 and was elected Speaker of the House in 1811 in his first term. He was thirty-four years old.

An ally of Madison and Monroe, Clay saw in himself the continuation of the Virginia Republican tradition. In 1824, when the old Republican Party split between support for John Quincy Adams and Andrew Jackson, Clay fatefully went with Adams. He became Adams's secretary of state during the Massachusetts native's single presidential term—and thus an enemy of Jackson's. In 1832, Clay ran for president against the incumbent Jackson, who beat him handily.

The formation of the Whig Party was intended to counterbalance the popular power of Jackson's Democrats. A Whig was, historically speaking, someone who stood for legislative power against executive usurpation—the way English Whigs had stood against the royalism of the Tory Party. As the American Whigs depicted it, Jackson had taken advantage of the broadening of the franchise and the rise of democratic, populist politics to make himself into a despot, one who defied the will of Congress and elevated the personal power of the presidency to an unprecedented and dangerous degree. The Whig Party was founded to take on Jackson.

Lincoln's attraction to Clay's Whigs above all reflected the younger man's admiration for Clay's particular cast of mind and distinctive political brilliance. There was some indirect personal connection. Lincoln had been born in Kentucky, Clay's political base. Andrew Jackson was much more a frontiersman than Clay, and a self-made man to boot— yet Lincoln did not choose to become a Jacksonian Democrat.

Lincoln also had policy reasons for his attraction to the Whig Party. Clay favored the development of the economy through what was called the "American system"—federal funding of transportation infrastructure. Running for office in 1832, influenced by his travels down the often difficult-to-navigate Mississippi, Lincoln had instinctively made the improvement of the Sangamon River into his sole campaign issue. Jackson had originally supported "internal improvements," as such policies were called, from the Senate. As president, however, he had reversed course. Swayed by Southern opposition to the tariffs needed to raise the money for internal improvements, Jackson vetoed federally funded infrastructure projects such as the Maysville Road, which would have linked Clay's hometown of Lexington to the Ohio River.

Jackson's Democratic Party probably had more supporters in the Illinois of 1834 than did Clay's Whigs. Plenty of aspiring Illinois politicians thought Jackson's veto of the Maysville Road was justified as a block on a project that would benefit only Kentucky, not the nation. Stephen Douglas, Lincoln's Illinois contemporary who would eventually become his greatest political rival, also entered state politics in 1834, winning his first local office (as a state's attorney in Jacksonville, Illinois) at precisely the same time as Lincoln. Douglas began his career as a Jacksonian Democrat, not a Whig.

Given the logical reasons that should have made Lincoln a Jacksonian, his preference for internal improvements cannot fully explain his attraction to Clay. What drew Lincoln most powerfully to Clay was his reputation as the Great Compromiser—the man who had held the union together. Clay had earned that nickname in 1819, at the age of forty-two, when he crafted the Missouri Compromise, a working solution to the first major constitutional crisis faced by the union.

Today it can be difficult to imagine the force of the great constitutional crises that preceded the Civil War: the Missouri crisis of 1819, the nullification crisis of 1832, the 1850 crisis precipitated by the acquisition of New Mexico and California, and the Kansas crisis that began in 1854 and never really ended. The main reason it is so difficult to retroject ourselves into the thought-world of these crises is that our conception of the Constitution is so profoundly influenced by the Civil War and its aftermath. We think we understand the prewar Constitution, because the Constitution remains for us a living document, evidence of a continued commitment to freedom and self-government under the rule of law.

Yet the Constitution had a different meaning and different functions before the Civil War than it did afterward. Above all, the antebellum Constitution was a blueprint for enabling the states to work together to preserve the union and expand it across the continent. At its core lay a central compromise: the compromise over slavery between the Southern states, whose economies and white culture depended on the practice, and the Northern states, where slavery had come to be seen as a relic of an outdated past. Clay was the self-appointed guardian of that compromise. Lincoln was, almost until the moment he ran for president, Clay's admirer and disciple.

This compromise over slavery dated back to the long, hot summer of 1787, when the Constitutional Convention in Philadelphia roughed out its initial contours. To be sure, the framers had spent most of the summer focused on a different compromise, the one between small and large states that resulted in the creation of a Senate in which all states had equal representation regardless of size. But as the summer progressed, some of the delegates to the convention had come to realize that the division between North and South was much more consequential and serious than the one between different-sized states.

In the original Constitution, the slavery compromise could be glimpsed in three provisions, each of them phrased in euphemism to avoid referring by name to enslaved persons or even persons of African ancestry. The three-fifths compromise specified that the number of congressmen in the House of Representatives, as well as the apportionment of direct taxes, should be determined "by adding to the whole number of free persons . . . three fifths of all other persons"—in other words, enslaved persons of African descent.

Another provision specified that, until 1808, Congress could not prohibit "the migration or importation of such persons as any of the states now existing shall think proper to admit," protecting the slave trade for twenty years. The provision was included in the Constitution at the insistence of South Carolinians (with the help of the Connecticut delegation) to keep down the cost of acquiring new slaves for their expanding rice fields.

Finally, the Constitution demanded that "no person held to service or labor in one state . . . escaping into another, shall . . . be discharged from such service or labor, but shall be delivered up upon claim of the party to whom such service or labor may be due." The infamous fugitive slave clause guaranteed that if enslaved persons should escape to free states, not only would they not become free as a matter of law, but the free states would be obligated under the Constitution to return them to their owners. In intent and effect, this clause superseded the Northern states' commitment to principles of abolition and freedom. It subordinated the courts and other legal institutions of the free states to the constitutional principle of sustaining slavery.

These three elements of the slavery compromise were necessary to get support from all the states for the original Constitution—a fact that was acknowledged at the time. At the New York ratifying convention, Alexander Hamilton defended the three-fifths provision against antislavery critics by saying that it "was one result of the spirit of accommodation, which governed the Convention; and without this indulgence, no union could possibly have been formed."[26] Yet these accommodations were only the beginning of much greater constitutional compromises still to come: compromises over whether and how slavery would be extended to new states as the United States grew and expanded.

In 1787, it was still not clear that the United States would seek to extend its territory across the whole of the North American continent. The first aim of the framers was to ensure that the states would stay together as part of a single political entity, a circumstance that seemed increasingly uncertain when the end of the Revolutionary War took away the overwhelming necessity of unity in order for the new republic to survive. The Constitution said very little about the acquisition of territory. It did, however, provide for the possibility of new states, and it discussed the direct administration of territory by the federal government, which meant it contained a mechanism for any expansion that might occur.

In 1803, Napoleon Bonaparte, then the first consul of France, made the potential for expansion into a reality. By offering to sell the United States the right of settlement through the vast Louisiana Territory, Napoleon opened the door to expansion across the continent. Gradual at first, expansion would come to seem so inevitable that it would eventually be described as "manifest destiny." The Constitution was originally designed for a union focused on the modest objective of surviving along the Eastern Seaboard. It would have to evolve to fit the needs and interests of a union committed to the project of conquering and settling a continent.

It was pure coincidence that the French offer came during the presidency of Thomas Jefferson, the first Republican to hold the office after the Federalist administrations of George Washington and John Adams. Napoleon was motivated by the ending of his own aspirations to an American empire, not by any factor in U.S. domestic politics. His troops had failed to recapture the independent republic created in Haiti under Toussaint L'Ouverture, and he needed money to finance his wars with Britain and its European allies.

Yet it mattered decisively for domestic American politics that the party in office in 1803, the time of the Louisiana Purchase, was the only party that might credibly have opposed expansion in the name of preserving the republic from the dangers of becoming an empire. Once Jefferson and his secretary of state, James Madison, had agreed to the plan of expansion, there was no meaningful opposing constituency left to resist the objective of continental empire. Expansion became American orthodoxy. The War of 1812, mocked by its opponents as "Mr. Madison's War," was ultimately a Republican-led war of expansion. Even though Madison first conceived it to force Britain to allow U.S. shipping, he justified the war as an opportunity to conquer Canada (which failed) and to gain power over the port of New Orleans and Florida (which succeeded).

The expansion of the United States—exemplified by Lincoln's own early life—posed a fundamental problem for the slavery compromise reached by the framers in Philadelphia. They had done their best to balance the relative power of free and slave states. The fact that all the states then existing had ratified the Constitution showed that their compromise was satisfactory for white voters in their generation.

But each time a new state was added, it had the potential to change the balance of power between the free and slave states. The size of the new state did not matter, at least in the Senate, where the Constitution guaranteed each state two votes. By definition, states had to be either free states (outlawing slavery) or slave states (enshrining the practice in their statutes). There could be no in-between. There was inevitably uncertainty about which way a new state would go, because the decision rested on a combination of the desires of the state's white citizens and the agreement of Congress, which had to be obtained for a state to be admitted to the union.

The result was nothing short of a paradox at the heart of the constitutional structure of the union. On the one hand, the practical purpose of the union under the Constitution had evolved into enabling the nation to expand. The states needed to stay together in order to muster the military capacity to conquer and consolidate territory, defeating Native American tribes and anyone else who might stand in the way. Expansion had become the raison d'être of the union itself.

On the other hand, each act of expansion threatened the very unity that was necessary to keep the project of expansion alive. Every time new territory was acquired and entered into the process of statehood, everyone in the country—not only the residents of the new state— had to focus on whether the new state would fall into the free or slave column. Each decision guaranteed new conflict. And each conflict increased the possibility that the union would not hold.

The Missouri crisis caused by the interaction between expansion and slavery—and the resulting compromise, which made Clay's reputation—came in early 1819, thirty years after the Constitution was ratified. The crisis was precipitated by the proposed admission to the union of Missouri, which would be the first state created out of territory acquired in the Louisiana Purchase. Many white residents of the would-be state wanted to allow slavery there. A little-known New York congressman, James Tallmadge, Jr., responded by proposing legislative amendments to the bill allowing admission that would have gradually abolished slavery in Missouri and barred new slaves from being brought there.

At stake was the composition of the Senate, which at the time was evenly split between eleven slave states and eleven free states. Northerners controlled the balance of power in the House, where population (modified by the three-fifths compromise) determined the number of representatives. The House supported Tallmadge's proposal. In the Senate, where every state had equal representation, the Southern interest held sway, and the Senate flatly refused to force abolition on Missouri.

In the congressional debates that followed, the most vociferous speakers openly acknowledged that war and disunion were realistic possibilities. A Georgia congressman charged that Northerners had "kindled a fire which all the waters of the ocean cannot put out, which seas of blood can only extinguish." Tallmadge, the New Yorker who had moved to block slavery in Missouri, shot back, "If a dissolution of the Union must take place, let it be so! If civil war, which gentlemen so much threaten, must come, I can only say, let it come!"

The debate about extending slavery also bled into a debate about the morality of slavery itself—a topic that had been almost completely suppressed in Philadelphia more than thirty years before. Northerners could not quote the Constitution to oppose slavery, because the Constitution said nothing against the practice and, indeed, contained the three compromise provisions that effectively protected it. So they appealed to the Declaration of Independence, particularly to its promise that "all men are created equal." This, they said, was the basis for all republican government—the kind of government that had to be created in the new states. Although they had to admit that the Constitution preserved slavery where it already existed, Northerners in Congress claimed, with some justification, that the framers had hoped for its gradual abolition everywhere.[27]

Whatever Madison might have imagined about the future end of slavery in 1787, by 1819, the cotton gin and the cotton boom that followed it had utterly transformed the prospects for slavery in the South. Southerners defended the admission of Missouri as a slave state with full recognition that they were facing for the first time an existential threat to the institution that underwrote their entire way of life. They defended slavery itself not as a necessary evil, but as a patriarchal institution that benefited slaves.[28] Their best argument, however, was neither to focus on slavery nor to argue against the Declaration of Independence. Rather, Southerners focused on the Constitution—which they understood and depicted as a framework for protecting the rights of states, including those of states like Missouri that were still in the process of joining the union. The Constitution protected slavery because it protected slave states.

The conflict did not seem resolvable, stretching through the summer recess of 1819 and into the new Congress that convened and began arguing afresh in 1820. Into the breach stepped Henry Clay, assisted by President James Monroe, who strongly favored admitting Missouri as a slave state. Clay's Missouri Compromise had two components. Maine, which had sought independence from Massachusetts, was admitted as a free state to provide a Senate counterbalance to Missouri, admitted as a slave state. Even more consequentially, Congress drew a line through the territory acquired in the Louisiana Purchase at the latitude of 36°30'. With the exception of Missouri, which lay in large part above the line, there would be no slavery allowed north of the line as new states were admitted. Below the line, slavery would be permitted.

The goal of drawing the line was to head off future controversies that would accompany the admission of new states by creating a rule that could and would be followed. Like all compromises, it did not fully satisfy either side—not Northerners, who would now have to live with the extension of slavery, and not Southerners, who would have to admit that Congress could in principle block slavery in newly admitted states. Writing in his diary for no immediate audience but himself, John Quincy Adams, serving as Monroe's secretary of state, blamed "the Constitution of the United States, which has sanctioned a dishonorable compromise with slavery." As he saw it, "the cement of common interest produced by slavery is stronger and more solid than that of an unmingled freedom."[29]

For a nation willing to see the original Constitution as a compromise, the Missouri Compromise could be recognized as a further, quasi-constitutional extension of the original compromise to new circumstances. The Missouri Compromise might be enshrined in a statute rather than a constitutional amendment, but that was a technicality. The federal Constitution was being reconceived as a compromise designed to hold the union together *and* enable expansion.

The Missouri Compromise became an integral part of that structure. This was Clay's doing—and it made him, in a certain sense, a second Madison.

THE JACKSON OPTION

For Lincoln to opt for the Whigs in 1834 meant embracing Clay's version of the compromise Constitution. At the same time, it also meant that Lincoln, like Clay, was not prepared to adopt the most extreme view of the federal government's power over the states—a view that was expressed by President Andrew Jackson in response to South Carolina's threat to nullify federal legislation during the second great crisis to threaten the constitutional fabric of the union. It is important to see the difference because, when Lincoln himself faced the secession crisis nearly thirty years later, he ended up following Jackson's view—not the Clay compromise approach he had favored as a young man.

Nullification was the brainchild of John C. Calhoun, the brilliant South Carolinian who had been a congressman, Monroe's secretary of war, and then vice president for John Quincy Adams's single presidential term and Andrew Jackson's first. The occasion for Calhoun's idea was the passage by Congress in 1828 of the so-called Tariff of Abominations. A product of fevered and complex preelection negotiation in Congress, the tariff taxed almost all imported goods at 38 percent and imported raw materials at 45 percent. In the House, the tariff was supported strongly by the mid-Atlantic and Western states. It received a mix of opposition and support from the manufacturing New England states. It was overwhelmingly opposed by the Southern states, which would bear the brunt of the cost because they relied disproportionately on imported goods.

In a pamphlet published anonymously in 1828, Calhoun argued that, when Congress passed an unconstitutional law, individual states had the right to nullify those laws by refusing to enforce them. The logical basis for the claim was that the Constitution was a compact entered into by coequal states. The parties that entered into such an agreement should, Calhoun maintained, have the authority to judge when the agreement was violated by the passage of an unconstitutional law. Once they had so judged, the states should be able to refuse to enforce the law altogether.

As radical as Calhoun's idea might sound today, it had some powerful precedent behind it. In 1798, Thomas Jefferson had drafted (also anonymously) a series of resolutions adopted by the Kentucky legislature that made essentially the same argument. Jefferson had not been specific at the time about exactly what the states could or should do once they deemed the law unconstitutional, but his document certainly left room for Calhoun's conclusion that nullification should be followed by refusal to enforce the law. At the same time, working in parallel to Jefferson, James Madison had drafted resolutions adopted by Virginia that also affirmed states' capacity to declare laws unconstitutional—although Madison had tried to limit the effects of the idea by suggesting that states could only announce that the laws were unconstitutional, rather than doing anything practical about it.

To be fair to Jefferson and Madison, they deemed the law to which they were primarily reacting—the Sedition Act, passed by a Federalist Congress and signed and implemented by John Adams—a blatantly unconstitutional violation of the First Amendment.[30] In contrast, the 1828 tariff, however unpopular and however motivated by sectional interests, did not plausibly fall outside the powers of Congress or otherwise violate the Constitution. Just the same, the fact that Jefferson and Madison could be cited in support of nullification made the doctrine all the more threatening to constitutional unity. If states could effectively decide on their own which laws they wanted to obey, the power of the national government would be undercut to the point of potential collapse.

Jackson, newly elected as president, took steps to reject nullification.

He started symbolically. On April 13, 1830, just a month after Lincoln had crossed into Illinois with his family, Jackson and Calhoun were attending the Jefferson Day dinner at Brown's Indian Queen Hotel in Washington, D.C. Calhoun, Jackson knew, intended to use the occasion to invoke Jefferson's love of states' rights. In particular, Calhoun wanted to make the point that the union was worth maintaining only if it enabled the Southern states to protect their interests.

Jackson sought to repudiate Calhoun's words before they had even been spoken. The president opposed nullification and rejected the idea that the union should be subordinated to the interests of the states. He certainly would have rejected any claim that states had a right to secede. Jackson rose first to offer a toast of his own: "Our federal Union: It must be preserved." Those in the audience—and the public who read reports in the newspapers—understood that by this ultimatum Jackson had all but accused his vice president of favoring disunion. That, Jackson implied, was the greatest political crime possible in the United States of 1830.

In the months and years that followed, an extended national debate developed about the essential nature of the union: whether it was a good in itself or a means to the end of liberty, and whether it was worth preserving at all costs. The debate raged while Lincoln was making his second trip down the Mississippi, fighting in the Black Hawk War, and running unsuccessfully for state legislature. Although we do not know to what extent he was aware of it at the time, the debate would structure Lincoln's political future. The positions taken in it would become the central topics of debate in the early days of his own presidency in 1861, as he tried to decide whether to go to war— and as he gravitated toward Jackson's view instead of Clay's.

There were, roughly, three points of view at the time of the nullification crisis. Calhoun embraced states' rights—and suggested that if the federal government threatened liberty, national government should be set aside. This view was captured in the toast Calhoun gave after Jackson had spoken preemptively. "The Union, next to our liberty, most dear," Calhoun said. "May we all remember that it can only be preserved by respecting the rights of the States and by distributing equally the benefits and burdens of the Union." Calhoun's toast did not put union first. It made union secondary to liberty. And Calhoun's version of liberty was very close to regional self-interest. To him, Southerners who could not prevail in Congress were implicitly being denied liberty. A union that failed to respect states' rights and distribute the costs and benefits of government equally across regions might no longer be worth preserving.[31]

The second view, midway between Calhoun and Jackson, was that while liberty was important as a purpose of the union, the union was also a good in itself. Senator Daniel Webster of Massachusetts gave the classic formulation of this idea in an important speech against nullification in the Senate on January 26–27, 1830. In the final, rousing words of the speech, the greatest orator of the age condemned the notion of "Liberty first and Union afterwards." Those were, he said, "words of delusion and folly." Instead, Webster proclaimed what he called "that other sentiment, dear to every true American heart": "Liberty and Union, now and for ever, one and inseparable!"

To promote the inherent value of the union, Webster had to offer at least an implicit explanation of its importance. The answer, understood by listeners across the country, lay in what the union had accomplished by 1830, and still had yet to accomplish. "While the Union lasts," Webster told his fellow citizens, "we have high, exciting, gratifying prospects spread out before us and our children." The "prospects" were not abstractions but actual views of a real landscape—the landscape of the North American continent, "spread out" for conquest and settlement by white Americans and their offspring. The true and ultimate value of the union was its capacity to enable the United States to become a continental empire.

The union had been transformed from a tool of last resort for maintaining independence into a machine for vast expansion. The shift reflected the changed fortunes of the United States itself between 1787, when the Constitution was proposed, and 1830, when the country faced the constitutional crisis of nullification. The United States no longer had any serious European opponents on its own continent. The path to the Pacific was visible, if not yet open. The only serious barrier to expansion lay within—in the possibility of discord that, Webster warned, would leave the states "dissevered, discordant, belligerent; on a land rent with civil feuds, or drenched, it may be, in fraternal blood!"[32]

Clay, Lincoln's model, took something like Webster's middle view. But he remained cautiously silent as the nullification debate raged. Instead, true to his reputation as a compromiser, he worked in the background to get the tariff of 1828 repealed. In 1832, Clay seemed to have succeeded. Congress rolled back the "abominations" of 1828 and enacted a new tariff, one that garnered a significant number of Southern votes in the House.

Unfortunately, South Carolina continued to reject the new tariff. The lesson its political elite had taken away from the debate of the previous two years was that the threat of nullification had worked. In November 1832, the South Carolina legislature passed a fresh ordinance of nullification, relying on Calhoun's theory that the state could declare a law to be unconstitutional, null, and void within the sovereign boundaries of the state. The ordinance went so far as to declare that if the federal government were to try to enforce its tariffs by closing ports or otherwise coercing South Carolina, the people of the state would "hold themselves absolved from all other further obligation to maintain or preserve their political connection with the people of the other states." Indeed, the state asserted, its people would "forthwith proceed to organize a separate government, and do all other acts and things which sovereign and independent states may of right do."[33] South Carolina was now threatening secession. The rumbling thundercloud of national concern around nullification had emitted a thunderbolt of crisis.

Now, in December 1832, Jackson decided things had gone far enough. He issued a presidential proclamation aimed squarely at South Carolina, which, he said, intended "the destruction of the Union." When Lincoln came to confront the secession crisis in 1861, Jackson's proclamation would be the single most important state paper he would have before him—and the only direct precedent for how a president of the United States had dealt with a similar threat. Northern newspapers would reprint Jackson's proclamation and urge Lincoln to adopt his model.[34] It is therefore worth examining Jackson's arguments in some detail—and recalling that the young Lincoln supported not Jackson, but Clay, who had advocated for a softer, compromise approach rather than Jackson's path of confrontation.

Jackson went further than Webster had gone in describing the union as equal in importance to liberty. He depicted the union as the central element of American political life. It was, he said, "coeval with our political existence"—exactly as old as the idea of America. The union was "sacred." It was "hitherto inviolate," or unbroken. It had been "perfected by our happy Constitution," not created by it. And the union had brought the United States "to a state of prosperity at home, and high consideration abroad, rarely, if ever, equalled in the history of nations."[35]

Jackson did not only defend the union with high rhetoric. He also offered a review of how the union had come into existence. Remarkably, he started before the Declaration of Independence, a document to which he paid almost no attention. Rather, Jackson asserted that even before the Declaration, "leagues were formed for common defense." In that moment, "we"—he used the first-person plural as though it obviously applied—"were known in our aggregate character as *the United Colonies of America*." Presumably Jackson was referring to the acts and declarations of the first Continental Congress, which met in 1774. He provided no detail but stated simply that "we declared ourselves a nation by a joint, not by several acts." Then, in the very same sentence, he moved immediately to the Articles of Confederation, which were, he said, "a solemn league of several states, by which they agreed that they would collectively form one nation for the purpose of conducting some certain domestic concerns, and all foreign relations." From the Articles, Jackson passed to the Constitution. It was, he said, "made in the name and by the authority of the people of the United States, whose delegates framed, and whose conventions approved it." He invoked the preamble's goal of forming a more perfect union.

Jackson was building to a crescendo. "The power to annul the law of the United States, assumed by one state," he declared, was "incompatible with the existence of the Union." Nullification "contradicted expressly the letter of the Constitution." It was "unauthorized by its spirit" and "inconsistent with every principle on which it was founded." Nullification was therefore "destructive of the great object for which it"—the Constitution—was "formed."[36] The great object of the Constitution—its purpose and goal—was the union.

As a legal argument, Jackson's approach was of limited use. He had done nothing to refute Calhoun's compact theory of the Constitution—a theory that could be traced back to Jefferson and even, with a little effort, to Madison, the Constitution's chief drafter. What was powerful in Jackson's argument was its appeal to the idea that the Constitution had value only insofar as it created and preserved the union. If nullification had the capacity to break the union, then it could not be permitted by a Constitution devoted to that end.

Jackson therefore focused on the claim that the Constitution had to be understood as the blueprint for the preservation of the union. "We have hitherto relied on it as the perpetual bond of our Union," he insisted. That reliance could not have been "mistaken." "Did we pledge ourselves to the support of an airy nothing?" he asked rhetorically. "Did the name of Washington sanction . . . such an anomaly in the history of fundamental legislation?" The obvious answer was "No, we have not erred!" The Constitution was and remained worthy of worship. It was "still the object of our reverence, the bond of our Union, our defence in danger, the source of our prosperity in peace."[37]

Such a constitution did not countenance nullification, Jackson made clear. Nor did it tolerate a "right to secede." By entering into the Constitution, the people had created "a single nation," not merely a "league" of states. Secession, he said, "does not break a league, but destroys the unity of a nation." Injuring the unity of the United States would be "an offence against the whole Union." Secession was a "revolutionary act." It was not, and could not be called, "a constitutional right."[38]

Jackson understood that argument and rhetoric might not be enough to force South Carolina to back down from nullification. He therefore ended with a direct threat. Although South Carolina had not yet committed any "act of violent opposition to the laws," he intended "to warn the citizens of South Carolina" that they were on their way to "ruin and disgrace."[39] If they continued on the path they had chosen, they were headed for violence. Their "fertile fields" would be "deluge[d] with blood."[40] Jackson was no great Shakespearean, but the reference to Henry V's threats of destruction in France was at least implicit. Jackson finally invoked the Bible so as to leave no doubt about what he was threatening. "[I]f it be the will of Heaven, that the recurrence of its primeval curse on man for the shedding of his brother's blood should fall upon our land,"[41] it would not be the fault of the United States, but of South Carolina. Jackson was signaling a willingness to undertake a civil war, even at the risk of invoking the curse of Cain.

In the days that followed, Jackson would ask Congress to pass a law authorizing use of military force against any state that sought to resist the enforcement of the federal tariff. His call for the Force Act showed that Jackson recognized that Congress had a role in taking on South Carolina. But his proclamation also demonstrated that Jackson believed his position as president enabled him to retaliate against the state even absent congressional authorization. "The laws of the United States must be executed," he said bluntly. "I have no discretionary power on the subject—my duty is emphatically pronounced in the Constitution." If South Carolina were to resist the enforcement of the law, that would be "disunion." And "disunion, by armed force, is *treason*." He, the president of United States, the "First Magistrate," would enforce the law against treason. He would not "accede to the mad project of disunion."[42]

The conception of presidential authority contained in this passage, and elsewhere in the proclamation, was extraordinarily wide-ranging. Jackson was saying that, as president, with the obligation to execute the laws, he could and would order the use of force against South Carolina, even without Congress. The proclamation was meant as a warning, as a threat, and as an assertion of presidential power.

The breadth of the presidential authority asserted by Jackson in the nullification crisis resonated with his more general view of his powers— exactly the view that led Clay to organize the Whig Party against what he perceived as Jackson's overreach. Daniel Webster came out in strong support of Jackson's proclamation, telling a Boston audience that the president had captured "the true principles of the Constitution." Webster embraced the Force Act, taking on Calhoun in the Senate debate over the bill. Clay, in contrast, went to work negotiating with Calhoun, and produced the Tariff Act of 1833, also known as the "compromise tariff." The law ensured the gradual lowering of tariff rates until 1842, when they would return to the earlier norm of 20 percent.

It was Clay's compromise tariff, not the Force Act or Jackson's proclamation, that ended the nullification crisis. The compromise negotiation took place against the backdrop of Jackson's threat of force, which influenced the environment for it. But Clay's approach eschewed the confrontational approach in favor of the oblique compromise.

And as if to vindicate Clay's worries, Jackson wasted no time after the nullification crisis in once more asserting his radical conception of presidential authority. In the summer of 1833, he ordered the secretary of the treasury to remove all federal deposits from the Bank of the United States and put the money in a series of state banks—effectively killing the national bank, which had been chartered by Congress. When the secretary of the treasury refused, Jackson fired him and replaced him with his attorney general, a Maryland lawyer named Roger Taney, who undertook the operation. Clay denounced Jackson, whom he had long considered a would-be Caesar who threatened the republic with dictatorship.[43] The bank affair was the chief justification for the formation of the Whigs. Even Webster, who had supported Jackson's approach to nullification, joined the new party.

Seen from the perspective of the young Lincoln, Jackson's extremity in addressing nullification was little different from his extremity in destroying the Bank of the United States. Clay's compromise approach was the model to be followed. Lincoln's preference was grounded in his personal preference for compromise and accommodation. As a recent writer on Lincoln's early years has observed, "No Jacksonian better fit the Jacksonian ideal than New Salem's Whig plebeian."[44] By biography, Lincoln should have been a Democrat. Becoming a Democrat would also have been good politics. "The tendency in Illinois was for every man of ambition to turn Democrat," noted John Todd Stuart, Lincoln's law partner in later years.[45] But Lincoln was a Whig and a Clay man by temperament and belief. And Clay was not an extreme unionist—if that meant threatening force to hold the states together. As a follower of the Virginian framers, Clay believed that the Constitution was a blueprint for compromise that would preserve the union.

A PORTRAIT OF THE WHIG AS A YOUNG MAN

Lincoln thought so, too. Most of his efforts during his three terms in the Illinois state legislature were focused on pushing for state-funded internal improvements. But on March 3, 1837, the day before the Democrat

Martin Van Buren was inaugurated president, Lincoln and another state representative, Daniel Stone of Springfield, took up the question of slavery in a way that displayed his point of view—the first direct evidence we have of Lincoln's thoughts on the subject. The occasion was a debate in the state legislature about resolutions for and against slavery received from other states—Virginia, Alabama, and Mississippi in the South, and New York and Connecticut in the North—a not uncommon catalyst for national political conversation in the prewar republic. The Illinois legislature offered a four-part resolution in response. Lincoln and Stone were not satisfied with its language, and so offered their own protest to be read into the legislative record.

Lincoln's protest started with a complex statement that summed up his objective of compromise. Lincoln and Stone, it read, "believe that the institution of slavery is founded on both injustice and bad policy; but that the promulgation of abolition doctrines tends rather to increase than to abate its evils."[46] Lincoln and Stone were saying that slavery was morally wrong, a view that was not unimaginable for white Illinoisans at the time, even if it was not mainstream. Yet in almost the same breath they were saying that abolitionist opposition to slavery would lead to more slavery, not less. The statement did not contain a formal logical contradiction: both halves technically pointed to the goal of reducing slavery. But no rational reader could have missed the point that Lincoln and Stone were urging abolitionists to remain silent—a goal sought by proslavery advocates. Their somewhat tortured formulation was intended to steer a middle course between slave states and free states.

In the years just before Lincoln and Stone issued their statement, the advocates of abolition (still seen as a radical doctrine almost everywhere in the union) had nevertheless become increasingly vocal and demanding. In December 1833, a large group of abolitionists, including three African Americans and four women, held a convention in Philadelphia and established the American Anti-Slavery Society. In its founding document, the society claimed "that each State in which slavery exists, has, by the Constitution of the United States, the exclusive right to *legislate* in regard to its abolition in said State."[47] The society was therefore demanding immediate emancipation not by Congress, but by slaveholders and slave-state legislatures.[48]

To the most radical of the abolitionists, like William Lloyd Garrison, the fact that the Constitution protected slavery in the states was a reason to condemn the Constitution itself. As Garrison put it in an 1832 article in his newspaper, *The Liberator*, the Constitution "was a compact formed at the sacrifice of the bodies and souls of millions of our race, for the sake of achieving a political object—an unblushing and monstrous coalition to do evil that good might come." The compact was not "sacred," but "wicked" and "ignominious." It followed that "such a compact was, in the nature of things and according to the law of God, null and void from the beginning . . . It was not valid then—it is not valid now."[49] Garrison put that same idea into the Declaration of Sentiments he wrote for the American Anti-Slavery Society: "All those laws which are now in force, admitting the right of slavery, are therefore before God utterly null and void."[50] This was the sort of bold challenge to the validity of the Constitution and its laws that Lincoln and Stone were labeling as harmful, likely to promote rather than hinder the cause of slavery. It was a challenge grounded in morality. And as Garrison's appeals to God made clear, the moral condemnation of slavery and the Constitution was squarely founded on religious values and ideals.

On the other side of Lincoln's position, the resolutions ultimately adopted by the Illinois state legislature were significantly more proslavery than Lincoln and Stone's proposal. Those resolutions stated "that we highly disapprove of the formation of abolition societies, and of the doctrines promulgated by them."[51] That went well beyond Lincoln's pragmatic statement that abolitionism would undercut its own objectives. The state legislature was outright condemning the principles of abolition, whereas Lincoln was in fact weakly endorsing abolition by saying that slavery was unjust and impolitic.

Lincoln and Stone's second assertion was that they believed "that the Congress of the United States has no power, under the constitution, to interfere with the institution of slavery in the different States."[52] This formulation treated the Constitution itself as the blueprint for compromise between North and South. Nothing in the Constitution said explicitly that Congress could not interfere with slavery using federal law. Lincoln and Stone must have been referring to the protection of property, and perhaps more broadly to the fugitive slave law and the three-fifths compromise. The two lawyers—for Lincoln had just earned his law license a few months earlier—were offering an implicit interpretation of the letter and the spirit of the Constitution. And in their interpretation, the Constitution protected slavery.

It is again instructive to compare the more proslavery resolutions adopted by the full legislature. Those declared that "the right of property in slaves, is sacred to the slave-holding States by the Federal Constitution, and that they cannot be deprived of that right without their consent." Like Lincoln and Stone's statement, this resolution identified the Constitution as the protector of slavery. But it featured an overt defense of the idea of "property in slaves," which was subtly different from the "institution of slavery" to which Lincoln and Stone referred. What was more, the state legislature's statement used the religiously infused language of "sacred" to describe the right to property holding.[53]

More important, the Illinois resolutions also added an element that was wholly lacking in Lincoln and Stone's statement: the assertion that slavery could not be abolished without the slave states' consent. The fact that they omitted this point altogether strongly suggests that Lincoln and Stone believed that slavery could be eliminated by a federal constitutional amendment—which in theory could be ratified and adopted without the consent of all the slave states. That was also why Lincoln and Stone spoke of the power of Congress under the Constitution, and not of the Constitution itself. They were saying that while the existing Constitution limited the power of Congress with respect to slavery, an amendment to the Constitution could accomplish what Congress could not.

As a matter of positive constitutional law, Lincoln and Stone were correct. Nothing in the Constitution put the institution of slavery outside of the bounds of amendment under Article V. The Constitution had exempted abolition of the slave trade from amendment for twenty years; that in turn implied that the other provisions of the Constitution were amendable. True, slaves had been considered property at the founding, and the Constitution stated that property could not be taken by the government without just compensation. A constitutional amendment, however, could change that state of affairs by, for example, denying that humans could be considered property, or making an exception to the requirement of just compensation.

The Illinois state legislature's resolution, in contrast, strongly hinted that an ordinary constitutional amendment could not bring about the abolition of slavery. The statement did not explain exactly why. The Constitution did specify one right that states could not lose without their consent, namely, the right to equal representation in the Senate. In practice, the Southern states' power in the Senate would effectively protect them against Congress passing an amendment and sending it out to the states for ratification. Probably the Illinois legislature meant to refer to that reality. As things stood, unless many free states were to be added until they swamped the slave states, the slave states in practice could not be deprived of slavery "without their consent."

Finally, Lincoln and Stone stated that they believed "that the Congress of the United States has the power, under the constitution, to abolish slavery in the District of Columbia; but that that power ought not to be exercised unless at the request of the people of said District."[54] Again they were offering a compromise. The state legislature had resolved "that the General Government cannot abolish slavery in the District of Columbia, against the consent of the citizens of said District without a manifest breach of good faith."[55] In substance, Lincoln and Stone on the one hand and the state legislature on the other agreed that Congress had the power to abolish slavery in Washington, D.C.; and both sides also thought that Congress should not do so. But Lincoln and Stone emphasized Congress's lawful power, then alluded to the reality that the white citizens of the capital would not embrace its exercise. The Illinois legislature's resolutions instead emphasized that the federal government could not abolish slavery in the capital without breaching the "good faith" of its white residents.

What was distinctive about Lincoln's approach to the Constitution was not the narrow fact that he understood the document as a blueprint for compromise. President Martin Van Buren, in the inaugural address he delivered the day after Lincoln and Stone submitted their protest, also praised the Constitution as a blueprint for compromise over slavery. "Our forefathers," Van Buren said, "were deeply impressed with the delicacy of this subject [of slavery], and they treated it with a forbearance so evidently wise that in spite of every sinister foreboding it never until the present period disturbed the tranquillity of our common country." If "this spirit of forbearance," this "generous and fraternal feeling" were to be neglected, Van Buren continued, it would be "injurious to every interest," inflaming the "violence of excited passions."[56]

But Van Buren's version of compromise was far more conciliatory toward slavery than was Lincoln's approach, which actively sought a middle ground between North and South, rather than conceding the rightness of slavery entirely. For the Democratic New Yorker Van Buren, the keyword "forbearance" stood for the idea that the Northern states would always hold back from trying to interfere with the Southern institution of slavery. In the same address, Van Buren reiterated that he would be an "inflexible and uncompromising opponent of every attempt on the part of Congress to abolish slavery in the District of Columbia against the wishes of the slaveholding States." And he boasted of "a determination equally decided to resist the slightest interference with [slavery] in the States where it exists."[57] The Democratic Illinois legislature was following its party's line in seeking total conciliation of the South. Lincoln was prepared to recognize the necessity and utility of compromise, but he also wanted to make sure that compromise in some way extended to include Northern opponents of slavery as well.

If Lincoln's proposed resolutions give us a view of the emerging politician's beliefs on slavery and abolition, his speech to the Young Men's Lyceum of Springfield provides a window into the development of his thinking about the Constitution. Delivered just a few months later, in late January 1838, the speech, now known as Lincoln's Lyceum Address, offered a critique of mob violence and a powerful albeit conventional defense of the importance of "the perpetuation of our political institutions."[58] The principle Lincoln chose to laud was the rule of law. The institution that he presented as most undergirding it was the Constitution itself, understood as a check on any excessive political passions—whether proslavery or antislavery. The Constitution supported a political order based on reason, not excessive feeling.

Some historians, seeking to highlight Lincoln's openness to the antislavery movement, emphasize that, in the speech, Lincoln mentioned the murder of the abolitionist journalist Elijah Lovejoy, killed by a mob in Alton, Illinois, in November 1837.[59] Lincoln did indeed condemn mobs who "throw printing presses into rivers" and "shoot editors." Yet he did not mention Lovejoy by name. In fact, Lincoln went to great lengths in the address to disclaim any pro- or antislavery sentiment. He was warning about a rise of disrespect for the rule of law that, he insisted, was "common to the whole country," and was not "confined to the slaveholding, or the non-slaveholding states."[60]

The substance of Lincoln's argument was that, when elements of the public began to regularize the imposition of punishments through lynching or riots, the result would be to break down and even destroy

"the *attachment* of the People" to their government. In Lincoln's depiction, this psychological attachment was necessary for government to
continue to operate successfully. Without it, "the feelings" of even "the
best citizens" would become "alienated" from the government. Left
"without friends," the government would become susceptible to the
ambitions of "men of sufficient talent and ambition" who would seek
to make their mark on history by overthrowing the existing constitutional order.

In a much-cited passage of the speech, Lincoln gave voice to a fantasy of what men of "towering genius" would aspire to accomplish.
They would not be satisfied with "a seat in Congress, a gubernatorial
or a presidential chair." Such men—he mentioned Alexander, Caesar,
and Napoleon—belonged to *"the family of the lion, or the tribe of the ea-
gle."* They would scorn the footsteps of their predecessors. They would
achieve distinction "whether at the expense of emancipating slaves, or
enslaving freemen."[61]

In the context of the speech, there was nothing meant to be
praiseworthy in Lincoln's depiction of dictatorial strongmen making
their mark on history. In no way was he telling his friends, colleagues,
and potential future constituents that he or they should aspire to the
accomplishments of a Caesar. And it was extremely significant that
the examples Lincoln gave of how such giants would break from the
precedents of good government was by emancipation or enslavement
of their fellow men. In Lincoln's presentation, the Constitution protected and preserved the status quo regarding slavery. To free slaves
would rend the fabric of the Constitution just as it would break the
traditions of American liberty to make free (white) men into slaves.

The way to preserve the existing political system and the Constitution, Lincoln argued, was to minimize the role of passion in politics.
Passion was useful in fighting for a revolution, he noted. But now, in
an era of uncertain national consolidation, passion must be replaced
by "sober reason." And reason—"cold, calculating, unimpassioned

reason"—was the most effective tool of strengthening the bonds of the Constitution and the rule of law. Reason, Lincoln announced in his peroration, must "be moulded into *general intelligence, sound morality*, and in particular, *a reverence for the constitution and laws.*"[62]

Reverence for the Constitution was the attitude that would restore popular attachment to government. Far from subjecting the Constitution to withering critique for its compromises with slavery, as abolitionists did, Lincoln was advocating for a political psychology that would shore up and perpetuate the Constitution as the one institution that could preserve and protect the existing order. The Constitution that deserved such reverence was itself a compromise. To revere it was to support a rule of law that precluded freeing slaves. Anyone who aspired to become a great man of history by emancipating or enslaving would be an enemy of the Constitution—and the reason on which it was based.

ABOLITIONISTS AND THE CONSTITUTION

The idea that the Constitution contained a compromise between North and South over slavery had been noted by observers at least since Alexander Hamilton had described the three-fifths compromise as an "accommodation" on the floor of the New York ratifying convention. The moral argument that this compromise rendered the Constitution illegitimate began to become prominent around 1840, when Madison's transcript-like notes on the constitutional convention of 1787 were published four years after his death. For the first time, the notes revealed the details of the negotiations over the slavery provisions, showing that Southern delegates had insisted on them as part of the price of the compromise that led to the adoption of the Constitution. It was not a coincidence that newly conspicuous moral concerns about the Constitution rested on the view that the Constitution should be interpreted in terms of its historical origins, origins that were highlighted by the newly available documents.

In 1839, William Jay, a lawyer and abolitionist, published a book called *A View of the Action of the Federal Government in Behalf of Slavery*. It opened with the declaration that "Our Fathers, in forming the Federal Constitution, entered into a guilty compromise on the subject of Slavery, and heavily is their sin now visited upon their children."[63] The reference to fathers and children was literal. Jay's father was John Jay, author of several of the Federalist Papers and later first chief justice of the United States.

In 1844, the American Anti-Slavery Society adopted the motto "No Union with Slaveholders" and officially announced a policy favoring the dissolution of the union. A few weeks later, the African American abolitionist Charles Lenox Remond (or Raymond) gave a speech expressing what he considered the proper perspective to be taken by African Americans on the Constitution. He felt, he said, "a deep interest in the question." He did not expect his comments "to make much impression upon the many—upon the body of this nation, for whose benefit the Constitution was made." He was addressing those "whom it entirely overlooks, or sees but to trample upon, and the fewer still, who identify themselves with the outcast."[64]

Remond acknowledged that it made sense "for nine-tenths of the people of the United States, to speak of the awe and reverence they feel as they contemplate the Constitution." But African Americans like him were "in a very different position," he pointed out. "What is it to *them* that it talks about peace—tranquillity—domestic enjoyment—civil rights? To them it is no such union . . . resting, as it does, upon all their dearest and holiest rights."[65] He recounted the case of Francis J. McIntosh, a free Black who had been lynched in 1836 for defending his wife's honor. "What was the Union to him?" Remond asked rhetorically. What was the union to the slave rebellion leader "Turner of Southampton," Remond then asked, saying Nat Turner deserved to be known by more than his slave name "Nat," and deserved to have his name glorified and a monument built to him.

Remond acknowledged the radicalism of his perspective. "[M]en say to me, 'Remond! you're wild! Remond! you're mad! Remond! you're a revolutionist!' Sir, in view of all these things, ought not this whole assembly—this whole nation to be revolutionists too?" Remond's point was that revolutionism was appropriate in the light of the realities of the Constitution and its concrete history:

> With all my knowledge of the origin and the progress, and my experience of the present practical workings of the American Constitution, shall I be found here advocating it as a glorious means to a glorious end? No! my fellow countrymen, I am here to register my testimony against it! Not because I do not feel how valuable it might be, were its provisions secured to the few as they are to the many— not because I wish to claim anything more for the few than an equality of privileges—not because I am not ready to "yield everything to the Union *but* Truth—Honor— Liberty" . . . but because (and I regret to say it) we have, as a people, yielded even these; and with such a people, I feel that I must not, as an individual, be numbered.[66]

In 1845, to bolster the historical case that the Constitution in its original context should be understood as "proslavery," the American Anti-Slavery Society published a book titled *The Constitution a Proslavery Compact*. The work consisted of extracts of Madison's notes edited by the prominent abolitionist Wendell Phillips. In an introductory essay, Phillips promised "all the details of that 'compromise,' which was made between freedom and slavery, in 1787; granting to the slaveholder distinct privileges and protection for his slave property, in return for certain commercial concessions on his part toward the North." The extracts, Phillips said, "prove also that the Nation at large were fully aware of this bargain at the time, and entered into it willingly and with open eyes." He concluded: "If then the Constitution be, what these Debates show that our fathers intended to make it . . . [then it] ought to be immediately annulled. No abolitionist can consistently take office under it, or swear to support it . . . To continue this disastrous alliance longer is madness."[67] Phillips was invoking the framers' intent in order to condemn the Constitution as immoral.

Even before the book with Phillips's introduction appeared, Garrison had expressed the essence of what would become the most famous and fiery condemnation of the Constitution—a condemnation that invoked the morality of biblical religion. "Slavery is a combination of DEATH and HELL," he wrote in *The Liberator*, "and with it the North have made a covenant, and are at agreement."[68] Garrison was paraphrasing Isaiah 28:15, in which the prophet denounces the sinful leaders of the Judean people: "Because ye have said, We have made a covenant with death, and with hell are we at agreement." To Garrison, the covenant with death was the Constitution itself. The biblical metaphor may have been suggested by an earlier usage that has been traced back to 1814, when a Connecticut Federalist critic of the War of 1812, contemplating disunion, wrote, "Had what has happened been foreshown to the men of New-England [in 1787], they would as soon have made a covenant with death, as a covenant of union with the states which have thus wantonly and cruelly oppressed them."[69] In 1854, Garrison would invoke the same verse at a Fourth of July rally outside Boston at which he burned a copy of the Constitution and declared it "a covenant with death, an agreement with hell."[70] The idea that the Constitution was morally illegitimate precisely because it had been designed and still functioned as a compromise with slavery—a "slaveholding bargain,"[71] in the words frequently used by Garrison's allies—became a distinctive aspect of the most radical abolitionism associated with the Anti-Slavery Society and its predominant leader.

True keepers of the Garrisonian flame considered the Constitution so morally repugnant that they even refused to vote in national elections, considering that the act would implicate them in the immorality of the compromise Constitution.

A variant on the moral condemnation of the Constitution was the observation that slavery contradicted the principles that the Constitution purported to uphold. Writing in 1838, the South Carolina–born Angelina Grimké, one of the first important women abolitionists and an ally of Garrison's, used the preamble to the Constitution to impugn slavery:

> We hold, that all the slaveholding laws violate the fundamental principles of the Constitution of the United States. In the preamble of that instrument, the great objects for which it was framed are declared to be "to establish justice, to promote the general welfare, and to secure the blessings of liberty to us and to our posterity." The slave laws are flagrant violations of these fundamental principles. Slavery subverts justice, promotes the welfare of the *few* to the manifest injury of the many, and robs thousands of the *posterity* of our forefathers of the blessings of liberty.[72]

Grimké also argued that slavery violated the Bill of Rights because, for example, slaves were "denied the right of a presentation by a grand jury, and a trial by a petit jury."[73]

A starkly different abolitionist view treated the constitutional compromise as a step in the direction of abolition—and insisted the Constitution could be considered "sacred" despite the compromise. This approach did not so much ignore the idea that the Constitution should be interpreted according to its history and origins as suggest that the framers' literal words mattered more than the fact that the Constitution in practice preserved slavery. In 1838, this text-focused, forward-looking argument was advanced by an African American abolitionist named Thomas Cole while addressing a meeting of the Massachusetts Anti-Slavery Society. "There is not a solitary word about slavery in that constitution," Cole pointed out. "The word slave is not in it. The constitution merely recognizes indirectly its existence, in some of its provisions."[74]

Cole went on to offer his own account of the compromise Constitution, acknowledging its recognition of slavery while offering a distinctive interpretation of how the framers had chosen their words:

> There was a compromise made, that the slave states should be entitled to a representation for three fifths of their slave population; and that slaves who escape should be delivered up to their masters. But so cautious were the framers of that instrument, to avoid recognizing slavery as a part of our systems; and so conscious were they of its repugnance to the very spirit of our institutions, that their provisions were made without introducing into that sacred instrument the word slave or slavery.[75]

According to Phillips and Garrison, the framers' use of circumlocution demonstrated their hypocrisy: they were seeking to avoid the embarrassment of using the word "slavery" even as they triply enshrined the practice. Cole was arguing, in contrast, that the framers were far-seeing, liberal men who wanted to ensure the eventual abolition of slavery and so kept the odious phrase out of the Constitution.* Indeed, Cole sought to interpret the compromise itself as a step along the path to eventual abolition:

---

* This perspective remains alive today. See Sean Wilentz, *No Property in Man: Slavery and Antislavery at the Nation's Founding* (Cambridge, Mass.: Harvard University Press, 2018).

And it is evident that this compromise, so far from amounting to a perpetual guarantee of slavery, was, on all hands, considered as but a *temporary* arrangement. This may be learned from the speech of Mr. Madison, in the Virginia convention, for the adoption of the federal constitution. Sir, the spirit of abolition was born in Virginia. If I am not mistaken, a resolution was introduced against this slave representation. Mr. Madison says, "The Southern states will not enter into this union, unless they are permitted a *temporary* continuance of this system."[76]

As a historical matter, Cole's proof was not precisely accurate. At the Virginia ratifying convention, Madison had in fact used the word "temporary" to describe one aspect of the slavery compromise in the Constitution. But he was speaking about the temporary preservation of the slave trade for twenty years, not slavery itself. George Mason, who opposed ratification at the Virginia convention, had just attacked the proposed Constitution for preserving the "disgraceful" slave trade while failing to "secure[] us the property of the slaves we have already." Madison replied that while the provision preserving the slave trade might be "impolitic," nevertheless "the Southern states would not have entered into the Union of America without the temporary permission of that trade."[77] Contrary to Cole's hopeful suggestion, the "spirit of abolition" was not born in Virginia—at least not in the person of George Mason, who had himself been accused by other Southerners at the constitutional convention of seeking to end the slave trade in order to enhance the sales value of the three hundred slaves he already owned.[78]

The implications of Cole's argument mattered much more than its historical accuracy, however. In a world where the Constitution was broadly seen as the bulwark of national unity, he was laying the groundwork for abolitionists to reject slavery without also rejecting the Constitution in the manner of Garrison. Following this direction, a still more radical abolitionist reading of the Constitution began to emerge in the 1840s. Grimké had suggested that slavery was inconsistent with the aspirational values of the Declaration of Independence, but she had not mounted a legal argument against slavery. According to this newer, radical view, the Constitution, properly interpreted as a legal document, did not sanction slavery—it outlawed it.

Several thinkers helped shape and promote this argument, including Gerrit Smith, a wealthy abolitionist and patron of other abolitionists. Smith, who developed close friendships with African American activists, was a founder of the Liberty Party, formed in 1840 as an alternative to the Garrisonian American Anti-Slavery Society's rejection of electoral participation as morally illegitimate.[79] The most sustained version of the thesis was developed by Lysander Spooner, a genuinely strange and fascinating combination of abolitionist, libertarian, and anarchist. Spooner was an autodidact who set up shop as a lawyer without attending university or spending the required five years of training in a law office. Among other exploits, he started a private letter delivery company in the hopes of challenging the monopoly of the U.S. mail. But he found his measure of immortality with his writings on slavery and the Constitution.

In 1845, the same year Phillips published his extract of Madison's notes on the constitutional convention, Spooner published *The Unconstitutionality of Slavery*, a densely packed, 129-page work devoted to the proposition "that slavery neither has, *nor ever had* any constitutional existence in this country."[80] Spooner's argument began with the principle that slavery was a violation of natural law, and could be legally established only by the valid legal act of some legislature or convention.* He then pointed out that the state constitutions that existed in 1789 did

---

* This principle was not itself original to Spooner. It had been enunciated by the great common law judge Lord Mansfield in the important case of *Somerset v. Stewart*, 98 Eng. Rep. 499, in 1772.

not mention slavery. (He neglected to mention state laws, which did.) The federal Constitution, Spooner continued, also did not mention slavery. Consequently, he reasoned, the Constitution did not and could not recognize slavery. Taking this astonishing argument a step further, Spooner insisted that the Constitution "denies the right of property in man; and that it, *of itself*, makes it impossible for slavery to have a legal existence in *any* of the United States."[81]

If Phillips and Garrison relied on historical evidence to depict the Constitution as a compromise with slavery, Spooner insisted that the words of the Constitution be given primacy over the intention of its drafters. This interpretive move enabled Spooner, following the argument made by Cole, to take advantage of the undoubted fact that the drafters of the Constitution had self-consciously avoided using the word "slavery." There was, at the time, no well-established debate over whether the Constitution should be interpreted according to its original meaning or by some other method. The abolitionists were pioneers in charting different paths of constitutional interpretation—as would be proslavery Southerners who came to rely on the original meaning of the Constitution to insist on their right to hold slaves.

BLACK ABOLITIONISTS DEBATE THE MEANING OF THE CONSTITUTION

As arguments over the Constitution escalated, African Americans took both sides. A fascinating debate on whether the Constitution should be understood as a proslavery or antislavery document played out on January 16, 1851, the second day of the sixth State Convention of the Colored Citizens of Ohio, held in Columbus. (The first Ohio convention had taken place in 1837; conventions of educated African American freemen had spread from Philadelphia in the 1830s to roughly a dozen states in the 1850s, and would continue for decades.)[82] Hezekiah Ford Douglas of Cuyahoga County, an abolitionist who had escaped enslavement at fifteen and would go on to command his own unit in the Civil War, opened the debate by proposing a resolution "that no colored man can consistently vote under the United States Constitution." His point was that it would be immoral for a free African American citizen to vote in a federal election, even where state law allowed it, as in Ohio and many other Northern states.

Douglas's logic began with history: "I hold, sir, that the Constitution of the United States is pro-slavery, considered so by those who framed it, and construed to that end ever since its adoption."[83] Moving to moral argument, Douglas discussed the provision prolonging the slave trade. Citing the fugitive slave clause and federal law enacted pursuant to it, he declared, "We are all, according to Congressional enactments, involved in the horrible system of human bondage."[84] To vote was to acknowledge the legitimacy of a constitutional order based on slavery; it followed for Douglas that it would be immoral for a free African American to exercise his franchise.

William Howard Day of Lorain County, a New York–born free African American and graduate of Oberlin College who would soon found and edit a weekly Cleveland newspaper called *The Aliened American*, rose in reply. Douglas's remarks contained an "error," Day argued, "namely, of making the *construction* of the Constitution of the United States, the same as the Constitution itself." There was, he acknowledged, "no dispute between us in regard to the proslavery action of this government, nor any doubt in our minds in regard to the aid which the Supreme Court of the United States has given to Slavery, and by their unjust and . . . illegal decisions; but *that* is not the Constitution—they are not that under which I vote." The Bible had been frequently misinterpreted, Day went on, but that should not lead anyone to abandon the Bible itself. It was "so in regard to the Constitution." When it came to voting, he said, "with judges' decisions we have nothing to do. Our business is with the Constitution."[85]

Day's distinction between the text and interpretation of that text—

and his comparison to the Bible—implied that the Constitution itself
should not be understood as proslavery, however it might be construed
in practice. He went on to make his vindication of the Constitution
explicit. If the Constitution stated that "it was framed to 'establish
justice,'" he said, "it, of course, is opposed to injustice; if it says plainly
[']no person shall be deprived of life, *liberty*, or property, without due
process of law,'—I suppose it means it, and I shall avail myself of the
benefit of it."[86] The text and language of the Constitution were what
mattered, not its historical origins or subsequent application. Day,
who would years later become an ordained minister of the African
Methodist Episcopal Church, was proposing that African Americans
should read the Constitution the way they should read the Bible: as
good Protestants, making its meaning relevant and liberatory for their
own lives.

This analysis led Day to a crescendo in which he confronted the
realities of slavery and racial discrimination while simultaneously explaining why he would use the Constitution as a weapon to fight them:

> Sir, coming up as I do, in the midst of three millions of
> men in chains, and five hundred thousands only half free,
> I consider every instrument precious which guarantees to
> me liberty. I consider the Constitution a foundation of
> American liberties, and wrapping myself in the flag of the
> nation, I would plant myself upon that Constitution, and
> using the weapons they have given me, I would appeal to
> the American people "for the rights thus guarantied."[87]

To this patriotic appeal, Douglas offered a powerful, dramatic riposte:

> The gentleman may wrap the Stars & Stripes of his country
> around him forty times, if possible, and with the Declara-
> tion of Independence in one hand, and the Constitution of

our common country in the other, may seat himself under
the shadow of the frowning monument of Bunker Hill,
and if the slave holder, under the Constitution, and with
the "Fugitive Bill," don't find you, then there don't exist a
Constitution.[88]

To Douglas, the systemic reality of slavery and oppression under the
Constitution trumped any possible appeal to constitutional ideals.

A practical compromise between Douglas and Day was then offered by Charles Henry Langston, himself one of the two first African
American Oberlin graduates, and (eventually) the grandfather of Har-
lem Renaissance poet Langston Hughes. Langston began by saying
that he "perfectly" agreed with Douglas "that the United States' Constitution is pro-slavery. It was made to foster and uphold that abominable,
vampirish and bloody system of American slavery." Langston observed
that members of the constitutional convention of 1787 "on returning to
their constituents, declared that Slavery was one of the interests sought
to be protected by the Constitution." The Constitution "was so understood and so administered all over the country."[89]

Yet, Langston continued, it did not follow from this historical and
ongoing reality that African Americans should not vote. "[W]hether the
Constitution is pro-slavery, and whether colored men 'can consistently
vote under the Constitution,' are two very distinct questions; and while I
would answer the former in the affirmative, I would not, like [Douglas],
answer the latter in the negative." He explained his position: "I would
vote under the United States Constitution on the same principle . . . that
I would call on every slave, from Maryland to Texas, to arise and assert
their *liberties*, and cut their masters' throats if they attempt again to reduce them to slavery." Voting was justified as an act of revolution. The
doctrine that "Resistance to Tyranny is obedience to God" was "equally
true in regard to colored men as white men." Langston concluded, "I
hope . . . that colored men will vote, or do anything else under the Con-

stitution, that will aid in effecting our liberties."[90] The complexity of the debate and the subtlety of the different positions taken demonstrate the contours of how history and morality were deployed among the abolitionists who held the highest stakes in it.

Frederick Douglass, ultimately the most important abolitionist of them all (no relation to the Ohio Douglas), began his career speaking and writing alongside Garrison, and for some years he shared the view of the Constitution as a morally bankrupt covenant with death. Over time, however, Douglass's close personal and professional ties to Garrison weakened—partly because Garrison did not want Douglass to found his own newspaper—and Douglass gradually moved away from Garrison's interpretation. In April 1850, Douglass wrote bluntly (and to my mind, accurately) that "Liberty and Slavery—opposite as heaven and hell—are both in the Constitution, and the oath to support the [Constitution] is an oath to perform that which God has made impossible." Douglass's insistence on the self-contradictory nature of the compromise Constitution was reminiscent of Grimké's observation more than a decade earlier that slavery contradicted the ideals of the preamble. The Constitution was, Douglass concluded, "at war with itself."[91]

This would turn out to be a transitional position for Douglass. In 1851, a few months after the debate at the African American convention in Ohio, the American Anti-Slavery Society officially resolved that all its members must subscribe to the Garrisonian position. Douglass balked. In his own newspaper, *The North Star*, he issued a statement headlined "Change of Opinion Announced." In it, Douglass declared that reading Lysander Spooner, as well as Gerrit Smith, who had become his chief financial supporter, had convinced him to alter his stance. He now believed that slavery "*never was lawful, and never can be made so.*"[92] He repeated the observation that the Constitution did not use the word "slavery." Douglass would go on to make the argument even more forcefully and famously for the next decade, until the war came. His move away from Garrison's rejection of the Constitution toward Gerrit Smith's engagement approach had now become a formal split from the American Anti-Slavery Society, which Garrison effectively still controlled.

Douglass's new view, descended from Cole via Spooner, did not convince all African American abolitionists, some of whom, still close to Garrison, continued to insist on the historical and ongoing realities of the Constitution as a compromise with slavery. Charles Lenox Remond had observed years before, "What if the word 'slave' is not in it? It does not matter to me nor mine. Slavery was in the understanding that framed it—Slavery is in the will that administers it."[93] Remond continued to hold this view even after Douglass had abandoned it in favor of an emphasis on the literal words of the Constitution.

Robert Purvis, one of the most important early Black abolitionists, also maintained Garrison's condemnation of the Constitution against Douglass. As Purvis put it in a speech, "[T]his talk about the Constitution being anti-slavery seems to me so utterly at variance with common sense and what we know to be facts that . . . I have no patience with it." Purvis said that he had "no particular objection" when white people, "who have little to feel on this subject . . . amuse themselves with such theories." But, he went on in harsh terms meant for Douglass, "when I see them imitated by colored men, I am disgusted! Sir, have we no self-respect? Are we to clank the chains that have been made for us, and praise the men who did the deed? . . . Are we such base, soulless, spiritless sycophants as all this?"[94] A newspaper reporting on another speech of Purvis's described him as giving "one of his characteristic ultra harangues." It paraphrased Purvis: "This government was the meanest and foulest despotism that ever existed. Washington and Jefferson were slave-drivers and thieves [whose] memory should be held in detestation. The Constitution was an accursed scroll, which he trampled underfoot." When the crowd hissed, Purvis simply continued speaking, the newspaper said: "The audience might hiss until the crack of doom for all the speaker cared, the founders of this country were man-thieves and murderers; he despised them and those who upheld them."[95]

But Douglass was joined by James McCune Smith, another important African American abolitionist. The debate came to a head in 1855 at the Colored National Convention held in Philadelphia. With Purvis pushing the view of the Constitution as proslavery and Smith urging Douglass's stance, the convention voted to proclaim that the Constitution should be read to reject slavery.[96] The pragmatic interest in depicting the abolitionist movement as pro-Constitution, not anti-Constitution, prevailed over the weight of historical evidence and the impulse to moral clarity and condemnation.

LINCOLN'S MAINSTREAM WHIG PRAGMATISM

Lincoln, for his part, remained for the time entirely outside (and perhaps barely aware of) these dueling radical abolitionist views of the Constitution, whether expressed by African Americans or whites. As a Whig, he accepted Clay's understanding of the Constitution as a compromise over slavery—and saw the compromise as desirable, not sinful. He would likely have been as quick to reject Garrison's condemnation of the Constitution as morally invalid as he would have been to deny Spooner's opinion that the Constitution outlawed slavery. Both views were profoundly outside the American mainstream. Lincoln, as a Clay Whig, was swimming in the very center of it.

Lincoln stepped down from the legislature in 1842. For the next four years, as he maneuvered to get himself into Congress, he focused on building his law practice. His formal political activity consisted of campaigning in 1844 for the unsuccessful Whig presidential candidate—Henry Clay himself. Lincoln "spent much time and labor" on that election, as he had on William Henry Harrison's successful campaign in 1840, he later said in his own campaign biography.[97] The speeches he gave were mostly focused on the Whigs' compromise position on tariffs.

In 1845, Lincoln sent a letter to Williamson Durley, an Illinois antislavery activist who belonged to Gerrit Smith's Liberty Party. That party had indirectly helped defeat Clay the previous year by taking votes away from him in the swing state of New York, where the Democrat James K. Polk had won narrowly. The letter argued that if their true goal was to limit the extension of slavery, Durley and other Liberty Party voters should have adopted a pragmatic compromise approach and voted for Clay.

Lincoln recognized that Liberty voters must have been motivated by the purist moral principle "We are not to do *evil* that *good* may come." But Lincoln disputed the applicability of the proposition: "If by your votes you could have prevented the *extention*, &c. of slavery, would it not have been *good* and not *evil* so to have used your votes, even though it involved the casting of them for a slaveholder?" In support of this pragmatic argument, Lincoln quoted the biblical touchstone of all pragmatic adages: "By the *fruit* the tree is to be known . . . If the fruit of electing Mr. Clay would have been to prevent the extension of slavery, could the act of electing have been *evil*?"[98] Clay had been president of the American Colonization Society, with its quixotic goal of resettling American Blacks in Africa. In the tradition of Madison, Clay embodied a profound internal tension: he was a slaveholder who thought slavery was wrong. This was not the only possible worldview in Clay's Kentucky. His cousin, Cassius Marcellus Clay, had become an active abolitionist after attending Yale College and hearing Garrison speak there. But Cassius Clay was an ideologue, while Henry Clay was a pragmatic gradualist—and in Lincoln's view, it would have been pragmatically wise for abolitionists to have supported Clay's pragmatism.

Having stated the pragmatist premise of knowing the tree by its fruits, Lincoln went on to apply it to the structure of the union under the Constitution: "I hold it to be a paramount duty of us in the free states, due to the Union of the states, and perhaps to liberty itself (paradox though it may seem) to let the slavery of the other states alone." Slavery must be let alone to preserve the union. And because the union preserved liberty, he was prepared to suggest the "paradox" that slavery should be preserved to serve liberty itself.[99] As he had in 1837, however, Lincoln also wanted to emphasize the wrongfulness of slavery and his opposition to its being extended to new territories. "[O]n the other hand, I hold it to be equally clear," he told the abolitionist Durley, "that we should never knowingly lend ourselves directly or indirectly, to prevent . . . slavery from dying a natural death—to find new places for it to live in, when it can no longer exist in the old."[100]

Taken together, the two statements captured the essence of Lincoln's Whig compromise position: the Constitution was a framework for preserving the union by protecting slavery where it existed; but that framework was compatible with limiting the extent of slavery so that it might somehow die a "natural death." The Whig fantasy that slavery would pass away on its own echoed the hopes of Madison and Jefferson, Clay's idols. It had been an unlikely if not inconceivable possibility before the cotton gin. By 1845, when Lincoln was still repeating it, it was logically indefensible. Yet it remained part of Lincoln's compromise picture for the preservation of the Constitution, and with it, the union.

Two

THE BREAKING
CONSTITUTION

WAR AND REVOLUTION

More than any other event until Southern secession, the Mexican-American War of 1846–48 revealed that Clay and Lincoln's Whig compromise Constitution was in danger of collapse. In their view, the compromise over slavery had always been and remained necessary to preserve the union; and they understood that the union was being used as a tool to facilitate national expansion. The war, to them, reversed the logical order. To Whigs, the Mexican-American War was a case of expanding the union for the specific goal of extending slavery. Whigs did not oppose expansion per se. They objected to expansion that was designed to acquire more slave territory and entrench the institution of slavery more deeply in the structure of the union.

From the standpoint of geopolitics, the war itself was a fairly straightforward piece of imperial expansion. In 1845, the United States had annexed Texas, which nine years before had declared itself to be a republic independent of Mexico. Texas's independence rested on the strength of the collective will of its relatively small number of Anglo inhabitants and their successful resistance to General Antonio López de Santa Anna.

No American seriously disputed that the Republic of Texas could agree to be annexed by the United States. No one realistically doubted that when Texas ultimately became a state, it would be admitted to the union as a slave state—and paired with Oregon to maintain the slave/free balance in the Senate. At issue was what would happen to Mexican territory beyond Texas that the United States might conquer and annex in the war. Whigs understood the war as a pretext to acquire this territory and organize it into slave states. In their view, the benefits of expansion generally were exceeded by the costs of expansion aimed at increasing the slave interest.

President James K. Polk, sworn into office in 1845, acted as presidents before him, including Madison and Monroe, had done when acquiring new territory: he created a casus belli—an event taken as a justification for war—by asserting control over the maximum amount of land that could conceivably be claimed. The Republic of Texas claimed title to land extending all the way to what Americans called the Rio Grande and Mexicans called the Rio Bravo. Polk asserted U.S. sovereignty over all that Texas claimed as its own. Mexico, for its part, insisted that the territory of Texas extended only as far as the Nueces River, which reaches the Gulf of Mexico near what is today Corpus Christi.

The difference between the extent of the two claims was considerable, amounting to a large wedge of land between the two rivers and the gulf. Only force would resolve the controversy. Under the Constitution, Polk could have gone to Congress and asked for a declaration of war. But Polk knew that he would be unlikely to get such a declaration from a Congress wary of touching a subject that could only lead to controversy between the Northern and Southern states. The best strategy available to him was to provoke Mexico into attacking U.S. troops, then maintain that his inherent authority as commander in chief enabled him to fight back, even without a formal declaration of war from Congress.

Accordingly, Polk sent General Zachary Taylor into the disputed area with a force of 3,500 men. The challenge to Mexican sovereignty was obvious and could not go unmet. Santa Anna sent a force of 2,000. In April 1846, in the first encounter between the two sides, known as the Thornton affair, Santa Anna's cavalry routed a small U.S. reconnaissance patrol, killing eleven of them. The Mexican army then laid siege to "Fort Texas," an earthwork fortification built by Taylor's troops on the north bank of the Rio Grande. Taylor moved to relieve the siege. Two significant battles followed, featuring cavalry charges, light artillery, and hand-to-hand combat. The U.S. forces emerged with the advantage.

War had begun in earnest—and that changed the political situation in Washington. Although Whigs still opposed the war because they opposed the extension of slavery, they also did not want to expose themselves to the charge of failing to support U.S. troops who were already in combat. On May 13, 1846, Congress declared war on Mexico. Just two senators and fourteen congressmen voted no.

Lincoln was elected to Congress as a Whig for a single term in November 1846—the only national office he would hold until the presidency. Under the rules of the House as they then existed, he did not take his seat in Congress until December 1847. "All the battles of the Mexican war had been fought . . . ," as Lincoln would later note in his campaign autobiography, "but the American army was still in Mexico, and the treaty of peace was not fully and formally ratified."[1] In September 1847, General Winfield Scott and the U.S. Army had taken Mexico City. The final peace treaty would be signed in February 1848.

Lincoln's precise qualification of the chronology of his congressional term and the progress of the war was not happenstance. Running for president in 1860, Lincoln well knew that his record on the Mexican-American War subjected him to potentially significant criticism. The source of the danger was that, while in Congress, Lincoln had unrelentingly criticized Polk and the war's aims. That made him vulnerable to the claim that he had undermined the war effort while U.S. troops were in harm's way. Lincoln had understood the political risk at the time. The risk was realized when he ran for president years later.

The centerpiece of Lincoln's critique of the Mexican-American War, both while in Congress and fifteen years on, was the twofold claim that the war was unnecessary and that Polk had started it unconstitutionally. Lincoln broached this position in December 1847, just after taking his seat, by introducing a series of eight resolutions to Congress in the form of demands for Polk to answer a series of questions about the first moments of violence between Mexican and American troops, to which Polk had referred in asking Congress to declare war. They focused on "the spot of soil on which the blood of our *citizens* was shed." Lincoln demanded to know all about the history of who had governed that "spot"—a spot, he implied, that was not within the territory actually controlled by the Republic of Texas.[2]

Congress did not take any action on Lincoln's proposed "spot" resolutions, nor is there evidence to suggest that anyone then paid much attention to the first-term congressman's demands. Lincoln offered a lengthier and more detailed exposition of his position in a speech in Congress on the topic in January 1848, a bit more than a month later. The speech matters because it shows Lincoln grappling not only with the war's supposed violation of the constitutional compromise but also with the deep underlying questions of when and how a president could justifiably take up arms without congressional preapproval. Like other Whigs, Lincoln was trying to mount a critique of the Democratic incumbent in an election year. But he was also trying to make a name for himself in what he knew might be a short congressional career. Opining on the major constitutional issue of the day from a Whig perspective would be a way to earn national attention.

The occasion for the speech was discussion of a Whig resolution asserting that the war had been "unnecessarily and unconstitutionally commenced by the President." Lincoln began by explaining that his view since the beginning of the war had been that the right course for anyone who believed the war had been wrongly begun was to "remain silent on that point" until the war was over. He was speaking now, he said, only because Polk was trying to transform every vote to supply the troops "into an endorsement of the justice and wisdom of his conduct."[3]

Lincoln went on to assert that Polk had lied when he said that the war had begun on American soil. He made the case that Polk had "sent the army into the midst of a settlement of Mexican people, who had never submitted, by consent or by force, to the authority of Texas or of the United States, and that *there*, and *thereby*, the first blood of the war was shed."[4] Lincoln intended to show that Polk had overstepped the constitutional bounds of the presidency to provoke a war that was meant to extend slave territory.

To make his argument, Lincoln offered an explanation of how the Republic of Texas had come to exercise control over any territory at all. A more experienced politician might have held back from offering a grand theory of sovereignty and self-government in the course of what was essentially a political speech. But the self-taught Lincoln, who had gained his legal qualifications while in the Illinois state legislature and had been building his legal career ever since, was drawn to the opportunity.

In Lincoln's account, Texas's claim to territory—and hence the claims of the United States, which had annexed Texas—depended not on a treaty, "but on revolution." He explained what he meant:

> Any people anywhere, being inclined and having the power, have the *right* to rise up, and shake off the existing government, and form a new one that suits them better. This is a most valuable, a most sacred right—a right, which we hope and believe, is to liberate the world.[5]

Lincoln was speaking of the white Texans who had risen up against Mexico and declared independence. His listeners would all have understood perfectly that the Texans' actions paralleled those of the colonial Americans who had declared independence from Great Britain. That was what made the right "sacred": it applied to anyone living anywhere. It would "liberate the world" insofar as people around the globe might themselves throw off the yoke of tyranny. And it foreshadowed, unintentionally to be sure, an argument that would be made in favor of the legitimacy of Southern secession.

So far, Lincoln's analysis was entirely conventional. Yet he went on to add details that were to a degree original. The right to revolution, he explained, could not be "confined to cases in which the whole people of an existing government may choose to exercise it." Revolution could be made by a part of the population:

> Any portion of such people that *can*, *may* revolutionize, and make their *own*, of so much of the territory as they inhabit. More than this, a *majority* of any portion of such people may revolutionize, putting down a *minority*, intermingled with, or near about them, who may oppose their movement.[6]

Revolutions could not be analyzed in purely legalistic terms, Lincoln further explained: "It is a quality of revolutions not to go by *old* lines, or *old* laws; but to break up both, and make new ones." The only limit on the territorial claims of a revolutionary body was that those who made the revolution must actually control territory that they claimed. The Republic of Texas could claim to own only those areas that had actually been subjected to revolutionary control. "In my view," he concluded, "just so far as [Texas] carried her revolution, by obtaining the *actual*, willing or unwilling, submission of the people, *so far*, the country was hers, and no farther."[7] Lincoln was treating revolution as a form of absolute rupture in the political fabric, rupture that permitted a basic transformation in who governed, and how. At the same time, he was insisting that the rupture model applied only where revolution had in fact been accomplished. He could thus embrace the Texans' declaration of independence while still rejecting a war fought by the United States to take territory that was not subject to the Texans' revolution. One could defend the Texan Declaration of Independence, but the war the United States was allegedly fighting on Texas's behalf was another matter.

With respect to that conflict, Lincoln was making the point that Texas did not in fact control the spot where Mexican and U.S. troops had clashed—and that Polk had therefore provoked a war illegitimately. Lincoln again challenged Polk to prove otherwise. "But if he *can* not, or *will* not do this . . . ," Lincoln went on, "then I shall be fully convinced . . . that he is deeply conscious of being in the wrong— that he feels the blood of this war, like the blood of Abel, is crying to Heaven against him."[8] The biblical allusion led directly to Lincoln's accusation: Polk "ordered General Taylor into the midst of a peaceful Mexican settlement, purposely to bring on a war."[9] Polk had "some strong motive" to do so, Lincoln insisted—one "I will not stop now to give my opinion concerning."[10] The motive, Lincoln implied, was conquest of Mexican territory, perhaps wrong in itself and certainly wrong insofar as it was motivated by the wish to extend slavery. That, for Lincoln, was what made the wrong so awful that it cried out to heaven.

In broader terms, Lincoln was articulating a theory of how sovereign political power could be justifiably destroyed, created, and extended. He was embracing a universal human right to revolution. Such a revolution transcended and broke legal and political borders and boundaries. It did not follow "old lines" or "old laws"; it formed new ones. Once released, the power of revolutionary government could be imposed on everyone proximate—whether they consented or not. The fact of submission, not respect for procedural niceties, was what mattered for determining the legitimacy of a functioning government. This account of the right to revolution would pose a conceptual challenge when Lincoln, as president, had to confront Southern secession.

CRISIS AND COMPROMISE

When Lincoln gave his speech on January 12, 1848, the negotiation of the treaty to end the war was nearing completion. In the Treaty of Guadalupe Hidalgo, signed February 2, the United States, then occupying Mexico City, promised to pay Mexico the token sum of $15 million in exchange for the Mexican provinces of Nuevo México and Alta California. The war had gained the United States a vast new territory of some 525,000 square miles. With that new territory came the certainty of new states eventually being formed—and from the war's inception, Whigs had feared that Polk would seek to admit the new territories to the United States as slave states.

It was essentially inevitable that a struggle over the character of the states to be formed from Mexican territory would precipitate a national political crisis. Since the Missouri Compromise, new states had been admitted in pairs of slave and free states, preserving the balance of the Senate. The Missouri Compromise had come to function as a quasi-constitutional guarantee that North and South would have equal Senate representation. That was not the framers' design, to be sure. But the Senate had after all been composed as a compromise to guarantee parity between small and large states. So in a sense it was a natural evolution for the institution to function as the compromise guarantor of parity between regions of the country.*

---

* Even after the Civil War and the passage of the Reconstruction amendments, the Senate would remain the quasi-constitutional site of sectional compromise over race until the Civil Rights Act of 1964. To the question "Why the Senate?" the answer surely is "Because it was born in compromise."

Until the acquisition of the new Mexican territories, it had been possible to predict and manage the accession of new states in this pairwise fashion. The new territories upended those predictions. All of Nuevo México and much of Alta California were beneath the 36°30' line specified in the Missouri Compromise, meaning that, in principle, states organized in them should be admitted as slave states. Such a development, at such a scale, would upset the balance in the Senate. Yet admitting new states carved out of the territories as free states would violate the terms of the Missouri Compromise.

The struggle might have taken many years to ripen. In the past it had taken decades—sometimes nearly half a century—for newly acquired territories to become organized as states. But on January 24, 1848, just twelve days after Lincoln's speech, gold was discovered near Sutter's Mill in what was then still Alta California. The gold rush that followed brought thousands of white settlers to California much faster than could otherwise have been anticipated. Meanwhile, as Texans sought to claim the province of Nuevo México as part of Texas, white settlers there hastened to organize themselves into a territorial government to seek separate statehood. The conflict could not be delayed.

The nature of the conflict was affected by the presidential election of 1848, which took place while Lincoln was in the House. Polk had promised to serve only one term and did not run again. To replace him, the Democrats nominated Lewis Cass, the Michigan senator who had been secretary of war under Jackson and, before that, the governor of the Michigan Territory. The Democrats called their candidate "General Cass" on the strength of his appointment to that rank in the War of 1812—and because they hoped to counteract the appeal of the Whig candidate, General Zachary Taylor, the hero of the Mexican-American War.

Taylor became the Whig candidate not because he was known to be a Whig, but because he was willing to accept the nomination. Clay, who lost a son in the war, would have liked to have been nominated.

But his public stance against the ultimately successful war made it seem likely that he would lose. It did not help that Clay had been defeated in three previous presidential elections or that he was seventy-one, considered very old for the presidency, given life expectancies of the era.

Voters understood that the future of the newly acquired territories was the major issue in the election. Yet Taylor managed to avoid taking a public stand on it. Lincoln, speaking in the House in support of Taylor, reflected the ambiguity in a speech in which he considered Taylor's position on the all-important Wilmot Proviso—a proposed piece of legislation first introduced in 1846 by the otherwise obscure Pennsylvania Democrat David Wilmot. The Wilmot Proviso stated explicitly that slavery would never be extended to territories acquired in the Mexican-American War, including California and New Mexico (the Republic of Texas had already been annexed before the war began). The House had passed the proviso when Wilmot introduced it, but the Senate blocked it. Although proposed by a Democrat, the proviso stood as the Whig fallback position now that the war was won and the territory acquired.

"I admit," Lincoln said on the floor of the House on July 27, 1848, "I do not certainly know what [Taylor] would do on the Wilmot Proviso." He was himself, Lincoln said, "a Northern man, or rather, a Western free state man," and so was "against the extension of slavery." On that basis, Lincoln explained, "with what information I have, I hope and *believe*, Gen. Taylor, if elected, would not veto the Proviso." That was only a wish, not a fact, Lincoln made clear: "I do not *know* it."[11]

Lincoln was echoing the nuanced Whig position, which was that Taylor was the Whig candidate despite his having taken no position on whether slavery could be introduced in any of the newly acquired territories. Lincoln went on to say that if he knew for a fact that Taylor would veto the Wilmot Proviso, and allow the extension of slavery into some of the new territory, he "still would vote for him." Taylor was preferable to Cass, Lincoln explained, "because, *should* slavery thereby go to the territory we now have, just so much will certainly happen by the election of Cass; and, in addition, a course of policy, leading to new wars, new acquisitions of territory and still further extensions of slavery."[12] Lincoln was not opposing the acquisition of new territory so much as its acquisition for purposes of extending slavery.

In the end, Lincoln's pragmatic view was that Taylor at his worst would be better than Cass at his best. "One of the two is to be President; which is preferable?"[13] Lincoln was certainly speaking as a Whig loyalist, supporting his candidate's preferred strategy. But the content of the strategy—like the choice of Taylor—reflected the core Whig philosophy that Lincoln shared: the philosophy that treated the Constitution as a mechanism of compromise. Electing Taylor would help preserve the union. Even if electing Taylor extended slavery, that extension could be justified because it would help reduce the probability of further extensions.

Taylor's ambiguity strategy worked, and he defeated Cass. He took office just as Lincoln was ending his sole term in Congress. Lincoln had been elected as part of an agreement among three Whigs that they would alternate as candidates, and he did not return home to seek the nomination. That said, it seems probable he would have lost even had he tried to run for reelection. The Democrat Cass carried Illinois, and Lincoln's Whig colleague lost in his congressional race in Lincoln's district.

Lincoln stayed in Congress until the bitter end of his term—7:00 a.m. on March 4, 1849, just hours before the new Congress would convene. The night was spent fighting over a bill that would have retained Mexican law in the new territories, including the Mexican law that barred slavery. The Congress that Lincoln left was in disarray. No Speaker of the House could be elected for three weeks. Deadlock was the order of the day.

As president, Taylor aimed to resolve the crisis by applying the substance of the Wilmot Proviso without it ever being adopted. His preferred course of action was for California and New Mexico to organize conventions for themselves, propose constitutions that banned slavery, and seek admission to the union on those terms. This approach was supposed to avoid any congressional opportunity to debate whether slavery would be introduced in the new states. The decision would be made at the state level—and it would be a decision against slavery. What made Taylor's approach realistic was that neither California nor New Mexico had a climate suitable for cotton, and neither had had legal slavery while under Mexican control. As a consequence, those who lived there had no strong economic or ideological interest in the introduction of slavery.

Taylor was successful in getting conventions going in both places. But the problem was not in California or New Mexico, but in Washington, D.C. The House and Senate would have to approve the admission of new states. Southern senators were not ready to allow California or New Mexico to enter as free states, breaking parity in the Senate, without significant concessions.

Enter Henry Clay. Clay's appearance at this critical juncture was almost that of a deus ex machina straightening out a convoluted stage plot. The Great Compromiser had left the Senate in 1842, planning to run for president from his plantation home, as his models Jefferson and Madison had both done. But he had lost the presidential race in 1844 and been passed over for the Whig nomination in 1848. Bitter about the selection of Taylor by the party he himself had founded, Clay declined to campaign for the nominee and had no prospect or intention of joining Taylor's cabinet. But he agreed to return to the Senate— perhaps sensing that the emerging national crisis would give him an opportunity for a third magnificent attempt at national reconciliation, thirty years after his first one had made his name as a statesman.

Clay waited until Taylor formally announced his preferred, state-based solution, in his State of the Union message in December 1849. Then, in January 1850, Clay introduced his own eight-part grand bargain. In structure it resembled the Missouri Compromise. It gave something to each side, finessed the logical incompatibility of proslavery and antislavery positions, and brought together apparently unconnected national issues in order to resolve them all.

Clay's proposed compromise was more favorable to the South than Taylor's. In brief, Clay suggested admitting California as a free state while organizing New Mexico (along with Utah) as a territory, not a state. Congress would not ban slavery in the District of Columbia, as some Northerners had been urging, but would instead bar the slave trade there. That would remove the embarrassing spectacle of slaves being bought and sold in the shadow of the Capitol; it also echoed the sentiment of the framers' generation, which considered the slave trade barbarous even as it found room for slavery itself. And to assuage Southerners' protest about the acceptance of a free state partly below the 36°30' line, Clay introduced a much-strengthened fugitive slave law. Northern states would have to acquiesce in the principle of enslaved people as property by returning escaped slaves to servitude.

It took most of 1850 for the compromise to become law. Taylor's opposition might have sunk it; but Taylor died and was succeeded by Millard Fillmore, his vice president. Fillmore fired Taylor's entire cabinet, and endorsed Clay's plan. However, even Fillmore's support was not enough to bring the opposing sides together. In late summer, frustrated with his apparent failure, Clay himself became ill with tuberculosis and had to leave Washington to convalesce in Newport, Rhode Island. Senator Stephen Douglas of Illinois then took up the task, shepherding the compromise through the Senate.

Douglas had presidential ambitions. He knew that effecting the compromise would make him a major national figure in the tradition of Clay—and that it would make him popular among pro-union moderates in the South. As finally agreed, the compromise also required adjudication of the borders of Texas, which among other things included setting the northern border of the state at 36°30'. Clay-inspired compromise had, it seemed, prevailed, albeit this time brought to fruition by Douglas.

Lincoln supported and celebrated the Compromise of 1850, depicting it not as Douglas's first national success, but as Clay's last accomplishment. When Clay died of tuberculosis in 1852, Lincoln eulogized him as "*the* man for a crisis." In the recent case of "our territory newly acquired of Mexico," as in 1819 and 1833, "the task of devising a mode of adjustment, seems to have been cast upon Mr. Clay, by common consent." And Clay had succeeded: "[H]is performance of the task, in each case, was little else than a literal fulfilment of the public expectation."[14] Lincoln made it clear that by preserving the union through compromise, Clay had made the United States what it was: "Our country is prosperous and powerful; but could it have been quite all it has been, and is, and is to be, without Henry Clay? Such a man the times have demanded, and such, in the providence of God was given us."[15]

Lincoln's position was not the only one possible, even among those who supported the new compromise. One view with important implications for the Constitution was expressed in a major speech by Daniel Webster, the same senator who, twenty years before, had laid out the case for the inherent worth of the union while emphasizing its necessity for continental expansion. In this, his last great Senate speech, titled "The Constitution and the Union," Webster threw himself behind Clay's compromise by offering a full-throated defense of the obligation to respect the fugitive slave clause—because of an "obligation" to follow the Constitution "as a question of morals and a question of conscience." Those who opposed the return of escaped slaves had no right to do so: "None at all—none at all. Neither in the forum of conscience, nor before the face of the Constitution, are they justified, in my opinion." Abolitionists were "very honest good people, misled, as I think, by strange enthusiasm."[16]

In Webster's account, the constitutional bargain of 1787 had first been struck by people on two sides who at the time agreed that slavery was a "moral wrong." Since then, opinions had "greatly changed," so that Southerners now embraced slavery as a "cherished institution" while Northerners viewed it with distaste. But the duty to uphold the original compromise was now driven by a moral obligation to uphold the union. "I hold the idea of the separation of these states . . . as a moral impossibility," Webster intoned.[17] Morality dictated that the Constitution be upheld—and slavery preserved. The speech was hailed by Southerners and Northern moderates as an act of statesmanship. Opponents of slavery considered it a betrayal. By making the continuation of compromise into a moral duty, Webster went much further than Lincoln did, then or ever.

Another pole of possible opinion expressed in the Senate came from William Seward of New York. As Webster was leaving the Senate, Seward, a Whig, was just arriving. His address, delivered four days after Webster's, was his maiden speech before the body. It was intended to accept the existence of past compromises while refusing the legitimacy of any future compromise over slavery—and insisting that California must remain a free state. "I AM OPPOSED TO ANY SUCH COMPROMISE, IN ANY AND ALL THE FORMS IN WHICH IT HAS BEEN PROPOSED, because . . . I think all legislative compromises radically wrong and essentially vicious," Seward maintained, against the received wisdom of Clay's Whig Party. A compromise over slavery would amount to the exchange of "some portion of liberty—some portion of human rights in one region, for liberty in another region."

Turning to the Constitution, Seward asserted "that the Constitution does not recognize property in man, but leaves that question, as between the states, to the law of nature and nations." He certainly did not claim, like Spooner, that the Constitution outlawed slavery. He did, however, say that slavery was "temporary, accidental, partial, and incongruous," while freedom was "perpetual, organic, universal" and "in harmony with the Constitution of the United States."

Seward acknowledged that the Constitution "regulates our stewardship" of newly acquired territory and "devotes the domain to union, to justice, to defence, to welfare, and to liberty." Then, in the passage that made the speech famous, he went on:

> But there is a higher law than the Constitution, which
> regulates our authority over the domain, and devotes it to
> the same noble purposes. The territory is a part . . . of the
> common heritage of mankind, bestowed upon them by
> the Creator of the universe. We are his stewards, and must
> so discharge our trust as to secure to the highest attainable
> degree, their happiness.[18]

By referring to a "higher law," one above the Constitution, Seward indirectly repudiated Webster's argument that the moral duty to obey the Constitution itself demanded compromise with slavery. And Seward hinted at the logical possibility that the Constitution itself might be immoral if applied so as to extend slavery to new territories.

Seward invoked "the Creator" as the source of the moral law. Yet he did not pit religious morality against the Constitution, as some abolitionists did. Read carefully, Seward's speech said only that the duty to God, which was higher than the Constitution, dictated the same result: the preservation of the new territories as free. But coming from a U.S. senator—not a radical, outlying abolitionist figure like Purvis or Garrison—the words were enough to open a vista of moral criticism of the Constitution. Printers produced a hundred thousand pamphlets containing the speech, and newspapers circulated perhaps another hundred thousand copies. Seward would always deny that the speech was intended to undercut the authority of the Constitution. The speech made him famous nonetheless, and started him on the course that would lead to his becoming Lincoln's secretary of state.

CLINGING TO COMPROMISE

After leaving Congress in 1849, Lincoln spent most of the next five years out of politics, building his legal practice in Springfield and across Illinois. During that time, his views on national political issues, including slavery, did not change appreciably. He remained squarely within the mainstream of Whig beliefs, continuing to oppose the expansion of slavery while rejecting the path of abolitionism. Illinois Whigs like Lincoln rejected slavery for multiple, overlapping reasons. They believed that slavery contradicted the right of all humans to control their own labor and to rise as a result—the "free labor" view Lincoln would eventually express publicly in a speech a decade later.[19] Its expansion therefore interfered with opportunities for free white laborers and enhanced the antidemocratic power of an aristocratic class of rich planters. White Illinois Whigs did not, however, feel any special solicitude for Black people, with whom they often had little contact. Although many Whigs in the Illinois legislature voted against the Black Exclusion Law in 1853, the law passed easily anyway.[20] Lincoln himself maintained an assiduous silence on what was a major issue in state politics at the time. Belief in white racial superiority or supremacy was compatible with opposition to the expansion of slavery.

Lincoln also remained committed to maintaining the compromise with slavery on which the union was based. His 1852 eulogy of Clay praised the father of the Missouri Compromise as still the guiding light for how national politics should be conducted. To Lincoln, the Compromise of 1850 essentially reaffirmed the Missouri Compromise. He described it carefully, and positively, in an important speech he gave in Peoria in 1854—the speech that heralded his return to political life:

> The south got their new fugitive-slave law; and the North got California, (the far best part of our acquisition from Mexico,) as a free State. The south got a provision that New Mexico and Utah, *when admitted as States*, may come in *with* or *without* slavery as they may then choose; and the north got the slave-trade abolished in the District of Columbia. The north got the western boundary of Texas, thence further back eastward than the south desired; but, in turn, they gave Texas ten millions of dollars, with which to pay her old debts. This is the Compromise of 1850.[21]

None of this altered the Missouri Compromise, Lincoln insisted. Responsibility for that momentous change Lincoln laid at the feet of Douglas, who in 1853, pursuing his ambition to become the Democratic candidate for president, had introduced legislation to break the Nebraska Territory into two parts, Kansas and Nebraska. In January 1854, Douglas had added an amendment declaring the Missouri Compromise inoperative and void, thus allowing Kansans (and in theory Nebraskans) to enact slavery in their territory should they wish to do so—even though most of Kansas and all of Nebraska lay above the 36°30' line. The legislation embodied for the first time the position that Douglas had held for some years: namely, that white residents of any federal territory should have the right of "popular sovereignty" to determine whether they wanted slavery in the states they would form. Douglas insisted that this principle was not inconsistent with the Compromise of 1850, which he had helped enact. He presented popular sovereignty over whether to introduce slavery in newly forming states as itself a compromise position. In any case, it was certain to boost his popularity in the South, which he needed to make a presidential run.

As a result, when Congress passed the Kansas-Nebraska Act, Clay's first great compromise came to an end. And despite Douglas's claims to the contrary, Clay's last compromise was similarly repudiated insofar as the crisis that ensued would not be resolved in the six years leading to the Civil War. Lincoln denounced Douglas's repeal—and the principle of popular sovereignty on which it was based—as an opening to the active spread of slavery: "I think, and shall try to show," he intoned, "that it is wrong; wrong in its direct effect, letting slavery into Kansas and Nebraska—and wrong in its prospective principle, allowing it to spread to every other part of the wide world, where men can be found inclined to take it."[22]

In the speech, Lincoln's goal was to argue for a return to his version of the principle of compromise—compromise that had been embedded in the Constitution. He described the compromise Constitution in tones so frank they were genuinely harsh: "[T]here are constitutional relations between the slave and free States," he told the Peoria audience, "which are degrading to the latter." The Constitution's first "degrading" provision was the fugitive slave clause: "We are under legal obligations to catch and return their runaway slaves to them—a sort of dirty, disagreeable job, which I believe, as a general rule the slaveholders will not perform for one another."[23]

Lincoln then turned to the three-fifths compromise. "[I]n the control of the government—the management of the partnership affairs—they have greatly the advantage of us," he told the free citizens of Illinois.[24] Reviewing the large numbers of slaves that gave Southern states greater representation per voter than Northern states, he explained:

> Thus each white man in South Carolina is . . . more than the double of any one of us in this crowd. The same advantage . . . is held by all the citizens of the slave States, over those of the free; and it is an absolute truth, without an

exception, that there is no voter in any slave State, but who
has more legal power in the government, than any voter in
any free State.[25]

Lincoln made it clear that the constitutional compromise was
"manifestly unfair." But as he also made clear, such unfairness was an
accepted part of the Constitution: "I do not mention it to complain
of it, in so far as it is already settled. It is in the constitution."[26] For
Lincoln, there was nothing inherently shocking about saying that the
Constitution was both unfair and also settled. The Constitution was a
compromise. Compromises often involve unfairness. And the mark of
a successful compromise is precisely that it becomes settled—agreed
upon and accepted by all the parties.

The "settled" nature of the compromise was, for Lincoln, the primary reason to maintain it despite its unfairness. "I do not, for that
cause [namely, its unfairness], or any other cause, propose to destroy, or
alter, or disregard the constitution," Lincoln said. "I stand to it, fairly,
fully, and firmly."[27]

Here was Lincoln's declaration of constitutional faith, stated in 1854
and summing up his whole career as a Whig up to that point in his
political life. The Constitution must not be destroyed, altered, or disregarded. It must be preserved and followed. Lincoln committed himself to following the Constitution "fairly"—even if its compromise was
unfair—"fully"—not partially—and "firmly"—not waveringly.

The speech was not quite finished. Having expressed his total commitment to the compromise Constitution, Lincoln concluded by clarifying that the Missouri Compromise, reaffirmed by the Compromise
of 1850, had become part of the constitutional structure. "The nation,"
he claimed, "was looking to the forming of new bonds of Union; and
a long course of peace and prosperity seemed to lie before us."[28] The
phrase "new bonds of Union" referred to the renewal of the constitutional arrangement in which compromise over slavery guaranteed

the union's continued existence. It was only the Kansas-Nebraska Act, Lincoln argued, that had revived the struggle between slavery and freedom, which threatened to upend the compromise and, with it, the union itself.

Lincoln's solution was remarkably straightforward: "The Missouri Compromise ought to be restored. For the sake of the Union, it ought to be restored. We ought to elect a House of Representatives which will vote its restoration." A compromise formula existed—and the only way to return to it was to reenact it officially. What would happen if the country failed to do so? He answered:

> [W]e shall have repudiated—discarded from the councils of the Nation—the SPIRIT of COMPROMISE; for who after this will ever trust in a national compromise? The spirit of mutual concession—that spirit which first gave us the constitution, and which has thrice saved the Union—we shall have strangled and cast from us forever.[29]

Again, Lincoln expressed his constitutional vision with breathtaking clarity. The "SPIRIT of COMPROMISE"—written in capital letters to capture Lincoln's emphasis—was nothing less than the animating spirit of the union itself.

The spirit of compromise "gave us the constitution" in 1787. The same spirit had saved the union in Clay's three great moments: the Missouri Compromise of 1820, the compromise tariff that ended the nullification crisis of 1832, and the Compromise of 1850. It was now in danger of being lost. "But restore the compromise, and what then?" Lincoln asked. "We thereby restore the national faith, the national confidence, the national feeling of brotherhood. We thereby reinstate the spirit of concession and compromise—that spirit which has never failed us in past perils, and which may be safely trusted for all the future."[30]

TOWARD REPUBLICANISM

The Peoria speech would be Lincoln's last major articulation of the Whig position on compromise—a constitutional understanding that traced through Henry Clay back to the founders themselves. A month after giving it, in November 1854, Lincoln got himself reelected to the Illinois state legislature, then almost immediately withdrew from office and presented himself to that body as the Whig candidate for the Senate. In February 1855, he lost to the Democrat Lyman Trumbull. The Whig Party itself was in collapse—a collapse that perfectly instantiated the failure of the party's compromise vision. Clay had died in the summer of 1852. Webster, whose speech in favor of the Compromise of 1850 had alienated many of his erstwhile New England admirers, died that autumn. Its revered compromisers gone, the Whig Party lost its Southern supporters, who favored Douglas's Kansas-Nebraska Act, to the Democrats. Whigs in the North looked elsewhere—to the newly founded Republican Party.

Lincoln took his time joining the Republicans. Nearly a year and a half passed between his unsuccessful Senate bid and May 29, 1856, when he gave a major speech to the Anti-Nebraska Convention held in Bloomington, Illinois—the convention that essentially inaugurated the Republican Party in the state. This was Lincoln's famous "lost speech," of which no reliable text remains. The loss may be because Lincoln's speeches at the time were not typically written down verbatim; because supporters feared its antislavery tone might harm the new party; or just possibly because, as legend has it, reporters in attendance were so mesmerized by the oratory that they stopped taking notes.[31]

During his journey to Republicanism, Lincoln began to take a stronger antislavery line than he had before. But his commitment to the Constitution as a compromise did not waver—even with regard to the constitutional obligation to return fugitive slaves to their masters. In his August 1855 letter to his friend Joshua Speed, a slaveholder,

Lincoln insisted, "I . . . acknowledge *your* rights and *my* obligations, under the constitution, in regard to your slaves."[32]

Lincoln's rhetorical reason for describing himself as morally troubled by slavery was to tell Speed that Northerners were paying a price in accepting the compromise Constitution. "It is hardly fair for you to assume," he wrote, "that I have no interest in a thing which has, and continually exercises, the power of making me miserable." The fact that he and other Northerners considered slavery morally wrong— yet accepted the practice under the Constitution—was meant as proof of their good faith: "You ought rather to appreciate how much the great body of the Northern people do crucify their feelings, in order to maintain their loyalty to the Constitution and the Union."[33]

It is worth pausing to notice how self-undercutting Lincoln's formulation was. Northerners opposed to slavery could only maintain loyalty to the Constitution and the union if they were prepared to "crucify" their feelings against slavery. Yet Lincoln was not saying that it was wrong for Northerners to sacrifice their moral beliefs. To the contrary, he was *praising* his own and others' sacrifice of their antislavery sentiments in order to emphasize his commitment to the structure of compromise.

This was almost the polar opposite of the Garrisonian abolitionists' moral condemnation of the Constitution or even the "higher law" theory articulated by Seward in his 1850 Senate speech. According to both of these approaches, moral duty superseded constitutional duty. The Constitution was a species of law, but morality dictated a law higher still. Slavery was a moral wrong, and so it was wrong to maintain a constitutional compromise on slavery. According to Lincoln, in contrast, loyalty to the Constitution demanded subordinating one's moral instincts to the necessity of compromise. Compromising one's moral principles was the price of union.

In his letter to Speed, Lincoln was for the first time expressly naming a conflict between morality and constitutional duty. Consciously or otherwise, he was moving toward a recognition of the impossibility of the compromise on which the Constitution rested. This was an emerging internal crisis that was being driven by external political developments. Webster's idea that there was a moral duty to enforce the slavery compromise could not be defended if slavery itself was acknowledged as a moral outrage. The "spirit of compromise" that Lincoln had so praised the year before in his Peoria speech was passing away. The death of the Whig Party, the party of compromise, demanded that Lincoln figure out where he now belonged politically.

Lincoln was honest with his old friend Speed about his transitional confusion. "You enquire where I now stand," he wrote. "That is a disputed point. I think I am a whig; but others say there are no whigs, and that I am an abolitionist."[34] Lincoln had never in the past merely "thought" he was a Whig. He had been a Whig politician for twenty years. His new uncertainty resulted from the disappearance of the party in the outside world, where "others"—not Lincoln—"say there are no whigs."

Lincoln certainly did not consider himself an abolitionist, whatever others might be saying. "When I was at Washington," he pointed out to Speed, referring to his time as a congressman, "I voted for the Wilmot Proviso as good as forty times, and I never heard of any one attempting to unwhig me for that. I now do no more than oppose the *extension* of slavery."[35] Lincoln was saying that the old Whig position simply opposed extending slavery to new territories, as the never-adopted Wilmot Proviso had specified for those acquired in the Mexican-American War. That was all he believed now—or so he thought.

Lincoln closed his letter by rejecting the rising Know-Nothing Party, with its anti-immigrant, anti-Catholic bias, which Lincoln said was inconsistent with the basic doctrine that "*all men are created equal.*"[36] Lincoln was looking for something else. And in the emerging Republican Party, he found it.

Lincoln's law partner and later biographer, William Herndon, inaugurated the tradition of identifying Lincoln's "lost speech" to the Illinois Republicans in May 1856 as a turning point in his thinking. Herndon took credit for getting Lincoln to agree to attend the gathering in the first place, claiming to have signed Lincoln's name without his knowledge to a public letter calling for the meeting. When Lincoln agreed to go, Herndon wrote years later, "the conservative spirits who hovered around Springfield no longer held control of the political fortunes of Abraham Lincoln." Once on the podium, according to Herndon, Lincoln "was newly baptized and freshly born"—baptized, that is, into the spirit of antislavery:

> Heretofore he had simply argued the slavery question on ground of policy . . . never reaching the question of the radical and the eternal right. Now he . . . had the fervor of a new convert; the smothered flame broke out; enthusiasm unusual to him blazed up; his eyes were aglow with an inspiration; he felt justice; his heart was alive to the right; his sympathies, remarkably deep for him, burst forth, and he stood before the throne of the eternal Right.[37]

Herndon's account was almost certainly an exaggeration, but it does capture the reality that as Lincoln embraced the new Republican Party, he also embraced for the first time a strong public repudiation of the morality of slavery.

In the months that followed, Lincoln attended the Republican National Convention in Philadelphia, where he finished second in the balloting for vice president. He campaigned for John C. Frémont, the Republican nominee. And after Frémont lost to the Democrat James Buchanan, Lincoln gave a speech to a Republican banquet in Chicago in which he insisted that the "'central idea' in our political public opinion, at the beginning was, and until recently has continued to be, 'the equality of men.'" In the 1856 election, Lincoln asserted, the Democratic Party had aimed to "discard that central idea, and to substitute for it the opposite idea that slavery is right." If that "central idea" were to prevail, Lincoln said, the result "may be the perpetuity of human slavery, and its extension to all countries and colors."[38] Lincoln was still treating the extension of slavery as embodied in the Kansas-Nebraska Act as the great wrong committed by the Democratic Party. But he was also making the point that the effect of the extension could be to keep slavery alive forever—an eventuality he no longer hesitated to call morally wrong in itself.

Buchanan was inaugurated on March 4, 1857. Two days later, the Supreme Court dropped a bombshell onto the continuing national debate over the extension of slavery into the territories. The court's decision in *Dred Scott v. Sandford* marked only the second time in the court's history that it found a federal law to be unconstitutional. Lincoln responded vigorously to the decision, not only condemning its reasoning but also questioning the binding nature of the Supreme Court's ruling for the nation as a whole. His reaction to the *Dred Scott* case remains a topic of constitutional debate to this day. It is crucial for understanding how Lincoln thought of the Constitution on the eve of the Civil War—and how his views evolved once the war began.

LINCOLN'S *DRED SCOTT*

The controlling opinion was written by the chief justice of the United States, Roger Taney, who would become Lincoln's antagonist in the struggle over the meaning of the Constitution during the Civil War. Taney, born in 1777 and just a few days shy of eighty years old, was a relic of another age. He had been appointed chief justice in 1836 by Andrew Jackson, whom he had served as attorney general and acting secretary of the treasury. A Maryland Catholic, born into a slaveholding family, and still a Jacksonian Democrat in ideology, Taney was deeply committed to the preservation of the union. Between 1818 and 1824, he had, on moral grounds, freed the eleven enslaved persons he owned, excepting only two who were too old "to provide for themselves."[39] Yet while serving as Jackson's attorney general, he had written an unpublished opinion taking the position that people of African descent "were not looked upon as citizens by the contracting parties who formed the Constitution."[40]

To understand the logic of the *Dred Scott* decision, generally considered one of the two or three worst in the history of the Supreme Court, it is necessary to keep in mind Taney's goal. The chief justice sought above all to avoid secession. To that end, he aimed at nothing less than resolving once and for all the roiling conflict over the extension of slavery to new territories—the conflict that, everyone knew, threatened the very existence of the union.

The case had begun when Dred Scott, an enslaved man, went to federal court and filed a lawsuit demanding freedom on behalf of himself and his family. The essence of the claim was that, when Scott's then master had brought Scott and his wife into the part of the Missouri Territory north of the 36°30' line, and then brought Scott into the state of Illinois, Scott's and his wife's presence in territories where slavery was prohibited by law had legally freed them. This claim in turn was based on a legal idea that went back to an English decision of 1772, *Somerset v. Stewart*. In that case, the Court of the King's Bench had held that because slavery did not exist legally in England, an enslaved African who had been brought there from Jamaica by his master could not be compelled to return to Jamaica against his will.

Taney's decision ran to fifty-five pages,* but it can be summarized briefly: Taney chose not to decide whether an enslaved person could become free by being brought into a territory or state where slavery was

---

* All eight of the other justices filed concurrences or dissents of their own.

not recognized by law. Instead, he made two different arguments. First, he held that Scott could not have his case heard in federal court. Second, he denied that the Missouri territory north of the 36°30' compromise line was actually free territory at all.

The first of these arguments is the one that remains today so morally offensive and legally indefensible that it continues to stain the court's historical legacy. In order to argue that Scott could not bring a lawsuit in federal court, Taney held that Scott could not be considered a "citizen" under the provision of Article III of the Constitution that gave the federal courts jurisdiction over suits between citizens of different states.* To reach that conclusion, Taney held that no one of African descent—whether slave or free—could ever be a citizen of the United States.

As a legal argument, this assertion was extremely weak. Justice Benjamin Curtis pointed out in his sixty-seven page dissent that Northern states had long recognized African Americans as citizens. Several states had allowed free African Americans to vote as early as independence. When the Constitution referred to *citizens*, there was no good reason to think it meant to exclude people of African descent.

Taney ignored Curtis's point—and turned to the Declaration of Independence and its assertion that "all men are created equal." When that assertion was written, Taney observed, slavery existed in most of the newly formed United States. There were thus only two possible interpretations of the Declaration, according to Taney. Either the authors of the Declaration were hypocrites, or they never intended to include people of African descent in the category of "men" who would become citizens of the new nation. "It is too clear for dispute," Taney concluded, "that the enslaved African race were not intended to be included, and

---

* Enslaved persons were not legally considered citizens. But Scott's claim was precisely that he was not legally a slave and was therefore a citizen and a free man entitled to sue in order to have his freedom acknowledged and confirmed.

formed no part of the people who framed and adopted this declaration." Otherwise, "the conduct of the distinguished men who framed the Declaration of Independence would have been utterly and flagrantly inconsistent with the principles they asserted."[41]

Taney's historical argument that the framers must be understood as rejecting the very possibility of African American citizenship was, in a sense, the distorted mirror image of the Garrisonian condemnation of the framers' Constitution as irredeemably proslavery.* Like those abolitionists who insisted on interpreting the Constitution in the light of the framers' personal slaveholding and their compromise over slavery, Taney was offering a reading of the Declaration and the Constitution based on what he claimed was their original meaning in historical context. Like Garrison, Taney argued that this originalism yielded a Constitution committed to racial inequality. Both were advancing a relatively new approach to interpreting the Constitution. The difference was that while Garrisonian abolitionists condemned this white-supremacist Constitution, Taney lauded it.

Taney understood that not only abolitionists but even more moderate opponents of slavery, like Lincoln, frequently appealed to the Declaration of Independence to prove an American commitment to what Lincoln had called the "central idea" of equality. By reinterpreting the Declaration of Independence to exclude African Americans, Taney was trying to rob slavery's opponents of the best—really the only—text they could invoke to claim an official pedigree for their moral stance.

Yet notwithstanding the moral repugnance of Taney's insistence that people of African descent could never be part of the American political community, it was the second part of his decision that created

---

* As Frederick Douglass once put it in a different context, "Garrison sees in the Constitution precisely what John C. Calhoun sees there—a compromise with Slavery." Douglass, "Oath to Support the Constitution," *The North Star*, April 5, 1861, 2.

much greater political uproar in the three years that followed. In this part, Taney explained that Scott could not claim to have been free by virtue of having been brought into territory from which the Missouri Compromise had barred slavery. Scott could not have been freed because, Taney held, slavery had never been constitutionally outlawed above the 36°30' line. The Missouri Compromise had been enacted in 1820, of course. But, said Taney, it had been unconstitutional from the day it was enacted and so had never actually applied as a matter of law.

It sounds bizarre that the Supreme Court would strike down a law more than a quarter-century after it was enacted—and three years after it had been repealed. And in fact it was bizarre. Taney did not even have to address the Missouri Compromise to ensure that Dred Scott would lose his case. Once Taney had determined that Scott was not a citizen, the federal courts lacked the legal authority to hear the case in the first place, and Scott's claims would have to be dismissed.

But Taney's objectives were forward looking, not backward looking. He wanted to issue a ruling that would make it constitutionally impossible for Congress *ever* to adopt a new version of the Missouri Compromise—as Whigs like Lincoln had wanted to do as early as 1854. Taney believed that the ongoing controversy over a possible new prohibition on the extension of slavery to some territories would destabilize the union to the point where it would provoke Southern secession, which he feared and opposed. His idea was to use the Supreme Court's power of interpreting the Constitution to put any new Missouri Compromise out of bounds entirely and forever.

The argument that Taney used to assert the unconstitutionality of the Missouri Compromise—or of any future law restricting slavery in territories controlled by the United States—was based on the idea of fundamental rights. The right Taney focused on was the slaveholders' right to own property, specifically property in enslaved humans. When slaveholders brought their human property from states where they lawfully possessed it into the territories, Taney asserted, they did not lose their constitutional property rights just by traveling. If that were so, according to Taney, the slaveholders would not have their full rights as citizens. "Citizens of the United States," he explained, "who migrate to a Territory belonging to the people of the United States cannot be ruled as mere colonists, dependent upon the will of the General Government and to be governed by any laws it may think proper to impose."[42]

From this logic it followed that the federal government lacked the legal power to prohibit anyone from owning slaves in any territory they wished. The Missouri Compromise had therefore been invalid, because it prohibited slavery in some parts of some territories. On the basis of Taney's logic, no future law passed by Congress could prohibit slavery in any of them.

To Lincoln and other former Whigs, who had for many years considered the Missouri Compromise not only to be lawful but also to have the status of a quasi-constitution, the *Dred Scott* decision represented nothing less than a repudiation of their entire constitutional vision. The Missouri Compromise had been, to them, the continuation and embodiment of the compromise Constitution. Now the Supreme Court was holding that compromise itself unconstitutional. Northern sentiment was outraged by the decision, which quickly became a political bellwether. Southerners hailed the decision as a great victory. Some critics tried to claim that the court had not really overturned the Missouri Compromise because doing so was not necessary to its holding once it had determined that Scott was not a citizen; but this awkward position required the critics to accept as binding the court's holding that African Americans could never be citizens.

Lincoln responded on June 26, 1857, in a speech in Springfield. He framed his remarks as an answer to Douglas, who had spoken on the subject two weeks earlier in the same place, with Lincoln in attendance. Lincoln told the audience the decision was wrong—and he suggested that it should not be taken to block any future congressional regulation of slavery in the territories. "We think the Dred Scott decision is erroneous," he stated baldly. "We know the court that made it, has often over-ruled its own decisions, and we shall do what we can to have it over-rule this." Douglas had accused Republicans of seeking to resist the Supreme Court's authority. Lincoln denied the charge. "We believe, as much as Judge Douglas, (perhaps more)," he said, "in obedience to, and respect for the judicial department of government."[43]

Lincoln offered a subtle, lawyerly argument about how Supreme Court decisions become binding precedents for the future. "Judicial decisions," he began, "have two uses—first, to absolutely determine the case decided, and secondly, to indicate to the public how other similar cases will be decided when they arise." Lincoln acknowledged that, when it came to the situation of Dred Scott himself, the Supreme Court's decision was binding: Scott would remain a slave. But when it came to setting "the general policy of the country," he maintained, Supreme Court decisions "on Constitutional questions" became controlling only "when fully settled."[44]

But the *Dred Scott* decision was not "fully settled," according to Lincoln:

> If this important decision had been made by the unanimous concurrence of the judges, and without any apparent partisan bias, and in accordance with legal public expectation, and with the steady practice of the departments throughout our history, and had been in no part, based on assumed historical facts which are not really true; or, if wanting in some of these, it had been before the court more than once, and had there been affirmed and re-affirmed through a course of years, it then might be, perhaps would be, factious, nay, even revolutionary, to not acquiesce in it as a precedent.[45]

Lincoln was claiming that the circumstances surrounding the *Dred Scott* decision were so unusual that the decision did not yet create a binding precedent for the future. By so arguing, he intended to dispute the notion that Taney's decision would bind the government, thus leaving room for Congress to prohibit slavery in federal territories, notwithstanding Taney's intent to do just that. Ordinarily, Lincoln acknowledged, constitutional decisions could not be changed except by amendment or revolution. But in this unique circumstance, he insisted, "it is not resistance, it is not factious, it is not even disrespectful, to treat [the decision] as not having yet quite established a settled doctrine for the country."[46] Lincoln was not prepared to accept the validity of either part of the ruling. He was, somewhat creatively, seeking a way to undercut the whole of it without openly flouting the authority of the Supreme Court.

Lincoln's claim that the *Dred Scott* decision was not yet settled constitutional law is sometimes invoked as justification for government actors outside the judicial branch to ignore judicial precedents that would seem to bind them. The judiciary, however, has never embraced the theory, for the obvious reason that judges want to strengthen their authority, not weaken it. What is significant for our purposes is that Lincoln had little choice but to argue against Taney's attempt to prevent future compromise over slavery in the territories—because the decision was aimed at ruling unconstitutional Lincoln's entire political program as it had existed up to the time he became a Republican.

Only after he had rejected the *Dred Scott* decision's bar on future compromise did Lincoln set out to rehabilitate the Declaration of Independence: "I think the authors of that notable instrument intended to include *all* men, but they did not intend to declare all men equal *in all respects*." Rather, they "defined . . . in what respects they did consider all men created equal—equal in 'certain inalienable rights, among which are life, liberty, and the pursuit of happiness.' This they said, and this meant." As for the reality of slavery, the framers had spoken aspirationally about the future: "They did not mean to assert the obvious untruth, that all were then actually enjoying that equality . . . They meant simply to declare the *right*, so that the *enforcement* of it might follow as fast as circumstances should permit." The framers' aspirational aim was intended as a long-term goal:

> They meant to set up a standard maxim for free society, which should be familiar to all, and revered by all; constantly looked to, constantly labored for, and even though never perfectly attained, constantly approximated, and thereby constantly spreading and deepening its influence, and augmenting the happiness and value of life to all people of all colors everywhere.[47]

Lincoln's view broke the binary choice that Taney had offered in his opinion, and endeavored to save the Declaration as a source of authority for the antislavery ideal. The framers were not hypocrites, according to Lincoln. Nor had they intended to exclude people of African descent from the assertion that "all men are created equal." Rather, the framers had intended to create an aspirational, evolutionary principle, one that could be improved and updated by future generations.

Whether this defense was historically accurate was beside the point. It showed Lincoln's creativity in connecting himself to the framers, as he had long done via the legacy of Clay. Channeling Jefferson, Lincoln recruited the slaveholder's Declaration into the emerging Republican project of opposing not only the extension of slavery but also slavery itself.

THE HOUSE DIVIDED

Lincoln gave his "House Divided" speech at the Illinois Republican Convention in June 1858, accepting the party's nomination to run against Douglas for his Senate seat. The whole purpose of the speech was to connect the *Dred Scott* holding to Douglas's doctrine of popular sovereignty—and to combine the two into a grand theory of a fundamental constitutional transformation at work. What matters for our purposes about the speech is that it revealed for the first time Lincoln's apparent belief that, taken together, the Kansas-Nebraska Act and the *Dred Scott* decision were part of a strategy to subvert the Constitution's compromise on slavery.

The place to begin, of course, is with Lincoln's famous biblical opening—his assertion that "a house divided against itself cannot stand,"[48] and that therefore "this government cannot endure, permanently half *slave* and half *free*."[49] This was an astonishing thing for a former Whig to say. The entire structure of the constitutional compromise, from the framing of the Constitution in Philadelphia in 1787 through the three great crises resolved by Clay, was precisely based on the idea that the union could endure *only* so long as it remained half slave and half free. The Senate was the institutional compromise intended to preserve the parity of half and half, and it had done so from the Missouri Compromise until the Compromise of 1850.

Now Lincoln was saying that the union would have to become all slave or all free: "I do not expect the Union to be *dissolved*—I do not expect the house to *fall*—but I *do* expect it will cease to be divided." The options were either that slavery would stop spreading and reach a point where "the public mind" would be satisfied "that it is in course of ultimate extinction," or that slavery would "become alike lawful in all the States, *old* as well as *new*—*North* as well as *South*."[50] Neither option reflected compromise. One side or the other would prevail.

What had brought the Republican Lincoln to the point of denying the essential constitutional compromise vision he had held for twenty-five years of public service? The answer lay in his interpretation of constitutional developments since 1854. As Lincoln depicted it, the combination of popular sovereignty and the *Dred Scott* decision was going to have the legal effect of forcing slavery not only into all federal territories but also into free states.

The basis for Lincoln's fear was that while Douglas's doctrine supposedly let the white citizens of territories decide whether their states should be free or slave, the *Dred Scott* decision had held that neither Congress nor a territorial legislature could bar slavery. From this it followed, Lincoln pointed out, that masters could bring enslaved people into new territories without compunction. That would establish slavery as a practical matter in those territories, and when they became states, they would be very unlikely to reverse themselves and abolish slavery.

But that was not all, Lincoln warned. Once the Supreme Court had held that slavery could not be prohibited in the territories, it could go on to hold "that the Constitution of the United States does not permit a *state* to exclude slavery from its limits."[51] In this scenario, free states would lose their capacity to be free states altogether.

Taney had said no such thing, of course, nor did the conclusion follow. Lincoln was pushing the limits of legal logic. The Bill of Rights as interpreted by the Supreme Court only restricted the federal government from taking property without compensation. It did not restrain the states from defining what counted as property within their borders. The *Dred Scott* decision had therefore only applied to federal law—whether enacted by Congress or a territorial legislature operating subject to Congress's authority. It did not necessarily follow, legally speaking, that if Congress could not bar slavery in new territories, states likewise could not bar slavery. Such an argument would have required a further step in constitutional reasoning.

To be sure, however, such a future step was not inconceivable. The Supreme Court, for example, could have held that owning property was a privilege or immunity of citizens of the states,* and could not

* Under Article IV, section 2, clause 1, of the Constitution.

be abridged by a free state. From that, it would have followed that no state could bar a slaveholder from bringing slaves within its borders and keeping them there. This constitutional theory had in fact been articulated by some radical proslavery advocates.[52] Another possible theory, which Lincoln himself sketched in order to warn against it, was that if the Constitution itself affirmed a right to hold slaves, then the clause of the Constitution making it the supreme law of the land would impose that right on the states.[53] But the likelihood of any such holding was surely remote. Lincoln was not so much warning his audience about the pressing practical danger of the spread of slavery to free states as he was trying to awaken them to how the constitutional ground had shifted since 1854.

The real reason Lincoln wanted to suggest that slavery could be extended even to free states was to bring home his main point: that Douglas, Taney, and Buchanan had together broken the structure of constitutional compromise that had existed since the adoption of the Constitution. In the past, the grounds of conflict *and* of compromise between free and slave states had been the question of extending slavery. Now popular sovereignty plus the *Dred Scott* doctrine meant that there could be no compromise over extension. Under these conditions, Lincoln was warning, slavery could actually win the battle—unless checked by the free states.

The weakest aspect of Lincoln's great speech was that it offered no solution to the existential problem it posed, except defeating Douglas. To avoid awaking "to the *reality* . . . that the *Supreme* Court has made *Illinois* a *slave* State," he could offer only the proposal that Republicans "meet and overthrow the power of that dynasty" of Democrats. It was "the work now before all those who would prevent that consummation."[54]

Lincoln was a candidate for office, and it was natural enough for the takeaway of his speech to be that Republicans should help him beat his Democratic opponent. Yet the speech had done much more than present Douglas himself as part of the problem. It had framed the challenge as a fundamental tear in the constitutional fabric. And Lincoln had not proposed any way to repair the tear. His stated expectation that the house would not fall, and the union would not be dissolved, had no concrete plan attached to it. In declaring that the constitutional structure was broken, Lincoln should have had some idea of what would rebuild it. In 1858, he did not.

In the seven Lincoln-Douglas debates that followed between August and October of 1858, the *Dred Scott* case came up repeatedly. The arc of the debates has become the stuff of legend, nearly inconceivable when viewed in the light of the debased candidate debates of our day: the crisscross travels of the two men across the state to reach all seven venues, the many thousands of spectators from inside Illinois and beyond, the national press attention to the nuances of the candidates' ideas and rhetoric, and above all the sustained attention by both men to the most crucial and pressing problems of the day. Lincoln hammered home the argument that Douglas was, with Taney, part of a broader Democratic "conspiracy" to make slavery national. Douglas denied any conspiracy (plausibly, it must be said), while continuing nevertheless to advance his popular sovereignty "solution" to where slavery could be established, an approach that could certainly have allowed slavery to expand much farther than it already had done. Douglas repeatedly attacked Lincoln for questioning the authority of the *Dred Scott* decision, accusing him of encouraging mob rule instead of respecting the ruling of the Supreme Court. And he subjected Lincoln's "House Divided" speech to the devastating critique that it rejected the framers' original constitutional compromise. Douglas asked the audience to imagine that Lincoln had been present at the Philadelphia convention. If he had convinced others of his claim that the union could not endure half-slave and half-free, Douglas asserted, there would have been no Constitution formed at all.

Douglas's criticism forced Lincoln to articulate his own constitutional vision as it then existed. His responses to Douglas made it clear that he still sought to preserve some version of the compromise Constitution, notwithstanding his new Republicanism. At the center of the compromise, where it had always been for Whigs, was the protection of slavery in slave states. As Lincoln put it bluntly in the first debate, "I have no purpose, directly or indirectly, to interfere with the institution of slavery in the States where it exists. I believe I have no lawful right to do so, and I have no inclination to do so."[55]

Lincoln was forced by Douglas to acknowledge that the Constitution protected slavery via the fugitive slave clause. "In regard to the Fugitive Slave law," Lincoln explained in the second debate, "I have never hesitated to say, and I do not now hesitate to say, that I think, under the Constitution of the United States, the people of the Southern States are entitled to a Congressional Fugitive Slave law."[56] In the third debate, he expanded on the point by insisting on his sworn loyalty to the Constitution:

> Let me ask you why many of us who are opposed to slavery upon principle . . . hold ourselves under obligations to pass such a law, and abide by it when it is passed? Because the Constitution makes provision that the owners of slaves shall have the right to reclaim them . . . And although it is distasteful to me, I have sworn to support the Constitution, and having so sworn I cannot conceive that I do support it if I withhold from that right any necessary legislation to make it practical.[57]

Lincoln thus understood himself to be bound by his oath to uphold the Constitution not only to follow its explicit commands but also to carry out those commands through the enactment of legislation that would facilitate slaveholders' constitutional right to reclaim fugitives. This was not precisely the same as Webster's argument that there was a moral imperative to preserve the Constitution and hence a moral duty to return fugitive slaves. Lincoln was, rather, deriving the weight of the obligation from the oath he had taken. The idea of a duty derived from an oath to the Constitution would become central to his thinking just a few years later, when he took the presidential oath of office.

Lincoln was furthermore forced to acknowledge that if a state should apply for admission to the union with slavery protected in its state constitution, he would vote as a senator to admit that state to the union. This, too, showed that Lincoln accepted the basic principle that the Constitution authorized and in fact protected slavery. Under pressure from Douglas, Lincoln said that Congress possessed the power to prohibit slavery in the District of Columbia, but should not do so unless it could be achieved gradually, with a majority vote of the district's residents, and with compensation to "unwilling owners." He did not, however, say that these conditions were constitutional requirements—only that as a senator he would not favor abolition in the district unless they were satisfied.[58]

Lincoln ducked the question of whether Congress had the constitutional power to prohibit the slave trade between states, claiming not to have thought sufficiently deeply about the matter. But he did say that even if the power existed, he would not be in favor of exercising it without the consent of the Southern states.[59] Again, this was the language of compromise with the realities of slavery.

With respect to the *Dred Scott* decision, Lincoln rejected Douglas's charge that he favored mob rule by explaining that he did not think Dred Scott himself should be set free in violation of the Supreme Court's judgment:

> We do not propose that . . . we will in any violent way disturb the rights of property thus settled; but we nevertheless do oppose that decision as a political rule, which shall be binding on the voter, to vote for nobody who thinks it wrong, which shall be binding on the members of Con-

gress or the President to favor no measure that does not actually concur with the principles of that decision.[60]

Lincoln was clarifying his position that Congress could, notwithstanding the *Dred Scott* decision, still enact legislation that restricted slavery in the territories—even if the Supreme Court would subsequently strike down the legislation. His justification was that the *Dred Scott* decision must not be treated as binding "as a political rule" because "it lays the foundation not merely of enlarging and spreading out what we consider an evil, but it lays the foundation for spreading that evil into the States themselves." The point of this intended political resistance was "to have it reversed if we can, and a new judicial rule established upon this subject."[61]

This was a stronger statement against the binding authority of the *Dred Scott* decision than Lincoln had articulated previously. It was based on an implicit distinction Lincoln was proposing between the legal aspect of a judicial decision, which Lincoln was restricting to the facts of the case, and the "political" aspect of the decision, which would bind the political branches of government—that is, Congress and the president. In terms that would have important implications for his later confrontation with Taney over habeas corpus, Lincoln was asserting that the political branches of government did not need to treat the principles embodied in an unsettled judicial decision as binding upon them when they made new laws.

Douglas did not miss the opportunity to attack Lincoln's position. "The decision in the *Dred Scott* case is binding on every American citizen alike," he asserted, "and yet Mr. Lincoln argues that the Republicans are not bound by it, because they are opposed to it."[62] The criticism was well made. Lincoln was trying to resist the Supreme Court's constitutional decision because he was trying to keep open the possibility of constitutional compromise, which the court had intentionally blocked.

Lincoln's final response to Douglas was to revert to the idea of the compromise Constitution—and repeat his commitment to it. In the last debate, he quoted himself on the topic:

> It may be argued that there are certain conditions that make necessities and impose them upon us, and to the extent that a necessity is imposed upon a man he must submit to it. I think that was the condition in which we found ourselves when we established this government. We had slaves among us, we could not get our Constitution unless we permitted them to remain in slavery, we could not secure the good we did secure if we grasped for more; and having by necessity submitted to that much, it does not destroy the principle that is the charter of our liberties. Let the charter remain as our standard.[63]

He went on to claim the legacy of Clay for the proposition that slavery was an "evil" that should be eventually eliminated.[64] And he attributed the aspiration to the framers, not only in the Declaration but also in the Constitution. Following an argument that was by now well-known, Lincoln insisted that the framers had omitted the word "slavery" from even those constitutional provisions that preserved the institution so that "when it should be read by intelligent and patriotic men, after the institution of slavery had passed from among us—there should be nothing on the face of the great charter of liberty suggesting that such a thing as negro slavery had ever existed among us." This choice of language was not euphemism but "part of the evidence that the fathers of the Government expected and intended the institution of slavery to come to an end. They expected and intended that it should be in the course of ultimate extinction."[65]

The upshot for Lincoln was that the difference between him and

Douglas was over whether slavery was wrong and ought ultimately to be made extinct. "That is the real issue . . . ," he asserted. "It is the eternal struggle between these two principles—right and wrong—throughout the world."[66] Lincoln the Republican was openly espousing and emphasizing the moral wrongness of slavery, while Douglas remained silent on the subject, thus implicitly endorsing slavery as morally right. Yet like the Whig position from which it was ultimately derived, Lincoln's Republican stance still had no credible account of how the extinction of slavery could practically be accomplished so long as the compromise Constitution remained in place.

TO THE PRESIDENCY

Lincoln raised his national profile with the publication of the proceedings of the seven Lincoln-Douglas debates. But the speech that made him a potential contender for the Republican nomination for the presidency in 1860 was the one he gave at the Cooper Union in Manhattan in February of that year. The story of Lincoln's preparation, his nervousness, and even his ill-fitting suit—purchased for the occasion in an unsuccessful effort to make him look less like an out-of-towner—has been frequently told. What is less commonly acknowledged is the strange content of the speech.

The first half of the Cooper Union speech consisted nearly exclusively of a fairly bland historical essay focused on the framers of the Constitution. There was almost no introduction. There were no inspiring quotations from the men on whom the speech focused. Instead, Lincoln presented a collection of congressional voting records, enmeshed and interpreted in the light of his mildly tendentious legal reasoning. The second half of the speech consisted of an address to the Southern people—primarily defensive and secondarily intended to tell them that if the union should collapse, it would be their fault.

To understand why this odd performance catapulted Lincoln to national prominence among Republicans, it is necessary to recognize the extent to which the debate over the crisis spurred by the Kansas-Nebraska Act had become explicitly constitutional—and the extent to which the Republicans were losing that debate. Ever since he completed Clay's work by passing the Compromise of 1850, Douglas had skillfully assumed Clay's mantle as a proponent of the compromise Constitution. Yet Douglas, whether in conscious conjunction with the Supreme Court or not, had fundamentally changed the terms of the compromise that had previously existed. The original compromise, going back at least to 1821 and arguably to 1787, had protected slavery while leaving it up to Congress to determine where it would extend. Douglas's version of the compromise shifted the responsibility for that determination away from Congress to the white residents of territories on the way to becoming states.

The reason Douglas could claim to be following Clay was that, as he had argued in his 1858 campaign against Lincoln, the framers' Constitution embodied both slavery and non-slavery at the same time. Douglas was not wrong when he argued that this structure, however contradictory, had been the basis of the constitutional compromise ever since. It was false, Douglas asserted contra Lincoln, that the union could not endure half-slave and half-free. Rather, Douglas argued, the union could not endure *unless* it was half-slave and half-free, as it had always been. Thus far, Douglas could claim to be following Clay. What enabled him to transform Clay's version of compromise into his own, different form of compromise was the theoretical justification that Douglas offered for the whole structure: popular sovereignty at the state level, construed as the right of the white citizens of each state to decide whether they would recognize slavery. The term "popular sovereignty" had an attractive, constitutional-sounding ring to it. It was the key element that enabled Douglas to suggest a new form of compromise, one in which slavery could potentially extend to new territories even without the consent of the Northern states.

At all costs, Lincoln and the Republicans had to regain the constitutional high ground from Douglas. The point of the first half of the Cooper Union address was to do exactly that. Lincoln turned to dry history because history had become the battleground for the fight over the meaning of the Constitution. The argument he pursued was modest in its form and substance. Yet it resonated for a Republican audience because it represented the best available path to claim the authority of the Constitution for their position.

Lincoln could not argue that the framers of the Constitution had not been slaveholders; many had. Nor could he argue that the framers had supported abolition; only a few did. He could not deny that the Constitution effectively acknowledged slavery via the three-fifths compromise, the temporary protection of the slave trade, and the fugitive slave clause. All of this was implicit in the Whig theory of the compromise Constitution that Clay had advocated and Lincoln had long accepted.

Instead, Lincoln settled on the argument that a majority of the framers—twenty-one of the thirty-nine, by his somewhat doubtful calculation—had taken official actions consistent with the view that Congress had the constitutional authority to limit slavery in federal territories.[67] Stated so simply, Lincoln's claim sounds mild enough to be almost insignificant. Lincoln's historical evidence said nothing about the rightness or wrongness of slavery generally. It also fell well short of the notion that a majority of the framers supported the gradual abolition of slavery.

In the context of 1859, however, Lincoln's argument was intended as a historical answer to Douglas's popular sovereignty and to *Dred Scott*'s holding that Congress lacked the constitutional authority to prohibit slavery in the territories. Lincoln was setting out to prove that under the Constitution, Congress could always limit the extension of slavery. This claim was meant to turn back the political clock and re-introduce the possibility of limiting the extension of slavery. The goal was to bring back the older version of the compromise Constitution, the one that had existed before Douglas: a compromise in which slav-ery would be allowed to continue in slave states, but not beyond.

Lincoln's proofs were more those of a lawyer than of a historian. Four framers had voted to prohibit slavery in the Northwest Territory in 1784, before the Constitution even existed; two more had cast simi-lar votes in 1787 while the constitutional convention was going on—at which point the entire document was still a secret. As a historical mat-ter, these votes could demonstrate nothing definitive about what the Constitution might mean.

Slightly better evidence came from the act passed by the first Con-gress in 1789 to adopt the Northwest Ordinance, including its ban on slavery in the Northwest Territory. Sixteen framers sat in the first Congress, and Washington had signed the law. Lincoln was on firm ground when he said this vote proved that, to these framers, noth-ing in the Constitution as it then existed "properly forbade Congress to prohibit slavery in the federal territory."[68] The technical problem with Lincoln's argument was that Taney had based his reasoning in the *Dred Scott* case largely on the Fifth Amendment's protection of the right to property; and when Congress had passed the 1789 law, the Bill of Rights still had not been enacted or ratified.

The rest of Lincoln's evidence came from laws passed in 1798 and 1803 in connection with newly acquired federal territory. Those laws did not prohibit slavery, but they did limit it in certain respects. That enabled Lincoln to claim five more framers who had voted for these laws. Finally, two framers, Rufus King and Charles Pinckney, had served in the Congress that passed the Missouri Compromise. King had voted in favor, and Pinckney against. That gave Lincoln his "to-tal" of twenty-one framers who had acted on the assumption that the

Constitution authorized Congress to block slavery in the territories, as against two framers who had had the opportunity so to vote but had gone the other way.

What worked in Lincoln's argument was less the detail than its overarching effect. The historical section of the speech brought home, at least to sympathetic Republicans, the truth that there was nothing historical about Douglas's popular sovereignty theory or Taney's theory that there was a constitutional right to hold slaves in the territories. As a historical matter, Lincoln was correct to suggest that these Democratic theories were anachronistic. By extension, Lincoln, not Douglas, should have been seen as the heir to Clay's compromise Constitution. The Republicans could claim to be following the framers—and could do so credibly.

Lincoln's conclusion to this discussion was to claim the old compromise Constitution as the Republican position—nothing more. "This is all Republicans ask—all Republicans desire—in relation to slavery," he explained. "As those fathers marked it, so let it be again marked, as an evil not to be extended, but to be tolerated and protected only because of and so far as its actual presence among us makes that toleration and protection a necessity."[69]

The extremely limited nature of Lincoln's claim was underscored by the remainder of the speech, in which he turned rhetorically to address Southerners—and blamed them for rejecting the traditional constitutional compromise and heading toward disunion. In perhaps the most significant passage, Lincoln depicted the Republicans as preserving what had always worked before:

[Y]ou say you are conservative—eminently conservative—while we are revolutionary, destructive, or something of the sort. What is conservatism? Is it not adherence to the old and tried, against the new and untried? We stick to, contend for, the identical old policy on the point in con-

troversy which was adopted by "our fathers who framed
the Government under which we live;" while you with one
accord reject, and scout, and spit upon that old policy, and
insist upon substituting something new.[70]

Lincoln's point—the one that made national Republicans notice
him—was that the imminent collapse of the constitutional compromise was the result of changes demanded by Southerners, not Northerners. In essence, Lincoln was reversing the structure of blame by
insisting that Republican policy followed the old Whig compromise
line. "Again," he addressed the South, "you say we have made the
slavery question more prominent than it formerly was." Lincoln acknowledged that the slavery issue had become more prominent. But,
he asserted, "we deny that we made it so. It was not we, but you, who
discarded the old policy of the fathers."[71]

The only solution Lincoln offered to the crisis was to "go back to
[the] old policy." He told the South, and his audience, "If you would
have the peace of the old times, readopt the precepts and policy of the
old times."[72] After quoting Jefferson in favor of gradual "emancipation,
and deportation" of former slaves to Africa, Lincoln went out of his way
to explain that "Jefferson did not mean to say, nor do I, that the power
of emancipation is in the Federal Government . . . [A]s to the power of
emancipation, I speak of the slaveholding states only."[73] He was insisting that the old compromise was still on offer, and acknowledging that
the old compromise rested on constitutional protection of slavery in the
states where it existed.

Yet despite insisting that the Republican position was a return to
the familiar compromise Constitution, Lincoln concluded his speech
with an extended passage in which he all but said that the old compromise would no longer work. What would satisfy the South? he
asked rhetorically. "Simply this: We must not only let them alone,
but we must somehow, convince them that we do let them alone."

Unfortunately, Lincoln went on to explain, the only way to convince Southerners that slavery would be protected would be to "cease to call slavery *wrong*, and join them in calling it *right*."[74] Now he was hinting at the central theme of his "House Divided" speech: the inevitability of moral conflict over the rightness or wrongness of slavery. Ceasing to condemn slavery might placate the South, "but, thinking it wrong, as we do, can we yield to them? . . . In view of our moral, social, and political responsibilities, can we do this?"[75]

In the peroration of his Cooper Union speech, Lincoln did not answer his own question with a resounding no. Rather, he drew back from the "House Divided" formulation and closed with hopes of reconciliation: "Wrong as we think slavery is, we can yet afford to let it alone where it is, because that much is due to the necessity arising from its actual presence in the nation." The "necessity arising" from the "actual presence" of slavery was, as always, the core justification for the compromise Constitution. Lincoln insisted only that the Northerners should prevent slavery from spreading to the territories and not allow it "to overrun us here in these Free States."[76]

The ambivalence of Lincoln's performance can hardly be overstated. On the one hand, he wanted to insist on the conservatism of Republicanism. To do that, he had to embrace the compromise Constitution, which allowed for slavery, "wrong" as it might be, and still promise "to let it alone where it is."[77] On the other hand, he could not help but predict that this compromise was going to be rejected.

Then and now, the ambiguity of Lincoln's position has fueled competing interpretations of the politics surrounding the election of 1860. Southern leaders like Jefferson Davis treated Lincoln's election as a justification for secession, reasoning that Republicans' objection to slavery and commitment to blocking its extension were tantamount to a guarantee that slavery would be somehow ended. Since then, some historians have maintained that the secessionists were correct in this assessment. To them, the several million Northern white men who voted Republican in 1860 represent a popular, democratic antislavery movement based on the benefits of free labor and free soil to working-class white people alongside the inherent moral wrongfulness of slavery.[78] Even the scholar James Oakes, who once saw Lincoln primarily as a pragmatist on slavery, has recently changed his view to argue that by embracing the Republican platform in 1860, Lincoln had come to believe that "the Constitution itself was an antislavery document."[79] Both the nineteenth-century secessionists and the twenty-first century historians emphasize Lincoln's warning of looming disaster over his insistence that the old compromise was still available to continue.

Meanwhile, many prominent historians, echoing Lincoln's mainstream supporters in the 1860 election, maintain that Lincoln meant what he said when he promised to protect slavery. They point to Lincoln's Whig political roots and to his resistance to emancipation even after the war began as evidence that he and most Republican voters in 1860 were not genuinely committed to eradicating slavery, regardless of its immorality. For them, the slogan "Free Labor," like the related slogan "Free Soil," indicated white opposition to the expansion of slavery to new territories, not necessarily white opposition to slavery continuing in the South. Such Republicanism reflected an economic-cultural ideology that also encompassed an early version of what today might be called a sense of "whiteness."[80] Thus, Southerners who advocated secession in response to Lincoln's election were either paranoid or seeking an excuse to strike out on their own in search of greater power, influence, and wealth. A middle view also exists: namely, that the limitations on the extension of slavery could have boxed in the slave states so as to threaten slavery itself, hence justifying secession based on a probabilistic judgment of risk to the institution.[81]

The best way to reconcile these different perspectives is to acknowledge that Lincoln's own position, the one that endeared him to Republican party leaders and voters in 1860, was itself all but logically incoherent. Lincoln's final prayer at the Cooper Union, "LET US

HAVE FAITH THAT RIGHT MAKES MIGHT,"[82] exemplified this self-contradiction. The faith that Lincoln invoked was supposed to save the union. But the Constitution of the union, to which Lincoln was expressing loyalty, was not "right." It was a compromise designed to achieve "might," based fundamentally on embracing what Lincoln was now openly calling a terrible moral wrong. Having faith in the "right" would not lead to the preservation of either the Constitution or the union. It would lead to the dissolution of both.

Three

THE CHOICE OF WAR

No other president has ever faced a crisis even vaguely comparable to the one that confronted Abraham Lincoln when he was inaugurated on March 4, 1861. It had been four months since he was elected in November, defeating three rivals in a highly regionalized race that remains the most polarized in U.S. history. During that time, seven states had held special secession conventions that resolved to repeal their ratifications of "the compact entitled the United States Constitution" and "dissolve" the union between them and the other United States. (In order of secession, these states were South Carolina, Mississippi, Florida, Alabama, Georgia, Louisiana, and Texas.) At a constitutional convention in Montgomery, Alabama, that began on February 4, 1861, the seven states had formed the Confederate States of America (CSA), adopted a provisional constitution, and drafted a permanent constitution they would soon ratify. Federal officials in the seceding states—including senators, congressmen, judges, U.S. marshals, and postmasters—resigned their positions. Many took up new ones in the new CSA. Almost overnight, the federal government ceased to exist as a practical reality in the seceding states.

The seven states were not seceding because they had any "hostility" against the U.S. Constitution per se, they insisted. Rather, as Alabama's secession convention put it, "the people and legislatures of the Northern states" had "set[] at naught" the fugitive slave clause of the Constitution

and subscribed to "other dangerous misrepresentations of that instrument." This led the Alabamians to "believe that the Northern people design, by their numerical majority, . . . ultimately to destroy many of our
most valuable rights"—in particular, their right to hold enslaved persons
as property.[1] By their account, the seven states were not breaking the
U.S. Constitution. They were exercising a constitutional right to withdraw from the compact in order to protect the rights they claimed to enjoy under it. Their central narrative was one of constitutionally legitimate
dissolution and legitimate re-formation. They hoped and anticipated
that other slave states—like North Carolina, Kentucky, Tennessee, and
Missouri, which bordered them, and Virginia, Maryland, and Delaware
in the Upper South—would follow suit by leaving the union and joining
the Confederacy.

To underscore that the seceding states had no quarrel with the
Constitution itself, the draft Confederate constitution was modeled
closely on the U.S. Constitution, with much of its language lifted directly from the original. Jefferson Davis, who resigned from the Senate
on January 21 and was inaugurated president of the Confederacy on
February 29, explained in his inaugural address, "We have changed the
constituent parts, but not the system of our Government. The Constitution formed by our fathers is that of these Confederate States." He
praised the original framers' "exposition" of the Constitution as well
as "the judicial construction it has received" from the Supreme Court;
together those provided "a light which reveals its true meaning."[2] The
Confederate constitution, in Davis's depiction, was a faithful successor
to the original Constitution, and the Confederacy was a newly and
duly constituted political union.

The main structural difference between the Confederate constitution
and the U.S. Constitution that Davis emphasized was a greater focus
on states' rights. According to a metaphor employed by Madison and
others at the Philadelphia constitutional convention in 1787, the federal Constitution was modeled on the solar system. At the center was

the sun—the federal government—while the states revolved around it. Through the magic of Newtonian gravity, the planets orbited in perfect balance with the pull of the sun in the center. Too much gravitational pull, and the planets would be drawn into the sun, losing their separate existence. Too little pull, and the planet-states would fly off into space, breaking away from the union.

To states that had just seceded in fear of the federal government, the solar-system image no longer applied. Davis compared the Confederacy to a "constellation." In this metaphor, there was no sun in the center. All the states in the constellation were stars of equal importance, and none bore any gravitational relation to any other. The implication was that the Confederate government would not feature an overweening central power that would dominate the interests of the member states. Driving home the primacy of the states, the preamble to the Confederate constitution started with "We, the People of the Confederate States," and then immediately added, "each State acting in its sovereign and independent character."[3] This language was intended to convey that the people of the states, not the people as a whole, were creating the new government. The seceding states held that the original Constitution was also a compact among the people of the sovereign states, which was why the people of the states had the constitutional right to withdraw from it. They were simply making sure that, this time, there would be no ambiguity about the question.

The Confederate vice president, Alexander Hamilton Stephens, echoed Davis: "All the essentials of the old constitution, which have endeared it to the hearts of the American people, have been preserved and perpetuated," he declared, and then added, "Some changes have been made." Those changes enshrined constitutional interpretations long favored by the South—Congress could not, for example, impose tariffs to help one class of economic interests over another, or spend money on "internal improvements." In another minor "improvement," the president would be elected for a single six-year term and could not run for reelection.

The most significant change, however, was this: "The new constitution has put to rest, *forever*, all the agitating questions related to our peculiar institution—African slavery as it exists amongst us." This change alone was basic, Stephens explained. "The prevailing ideas" held by the framers about slavery—namely, that it was wrong "socially, morally, and politically" and that it would "pass away" eventually—"were fundamentally wrong. They rested upon the assumption of the equality of races. This was an error." Stephens then stated baldly:

> Our new government is founded upon exactly the opposite idea; its foundations are laid, its corner-stone rests, upon the great truth, that the negro is not equal to the white man; that slavery—subordination to the superior race—is his natural and normal condition.
>
> This, our new government, is the first, in the history of the world, based upon this great physical, philosophical, and moral truth.[4]

The Confederate constitution instantiated this "truth" by prohibiting any law "denying or impairing the right of property in negro slaves," and guaranteeing slavery in any territory to be acquired in the future.[5] Despite keeping in place a ban on importing enslaved people of African descent (a sop to British public opinion as well as to slaveholders who did not want the value of their slaves to go down), the constitution expressly allowed the importation of slaves from the United States and its territories into the CSA—across what the CSA considered international borders. To Stephens, the Confederate constitution was essentially the U.S. Constitution—except that it was based explicitly upon the principle of white supremacy.

Secession posed a potential military challenge as well as a consti-

tutional one. In South Carolina, the epicenter of the secession movement, the U.S. Army responded to the creation of the Confederacy
by evacuating fourteen of its bases. Just 127 U.S. soldiers remained.
They were concentrated at Fort Sumter, an uncompleted structure in
Charleston Harbor. When the army sent a civilian steamer from New
York to resupply the fort in January, cadets from the Citadel, the state's
military academy, fired on the ship, thwarting the effort and serving
notice that the fort was under siege. The governor of South Carolina
officially demanded the fort's surrender. On taking office, Lincoln was
told that by April 15 the troops at Fort Sumter would run out of food
and begin to starve.

We know what happened next—or we think we do. Lincoln ordered five U.S. Navy warships and some tugboats to bring supplies and
some five hundred more troops to the fort. The first ship in the little
armada reached the harbor on April 11. Then, early on the morning of
April 12, 1861, General Pierre Gustave Toutant Beauregard, acting on
Davis's authority, began to bombard Fort Sumter from artillery batteries on the shore. The bombardment continued well into the next day.
The Union soldiers managed a symbolic response, enough to preserve
honor but no more. Thirty-four hours after the attack started, the U.S.
Army surrendered the fort. The Civil War had begun.

What this familiar story obscures is that, when he took office, Lincoln had no clear legal or constitutional ground to go to war to preserve the union. As secession loomed, President James Buchanan and
his attorney general, Jeremiah S. Black, had laid out a comprehensive
theory of what power the president had to respond to the creation
of the Confederate States of America. According to an official legal
opinion by Black, on which Buchanan relied in his State of the Union
message in December 1860, the answer was: not very much.

Black and Buchanan acknowledged that the seceding states were
engaged in a revolutionary act that was not authorized by the Constitution. They admitted that, if federal officials in the seceding states

needed help enforcing federal law, the president could send it. But the core of the view propounded by the president and attorney general of the United States as secession took place was that the executive could not make war on the people of one of the United States.

If this view sounds surprising to us, that is because Lincoln's rejection of it has come in retrospect to seem inevitable. Lincoln's decision to go to war to preserve the union—or, really, to re-create it, since the union was already broken by secession—today appears obvious and unproblematic. Lincoln would insist that the union could not be broken, that the seceding states were in rebellion, and that he as president possessed the inherent authority to put down the rebellion by force of arms. That theory of the Constitution was ultimately so successful that it does not seem like a theory at all, but merely a statement of the facts or perhaps a logical necessity.

Yet despite our retrospective judgment, Lincoln's decision did not follow ineluctably from the text of the Constitution, the structure of the government, or even the logic of the union itself. Rather, Lincoln had to break the Constitution as it had until then been understood in order to make war to "preserve" the union. In the process, he reinvented the meaning of the Constitution.

AN OATH REGISTERED IN HEAVEN

Lincoln's second inaugural address is, by common consent, one of the greatest speeches given in American history. Its words can be read high on the wall inside the Lincoln Memorial, opposite the words of the Gettysburg Address. Not so Lincoln's first inaugural address, which tends to be remembered, if at all, only for its final line, with its romantic invocation of the "mystic chords of memory" and its ultimately unfulfilled prayer for the return of "the better angels of our nature."[6]

The reason for contemporary neglect of Lincoln's first presidential address to the nation is immediately apparent from its first full paragraph. Quoting a statement he had made in the first of his debates with Stephen Douglas in 1858, Lincoln hastened to tell the nation that "I have no purpose, directly or indirectly, to interfere with the institution of slavery in the States where it exists. I believe I have no lawful right to do so, and I have no inclination to do so."[7]

Lincoln led with the protection of slavery because the point of the speech was to try somehow to reverse the Southern secession that had taken place over the previous several months. Failing that, Lincoln hoped to convince moderate Southerners and those in border states that secession was unreasonable and would not last. Secession had been precipitated by his election in November, and fueled by arguments that the Republican Lincoln would inevitably threaten the institution of slavery itself.[8] It therefore seemed imperative to Lincoln to take the opportunity of his inauguration to reassure the South that he believed he had no legal right to interfere with slavery in their states. What was more, Lincoln believed that Congress could not constitutionally interfere with slavery, either. Referring later in his remarks to a proposed constitutional amendment that would have expressly promised that the federal government would never interfere with slavery where it existed in the states, Lincoln said he would have no objection to making such an amendment "irrevocable," because what the amendment made explicit was already in his opinion "implied constitutional law."[9]

To assure Southerners that his compromise position was consistent with that of the Republican Party, Lincoln quoted the Republican platform of 1860. It restated the traditional premise of the compromise Constitution: "[t]hat the maintenance inviolate of the rights of the States, and especially the right of each State to order and control its own domestic institutions [i.e., slavery] according to its own judgment exclusively, is essential to that balance of power on which the perfection and endurance of our political fabric depend."[10] In this formulation, the continuing protection of slavery was a necessary, "essential" part of the constitutional arrangement. It ensured the "balance of power" between North and South. And on that balance depended the union itself—the "political fabric" that had to be saved from rending.

Still worse from the standpoint of history, Lincoln then turned to the fugitive slave clause of the Constitution—and gave it a ringing endorsement. He read out the clause in full. It was part of the Constitution, he said, and therefore binding on anyone who swore an oath to the Constitution: "All members of Congress swear their support to the whole Constitution—to this provision as much as to any other." He himself had, just moments before, taken an oath to support the Constitution of the United States. He had taken it "with no mental reservations," Lincoln said. He had thus sworn fealty to the fugitive slave clause. And he had taken the oath "with no purpose to construe the Constitution or laws, by any hypercritical rules."[11] By "hypercritical," Lincoln meant hairsplitting of the kind the seceding states attributed to Northerners with regard to that clause. The Constitution meant just what it said, and that included a commitment to the return of fugitive slaves.[12] It would be difficult to imagine a clearer repudiation of the idea that the Lincoln who was elected in 1860 and inaugurated in 1861 understood the Constitution as an antislavery document.

Having fully embraced the traditional compromise Constitution, Lincoln turned to secession itself. In the strongest sentence of an exceedingly weak speech, he stated plainly that the union could not be broken. "I hold," Lincoln asserted, "that in contemplation of universal law, and of the Constitution, the Union of these States is perpetual."[13]

Obviously, the seceding states did not agree. Their theory was, roughly, that the Constitution was a "compact between the States" comparable to an international treaty among sovereign nations.[14] Under the logic of "the law of compact," South Carolina explained in its public declaration of secession, "the failure of one of the contracting parties to perform a material part of the agreement, entirely releases the obligation of the other."[15] Northern states had violated the constitutional compact. It followed that the Southern states had the right to secede under the terms of the agreement itself. As a compact among sovereign states, the Constitution implicitly provided for its own dissolution.*

Lincoln was rejecting the Southern theory on two different grounds, and each of them mattered. The simpler of the two grounds was that the Constitution itself did not permit secession. Lincoln pointed out that the preamble to the Constitution stated that one of the purposes of the document was "*to form a more perfect union.*" In legal terms, *perfect* means "complete." The idea was that the union under the Constitution would be more complete than the one that existed under the Articles of Confederation. The Articles of Confederation, for their part, had explicitly stated that the union would be "perpetual." Southerners thought that because the union was among sovereign states, it could always be dissolved. Lincoln concluded to the contrary that "if destruction of the Union, by one, or by a part only, of the States, be lawfully possible, the Union is *less* perfect than before the Constitution, having lost the vital element of perpetuity."[16] Thus, the words of the preamble made secession unconstitutional.

Lincoln then got to his main point: the South had not seceded under the Constitution; it had engaged in an act of revolution—a rejection of the constitutional framework itself. As Lincoln put it, "It follows that no State, upon its own mere motion, can lawfully get out of the Union,—that *resolves* and *ordinances* to that effect are legally void; and that acts of violence, within any State or States, against the authority of the United States, are insurrectionary or revolutionary,

---

* As in international law, South Carolina asserted, there was no court that could adjudicate the fact that the compact had been violated: "[W]here no arbiter is provided, each party is remitted to his own judgment to determine the fact of failure, with all its consequences."

according to circumstances."[17] It was legally "impossible to destroy" the Constitution, "except by some action not provided for in the instrument itself."[18]

This last sentence was all-important. "I therefore consider that, in view of the Constitution and the laws," Lincoln asserted, "the Union is unbroken." It still included the Southern states, and so as president, Lincoln had an ongoing constitutional obligation to continue protecting the union: "[T]o the extent of my ability I shall take care, as the Constitution itself expressly enjoins upon me, that the laws of the Union be faithfully executed in all the States."[19]

Yet Lincoln was also acknowledging that the Constitution *could* be destroyed—by a revolutionary act that existed outside the Constitution.* If revolution was permissible under international law, and was even a basic human right according to received American wisdom going back to 1776, why did Lincoln not consider the possibility that the South's revolutionary act of secession should be respected?[20] His answer, subtly expressed, was also extraordinarily important. He would perform his "simple duty" to enforce the Constitution "so far as practicable," he explained, "unless my rightful masters, the American people, shall withhold the requisite means, or, in some authoritative manner, direct the contrary."[21]

Lincoln was saying that it was not up to him as president of the United States to determine whether the Southern act of secession was a legitimate revolution. That decision was up to the American people— acting, presumably, through Congress, the body that the Constitution had created to represent them. One possibility he expressly contemplated was that Congress would "withhold" the president's means to

---

* This position was reminiscent of what Lincoln had said in his 1846 speech in Congress about Texans' revolution against Mexican authority. Then he had insisted that there was a basic human right to make a revolution and establish sovereignty over territory where one lived. Such a revolution could, in principle, be entitled to respect under international law.

enforce the law, by denying him personnel. The other possibility was that Congress would "in some authoritative manner" tell him not to enforce the Constitution. That would mean Congress had acknowledged the success of the Southern revolution. If that happened, then as president he would have to follow the will of the people—and give up trying to enforce the Constitution on the South.

By claiming that he did not have the power to decide whether the South had made a successful revolution, Lincoln was actually asserting for himself and his presidency the power to take on the South immediately, by force if necessary. In effect, Lincoln was insisting that so long as Congress did nothing, he was bound to act on the assumption that secession was not a successful revolution deserving recognition, but an act of rebellion to be suppressed. As he spoke those words, Congress was not in session, and so "the people" could take no steps one way or the other regarding secession. The upshot was that Lincoln would treat secession as rebellion, not revolution.

As a practical matter, this was the most important consequence of the inaugural address. It showed that Lincoln was adopting a strikingly different stance when facing secession than the one his predecessor, James Buchanan, had adopted. In his State of the Union message in December 1860, Buchanan had, like Lincoln, taken the view that the Constitution did not provide a mechanism for its own dissolution. "Secession," he had argued, "is neither more nor less than revolution." But that was where the similarity between the two presidents stopped. Unlike Lincoln's address, Buchanan's message proceeded on the assumption that, if the Northern states violated the Constitution, the Southern states would in fact be justified in revolutionary resistance. "In order to justify a resort to revolutionary resistance," Buchanan said, "the Federal Government must be guilty of 'a deliberate, palpable, and dangerous exercise' of powers not granted by the Constitution."[22] Buchanan contended that the Northern states had not in fact violated the Constitution as the seceding states maintained—and that the election of Lincoln did not constitute grounds for secession. But he actively presented the scenario of justified secession, which Lincoln certainly did not.

Buchanan had then laid out his theory of what the president could and could not do on his own, without Congress—and here in particular his views were very far from Lincoln's first inaugural address. According to Buchanan, once there were no federal officials doing their jobs in a state that had seceded, there was almost nothing the president could do to fulfill his constitutional duty to take care that the laws be faithfully executed. There were a couple of statutes on the books, from 1795 and 1807, that authorized the president to call out the militia when federal officials could not get a court order enforced. But that, he said, required federal courts and marshals to be operating, which they were not in South Carolina when Buchanan was speaking.

Buchanan explained that it was up to Congress to pass new laws if it wanted to authorize him to take action vis-à-vis South Carolina. "Congress alone," he reasoned, "has power to decide whether the present laws can or can not be amended so as to carry out more effectually the objects of the Constitution." He could appoint new customs officers if those in office resigned. And if South Carolina should try to "expel" troops from federal forts in South Carolina, Buchanan said, he had ordered the troops "to act strictly on the defensive."[23] Beyond that, Buchanan claimed to be powerless without getting authorization from Congress.

Lincoln effectively flipped Buchanan's logic on its head. According to Buchanan, the default position was that the president could do almost nothing without Congress. According to Lincoln, the president had to act unless Congress actively told him not to.

But there was more to Buchanan's theory—and more that Lincoln therefore had to refute. In his State of the Union message, Buchanan had admitted, as Lincoln himself did, that it was up to Congress, not the president, to recognize the validity of secession. He went on, however, to address the more fundamental constitutional question that would now confront Congress: Did Congress itself have "the power to coerce a State into submission" when it purported to secede from the union?[24]

It is no exaggeration to say that the fate of the union rested on the answer to this question. If the answer was yes, Congress could commence a war to force the Southern states back into the union. If the answer was no, then secession was a fait accompli, constitutionally speaking—and the Confederacy would have to be allowed to exist in peace.

Today we hardly remember it. But the stunning fact is that, having posed this question in the aftermath of South Carolina's secession, the then president of the United States went on to answer it by saying no. "After much serious reflection," Buchanan said, "I have arrived at the conclusion that no such power has been delegated to Congress or to any other department of the Federal Government."[25] That is, neither Congress nor the president had the authority under the Constitution to make seceding states stay in the union. As a constitutional matter, Buchanan was saying, Southern secession had to be allowed to occur, even if it was itself an act of revolution in violation of the Constitution. This view (astounding to us) differed sharply from the approach that Andrew Jackson, a Democrat like Buchanan, had taken at the time of the nullification crisis, when he threatened South Carolina with military coercion. Yet in 1860, it was the position of moderate Democrats who had no interest in a coercive war to preserve the union—and the position of the commander in chief.

Buchanan went on to reason that there were no "specific and enumerated powers granted to Congress" to keep states in the union, and that it was "equally apparent" that coercing states to remain was not covered by the clause of the Constitution that gave Congress the power to do what was "necessary and proper for carrying into execution" its other powers. He pointed out that, during the constitutional convention of 1787, the delegates had discussed introducing a provision that would have authorized "an exertion of the force of the whole against a delinquent State." James Madison had spoken against the provision, explaining, "The use of force against a State would look more like a declaration of war than an infliction of punishment; and would probably be considered by the party attacked as a dissolution of all previous compacts by which it might be bound."[26] The framers had considered authorizing federal coercion of the states, and had rejected it.

Beyond his historical and textual arguments, Buchanan also based his reasoning on the spirit of the law. "[T]he power to make war against a State is at variance with the whole spirit and intent of the Constitution," he asserted. The spirit Buchanan had in mind was the voluntary nature of democracy: "Suppose such a war should result in the conquest of a State; how are we to govern it afterwards? Shall we hold it as a province and govern it by despotic power?" That scenario seemed to him completely at odds with the basic principle of popular consent: "In the nature of things, we could not by physical force control the will of the people and compel them to elect Senators and Representatives to Congress and to perform all the other duties depending upon their own volition and required from the free citizens of a free State."[27] Taken on its own terms, this observation had a powerful internal logic. Indeed, it was to a certain degree prophetic. After the Civil War, Reconstruction would confront precisely the contradiction of establishing and legitimating democracy under conditions of military occupation—and would eventually fail.

Ultimately, Buchanan believed that war would not preserve the union even if it were constitutionally permissible: "War would not only present the most effectual means of destroying [the union], but would vanish all hope of its peaceable reconstruction." The costs of "fraternal conflict"—in both "blood and treasure"—would make "future reconciliation between the States impossible." Because civil war could not achieve its goal of preserving the union, the North should urge the South to rethink secession, but should accept it if it could not be avoided. "The fact is," he concluded, "that our Union rests upon public opinion . . . If it can not live in the affections of the people, it must one day perish."[28] That outcome would be tragic, but it would be preferable to civil war.

Lincoln did not think so, and he intended his first inaugural address to signal that to the seceding South. Yet at the same time as he spelled out his constitutional alternative to the Buchanan view, Lincoln also strove to present the South with an impression of restraint. He cited the Republican platform: "[W]e denounce the lawless invasion by armed force of the soil of any State or Territory, no matter what pretext, as among the gravest of crimes."[29] The word "invasion" referred to an attack from the outside. The natural meaning of this passage was to condemn any invasion of seceding Southern states by the army of the United States. This platform plank might also have been interpreted to condemn Southern attempts to use armed force against federal targets. But its primary purpose as drafted, and certainly as invoked by Lincoln, was to tell Southerners that Lincoln did not intend to send the army against them. As Lincoln immediately glossed it, "the property, peace and security of no section are to be in anywise endangered by the now incoming Administration."[30]

Lincoln had insisted that he would fulfill his constitutional duty to execute the laws of the United States even in states that had seceded. But he emphasized, "In doing this there needs to be no bloodshed or violence; and there shall be none unless it be forced upon the national authority." This amounted to a pledge not to fire the first shots. "The power confided to me," he explained, "will be used to hold, occupy, and possess the property, and places belonging to the government, and to collect the duties and imposts." This meant that Lincoln would not give up on federal control of Fort Sumter. "[B]ut beyond what may be necessary for these objects, there will be no invasion—no using of force against, or among the people anywhere."[31]

A promise not to invade the seceding states was no small matter. To be sure, Lincoln was taking a far stronger stand than Buchanan had.

Unlike his predecessor, Lincoln did not say that using coercion against the seceding states was unconstitutional or unwise. But he was disclaiming any intent to use coercion, at least for the moment. Lincoln even said that where "hostility to the United States" had forced federal officials to resign, he would make "no attempt to force obnoxious strangers among the people for that object." Lincoln insisted that "the strict legal right may exist in the government to enforce the exercise of these offices." He acknowledged, however, that "the attempt to do so would be so irritating and so nearly impracticable" that it would be better "to forego, for the time, the uses of such offices."[32]

Ultimately, Lincoln was aiming to convey a firmness that Buchanan had not; to seek reconciliation via protection of slavery; and if reconciliation proved impossible, to justify in advance whatever steps he might have to take. He drew to a close with a threat wrapped inside of a plea:

> In *your* hands, my dissatisfied fellow countrymen, and not
> in *mine*, is the momentous issue of civil war. The govern-
> ment will not assail *you*. You can have no conflict without
> being yourselves the aggressors. *You* have no oath registered
> in Heaven to destroy the government, while I shall have
> the most solemn one to "preserve, protect, and defend" it.[33]*

The plea was for Southerners not to precipitate a war. The threat was that if they did, Lincoln would rely on his self-declared constitutional

---

* In his first draft, Lincoln wrote: "Fellow-citizens! the momentous case is before you. On your undivided support of your government depends the decision of the great question it involves, whether your sacred Union will be preserved, and the blessing it secures to us as one people shall be perpetuated." See Kenneth M. Stampp, "The Concept of a Perpetual Union," *Journal of American History* 65, no. 1 (June 1978): 32. The final draft de-emphasized the notion that the fate of the union lay in the hands of the public.

powers to fight back. His oath of office was to "preserve, protect, and defend" the Constitution, not the government. By announcing that the oath he had "registered in Heaven" was to protect the government of the union, Lincoln was declaring that he considered himself duty-bound not to yield to secession. In the days that followed, he would have the opportunity to prove that he meant it.

SUMTER

Because Buchanan had not successfully reinforced or resupplied Fort Sumter, Lincoln's military options were all unattractive. The day before the inauguration, Winfield Scott, the senior general and head of the army, laid out his view of what could be done in a letter to William Seward, whom Lincoln had asked to become his secretary of state.* Scott, almost seventy-five years old, was the dominant figure in American military life. He had been a general since the War of 1812 (he was just twenty-seven when made brigadier) and in 1856 had advanced to the rank of lieutenant general—the first American since Washington to be promoted to that level. Most relevant, Scott had seen it all before. He had been the general whom Andrew Jackson had sent to Charleston Harbor in 1833 with troops and naval support to show South Carolinians that any attempt to block collection of federal tariffs would be met by force.

The previous December, Scott had reminded Buchanan of Jackson's dual strategy of projecting power to South Carolina while making it clear that any attack on federal forces would mean that the state had

---

* Seward had not yet accepted, however; indeed, two days earlier, on March 2, he had told Lincoln he would not take the job. See Russell McClintock, *Lincoln and the Decision for War: The Northern Response to Secession* (Chapel Hill: University of North Carolina Press, 2008), 194. Scott's letter reflected Seward's preference for conciliation, and McClintock suggests it was written at Seward's request. Ibid., 193.

made war on the United States, not the other way around.[34] Now, however, Scott did not present the option of reinforcing the fort. He told Seward—and therefore Lincoln—that there were just four possible courses of action the president could take.

Scott's first choice, the one he clearly favored, was to conciliate the South by renaming the Republican Party as the "Union Party" and adopting a set of constitutional amendments that would restore the Missouri Compromise and protect the extension of slavery to all new territories south of the 36°30' line, all the way to the Pacific. There were two similar sets of such recommendations in play—the Crittenden compromise of December 1860, which had been proposed in Congress but blocked by Republicans, and the proposal of the so-called Peace Conference of February 1861, which had passed by a vote of nine states to eight states. Scott said that regardless of which one Lincoln embraced, there would be no further secessions from the states of the Upper South; and he predicted "on the contrary, an early return of many, if not all the states which have already broken off from the Union."[35]

Scott made it clear that this was partly a military recommendation, not a purely political one. If Lincoln did not take radical steps toward reconciliation, he explained, "the remaining slave holding states" of the upper South would "probably join the . . . confederacy in less than sixty days." Maryland and Virginia—the states surrounding Washington, D.C.—were both slave states. Once those states had seceded, Washington would be "included in a foreign country." To defend the city, Scott said, "would require [a] permanent Garrison of at least 35,000 troops." Scott remembered the War of 1812, when a detachment of battle-hardened British soldiers had sacked the capital in a daring two-day campaign, routing a much larger number of hastily mustered American militiamen at the Battle of Bladensburg. The estimate of thirty-five thousand men to defend the capital was high but not absurd. The problem was that entire regular U.S. Army then consisted of just sixteen thousand regular troops.[36] Scott was saying that the geographical position of Washington, D.C., provided a strong military reason for Lincoln to keep the Upper South from seceding.

Scott's second option for Lincoln was to use the navy to "collect the duties on foreign goods outside the ports of which this Government has lost the command."[37] That meant placing warships outside Charleston and other southern ports—in essence a blockade. It would take an act of Congress, he thought, but it was certainly a sensible recommendation. A naval blockade would be an approach to war that de-emphasized the grave limitations of existing Union manpower. Lincoln would in fact commence such a blockade once he decided on war; and it would remain in place until 1865. Scott himself would recommend using blockades as the linchpin of his own war plan—the "Anaconda plan"—once Lincoln demanded a concrete war strategy from him.

The third option was a massive land war. The Union, Scott wrote, could "conquer the seceded states by invading armies." It could be done in "two or three years," Scott estimated, if the Union forces were led "by a young able general—a Wolfe, a Desaix or a Hoche." These were famous generals of the eighteenth century—one Englishman and two Frenchmen. All three had died young, two on the battlefield and one quite near it. If Scott had a potential American candidate for martyrdom in mind, he did not mention his name. To win the land war would also take "300,000 disciplined men" and losses of more than 100,000 to "skirmishes, sieges, battles and southern fevers." In the South, "the destruction of life and property . . . would be frightful—however perfect the moral discipline of the invaders."[38]

Scott intended to describe a land war as pointless. "The conquest" would entail an "enormous waste of human life," he wrote, and would cost "at least $250,000,000." He then asked rhetorically, "Cui bono?" Who would benefit? The result would be "fifteen devastated provinces—not to be brought into harmony with their conquerors; but

to be held, for generations, by heavy garrisons—at an expense qua-
druple the net duties or taxes which it would be possible to extract
from them—followed by a Protector or an emperor."³⁹ The conquered
South would have to be occupied like a set of imperial provinces. As a
military matter, Scott was arguing, such an occupation would be out-
rageously expensive—and could not realistically lead to democratic or
republican reintegration.

That left Scott with his fourth option—to let the South go. The
general expressed himself poetically: "Say to the seceded—States—
wayward sisters, depart in peace!" Scott was no secessionist. But from
the standpoint of military strategy, it was perfectly plausible to conclude that war was not an option worth pursuing. Scott had explained
that in case of war, the capital would be vulnerable. A naval blockade
alone would not suffice to end secession. An invasion would be costly
and lengthy, and did not seem likely to end in a manageable peace. It
would be irrational not to consider simply allowing secession for lack
of a decisive military option.

Perhaps Scott did not mention the possibility of attempting to resupply Fort Sumter because he no longer favored it. But it seems more
likely that the reason Scott did not refer to the suggestion he had made
three months earlier to Buchanan was that, by March, he believed it
was no longer possible to resupply the fort to enable it to hold out. The
day after the inauguration, March 5, Scott told Lincoln that "the officers of the fort . . . now see no alternative but a surrender." There was
no time to send the troops "necessary to give them relief." He added,
"Evacuation seems almost inevitable . . . if, indeed, the worn out garrison be not assaulted & carried in the present week."⁴⁰ He repeated the
advice on March 11 and again on March 28.⁴¹

In an undated note, presumably from around the same time, Scott
told Lincoln, "The giving up of Forts Sumter and Pickens may be best
justified by the hope that we should thereby recover the State to which
they geographically belong by the liberality of the act, besides retain-

ing the eight doubtful States."[42] This sounds like advice for post hoc justification of the surrender that Scott assessed as militarily necessary. Scott did not believe that Lincoln could face down the new Confederacy with a resupply of Fort Sumter in the way that Jackson had faced down South Carolina in 1833—because the military situation had changed since December.

As a military matter, that was accurate. The morning after his inauguration, Lincoln arrived at his office to a note from the outgoing secretary of war, Joseph Holt, informing him that he had received a dispatch from Major Robert Anderson at Fort Sumter stating that Charleston had been fortified and that it would now take an army of twenty thousand to thirty thousand men to conquer the city. Anderson knew perfectly well that no such force existed. He was writing to say that, with his limited provisions, he would shortly have to surrender the fort.[43] Lincoln sent the information to Scott, who told the president that while Sumter could have been reinforced in December when he first recommended it, and even into February, it was now too late.

The first full day of Lincoln's presidency thus made it clear that he would need to adopt a policy on Fort Sumter immediately. The very next day, more news came from Anderson. A dispatch dated March 2 specified that he had exactly twenty-eight days' worth of flour and bread left to feed his garrison.[44] There was now a clear end date to the Fort Sumter showdown.

Lincoln may or may not have been surprised by the immediacy of the need for a decision. Certainly his cabinet members professed to be "astonished" when he told them about it at his first cabinet meeting on March 9.[45] The state of the garrison at Fort Sumter was not treated as a state secret—or if it was, it was the most poorly guarded secret imaginable. Newspapers almost immediately reported the inevitability of a surrender. A week into Lincoln's presidency, the public expected him to order Anderson to evacuate.

Lincoln thought otherwise. He now understood that resupplying

Sumter would not allow the fort to stand. But in the weeks after the inauguration, he gradually settled on the policy of ordering and announcing a resupply, with the full realization that it would likely provoke an attack on the fort by the nascent Confederacy. His reason for rejecting concessions in response to secession was essentially that concessions under conditions of threat would only lead to more concessions. He illustrated his view of the situation using Aesop's fable of a lion who wanted to marry "a beautiful lady" and so agreed to her relatives' demand that he cut off his "long and sharp claws and his tusks"—after which the relatives "took clubs then and knocked him on the head."[46]

That is not to say that Lincoln would have rejected conciliation if he had thought it would work. At the same meeting where Lincoln recounted the fable of the lion, William C. Rives of Virginia told Lincoln that if he tried to coerce the Southern states to stay in the union, Virginia would secede, and Rives would support the decision. According to the source who recounted the details of the meeting, Lincoln declared that "if Virginia will stay in, I will withdraw the troops at Fort Sumter."[47] Lincoln knew that no such guarantee from Virginia was likely to come. His comment reflected his openness to being met halfway, in the unlikely event that should happen.

At a cabinet meeting on March 15, Lincoln invited Gustavus Fox, a former naval officer, to present a plan for resupplying the fort. Then Lincoln asked his cabinet members whether it would be "wise to attempt" resupplying the fort, assuming it was possible to do so at all. The cabinet was divided. All agreed that Lincoln had the constitutional authority to attempt the resupply. No one, not even Seward, who most strongly opposed the attempt, claimed that an attempted resupply would count as an invasion of the South. But several cabinet members wanted the first blows of the war to come through South Carolinian resistance to a civilian attempt to enforce some concrete federal law— not in military defense of federal property.[48] Seward thought that, in practice, the action would spark a war, and he wanted more time to work out a peaceful solution. Montgomery Blair, the postmaster general from Maryland, urged that further concessions would only weaken the Union, and maintained that a show of federal force would "demoralize the rebellion"[49]—a rather hopeful comparison to Jackson's actions in 1833. Seward seemed to have the better of the argument. Much of the cabinet left the meeting thinking that Lincoln had decided to evacuate the fort.[50]

On March 18, three days later, Lincoln again asked his cabinet members for their views, this time on whether it was plausible to place warships outside Southern ports to collect duties on imports. Again, no one claimed that doing so was beyond Lincoln's power. The concern was that such a blockade would effectively count as an act of war. Lincoln was clearly looking for further options. He sent Fox to Charleston on March 19 to confirm the military situation. Fox returned with the information that Anderson could hold out until April 15 by feeding his soldiers half rations; he also proposed a nighttime tugboat landing of supplies. Anderson in turn sent word that the tugboat scheme was unrealistic. Lincoln told Fox to make a list of what supplies would be needed.

On March 29, Lincoln again sought his cabinet's views on resupplying Sumter. By now he had begun to lose faith in Winfield Scott's judgment, primarily because the general had recommended evacuating Fort Pickens in Pensacola, Florida—another island fortification, and one that Lincoln had not previously imagined giving up. Opinion in the cabinet had shifted slightly to favor resupplying Sumter, although the group was still divided. The secretary of the treasury, Salmon P. Chase, said explicitly that it was perfectly reasonable to let the war begin through Southern resistance to an attempt to resupply troops.[51] Lincoln issued orders to Fox to get an expedition ready to leave New York as soon as April 6.[52]

Less than a month into his presidency, Lincoln was under almost unimaginable stress. The day after the cabinet meeting, March 30, he lost his temper in a meeting with California politicians who had come seeking patronage appointments. He yelled at one of them, balled up a written copy of a speech, threw it into the fire, and told them to leave. After they were gone, Lincoln complained of a "sick headache"— presumably a migraine—and fainted.[53] Seward, perhaps emboldened by Lincoln's collapse to think that Lincoln would be unable to govern effectively, sent the president an astonishing memorandum on April 1 suggesting that if Lincoln was not up to choosing a policy and engaging in an "energetic prosecution" of it, perhaps he should delegate it to "some member of his cabinet," presumably Seward himself.[54] Lincoln said no—with a politeness that is remarkable under the circumstances.

On April 4, Lincoln held a meeting with John Baldwin, a Virginia unionist, who confirmed that even moderates in the Upper South thought Lincoln must abandon Fort Sumter (and, for good measure, Fort Pickens) as gestures of conciliation to keep them in the union. Lincoln asked whether conflict could be avoided if he sent only supplies to Sumter, not fresh troops. Baldwin told him it would make no difference. Another dispatch came from Anderson, this one dated April 1, asserting that supplies would run out in a week and asking for an order to leave the fort. Anderson, it transpired, had never put his men on half rations after all.

The time had come for action. Lincoln sent word to Anderson that he would be resupplied and instructed him to expect a shipment by April 11 or 12 and not to evacuate before then. On April 6, Lincoln notified the governor of South Carolina that he intended to provision Fort Sumter. As a compromise measure, he promised that no troops or weapons would be sent to the fort "without further notice, or in case of attack."[55] This assured that Lincoln would not fire the first shots in a war, or even assume a warlike footing by helping prepare the fort for battle. As a matter of military tactics, it made no sense to make such a promise. Lincoln was practicing politics. He expected South Carolina to attack. And he did not want the Union to be seen as the aggressor in whatever conflict followed.

As a Whig congressman, Lincoln had excoriated President James K. Polk for provoking Mexican troops to attack U.S. forces. As Lincoln saw it then, Polk had acted unconstitutionally. Only Congress had the power to declare war. For the executive to deploy U.S. forces so as to induce an attack overstepped presidential authority. Now Lincoln was embarked on a course of action that was tactically and strategically comparable. He had promised in his inaugural address that federal troops would not initiate hostilities. Instead, he would send the resupply mission—an action that he knew would provoke a Confederate bombardment of Fort Sumter.

The resupply mission left New York on April 10. On April 11, the Confederacy demanded Anderson's surrender and threatened to begin bombardment. Following Lincoln's orders, Anderson declined. On the morning of April 12, the batteries along the Charleston harbor turned on the fort and began to shell it. The ships arrived the same morning but could not approach the fort because of the shelling. On April 14, Anderson surrendered. No one had died. But the Confederacy had attacked a U.S. government fort.

The assault was "unprovoked," Lincoln told a group of unionist Virginians on April 13. It constituted "the commencement of actual war against the Government."[56] It was, in short, an act of war.

Yet Lincoln did not ask Congress to declare war in response, because a declaration of war under the Constitution might imply the recognition of the Confederacy as a foreign government. An invasion might be construed as breaking the union. Constitutional and legal considerations dictated something different—and unprecedented.

In place of seeking a declaration of war, on April 15, Lincoln issued a carefully worded, almost modest proclamation. It began with the announcement that "the laws of the United States have been for some time past, and now are opposed, and the execution thereof obstructed" in seven named states.[57] These were the same seven states that had seceded—but secession was not directly mentioned, since it was not an act to which Lincoln was prepared to give legal validity, even by reference.

There was no mention of treason or revolution. The blocking of the execution of the laws was being undertaken, the proclamation said, "by combinations too powerful to be suppressed by the ordinary course of judicial proceedings, or by the powers vested in the Marshals by law."[58] The word "combinations" was a euphemism for what Lincoln would not call governments. It was an extreme understatement to say that the federal courts and U.S. marshals could not enforce the law. There were no federal courts in operation. All the judges and marshals had long since resigned.

The operative clause of the proclamation was similarly concise:

> Now therefore, I, Abraham Lincoln, President of the United States, in virtue of the power in me vested by the Constitution, and the laws, have thought fit to call forth, and hereby do call forth, the militia of the several States of the Union, to the aggregate number of seventy-five thousand, in order to suppress said combinations, and to cause the laws to be duly executed.[59]

Lincoln was invoking his constitutional authority as president to take care that the laws be executed. More controversially, he was asserting that this power authorized him to call out the militia—seventy-five thousand troops, to begin with—to "suppress" the Confederate governments.

This asserted constitutional power to suppress the Confederate state governments in order to execute the law was precisely what Buchanan and his attorney general, Jeremiah Black, had claimed the executive lacked. Black had admitted that when federal courts and marshals were not being obeyed, the executive had the authority to use the army or a militia to enforce the laws. "Their agency must continue to be used until their incapacity to cope with the power opposed to them shall be plainly demonstrated," he wrote. Once that was demonstrated by "clear evidence," however, "a military force can be called into the field." Such a force fielded by the executive "must be purely defensive," Black insisted. "It can suppress only such combinations as are found directly opposing the laws and obstructing the execution thereof."[60] To this extent, Lincoln's proclamation sounded superficially as though it were invoking Black's language. His proclamation specified that the federal courts and marshals were not being obeyed—and it called out the militia to enforce the laws. Even the word "combinations," used in Lincoln's proclamation to refer to the seceding state governments, could be traced to Black's description of "combinations" opposing and obstructing the execution of federal law.

The constitutional divergence between Black's view and Lincoln's had to do with what would happen if the federal officials in the state resigned, so that no federal civilian authority existed—as had happened in South Carolina and subsequently in the other seceding states. According to Black, the militia, when called out, had to serve "in strict subordination to the civil authority, since it is only in aid of the latter that the former can act at all." Because the job of the militia was to enforce federal law, and because federal law was ordinarily administered by civilians, the militia could only be deployed at the command of the civilian officials: namely, the federal judges and marshals. Consequently, Black maintained, when the courts were closed and no federal civilian authority existed, "troops would certainly be out of place, and their use wholly illegal."[61]

This conclusion followed from the logic of civilian legal enforcement, Black reasoned. If the militia were "sent to aid the courts and marshals, there must be courts and marshals to be aided." The job of enforcing the laws belonged "exclusively to the civil service," he asserted. "Without civilians in charge, the laws cannot be executed in any event, no matter what may be the physical strength which the Government has at its command." If Black was correct, then it followed that "to send a military force into any State, with orders to act against the people, would be simply making war upon them."[62]

Lincoln's proclamation rejected the key elements of the former attorney general's reasoning. Unlike Black, Lincoln did not take the position that only civilian authorities could enforce the law. When civilian authority in the form of courts and marshals was absent because of resignation, Lincoln believed that he as the president of the United States still possessed the duty and power to execute the laws. He could call out the militia, and he could enforce the laws via military authority, without civilian intervention.

From the standpoint of formal constitutional logic, Lincoln's position could be defended. The president of the United States was the chief executive of the government. Under the text of the Constitution, his authority ran throughout the country—not only to places where local federal officials existed to enforce the law. Black insisted that the authority to enforce the laws belonged strictly to civilians, but no express constitutional provision supported that claim. And even if Black were right in principle, the president was himself a civilian, albeit one with the dual character of chief executive and commander in chief.

What made Black's argument powerful, however, was his concrete, pragmatic assessment that "to send a military force into any state, with orders to act against the people, would be simply making war upon them." A militia or an army sent from outside the state into that state in order to suppress the local government certainly seemed indistinguishable from an act of invasion or war. Nothing in the Constitution expressly authorized the federal government to invade a state. Madison had disclaimed any such intention at the constitutional convention. Buchanan had quoted Madison to that effect in his State of the Union message, citing Madison's observations that the use of force against a state would resemble "a declaration of war" and that the state would likely consider such force "a dissolution of all previous compacts by which it might be bound"—namely, the Constitution.*

Madison's trenchant observation seemed as true in April 1861 as it had been in the summer of 1787. It was one thing to enforce the laws by ordinary civilian means, even to the point of using a militia to make sure court orders were obeyed. It was quite another, practically speaking, to send an army to suppress state governments, while insisting that the only purpose was to enforce the law. A federal army from outside the state did look like an invasion of the kind that characterized a declared war. And a state thus invaded might very well claim that by invading, the federal government had broken the constitutional compact that bound the state to the union.

To these concerns Lincoln had no direct answer—either then or at any subsequent time in the war. At no point during the conflict would Congress ever declare war on the Southern states. In order to suspend the writ of habeas corpus—the subject of the next chapter—Lincoln would declare that the seceding states were in a state of rebellion. But when it came to the legal status of war, he would never be able to get around the Madisonian problem that making war on states was not contemplated by the original Constitution. Lincoln would of course come to speak of the conflict as a "war." The code of conduct eventually developed for the Union Army by the political theorist Francis Lieber would

---

* In late November 1860, Black's predecessor as attorney general, Caleb Cushing of Massachusetts, had cited Madison's comments in a speech, likely giving Buchanan his source. Not only did Cushing think that Madison's comments were proof that the federal government lacked the constitutional power to use coercion against the state. Cushing went further, claiming that, according to Madison's logic, the use of coercion would "itself produce the legal dissolution of the Union." See McClintock, *Lincoln and the Decision for War*, 30, n. 26. (Cushing's speech was given November 26, 1860, at Newburyport, Massachusetts. See *Boston Press and Post*, Nov. 29, 1860, 2. Thanks to David Heusel for finding the printed text.)

use the word "war" and invoke the international laws of war.[63] But a basic constitutional tension would remain at the heart of the conflict until its end, and beyond: to the Union, the Civil War could never be a war in the constitutional sense, because the moment it became a war, it would presume two nations fighting each other, not a single legitimate government seeking to execute the laws.

In his proclamation, Lincoln therefore avoided saying anything about war or invasion. He made only one concession to the warlike nature of the coming conflict. Having called up the militia "to cause the laws to be duly executed," he stated that "the details" would be "immediately communicated to the state authorities through the War Department."[64] The calling up of the militia was a state function to be performed at federal direction—and Lincoln would use the War Department to achieve it. More than anything, this necessity illustrated just how far the federal government was from the capacity actually to execute the laws. Lincoln needed militias from Northern states to get sufficient manpower to mount an attack on the Confederacy.

PERPETUITY AND CONSTITUTIONAL GOVERNMENT

Because Lincoln wanted to focus on his constitutional authority to execute the laws, he reduced the preservation of the union to subordinate status in the proclamation. He said only, "I appeal to all loyal citizens to favor, facilitate and aid this effort to maintain the honor, the integrity, and the existence of our National Union, and the perpetuity of popular government; and to redress wrongs already long enough endured."[65] Invoking loyalty implied that the seceding states were disloyal. It did not (yet) go so far as to declare them traitorous. Calling to maintain the "integrity" and "existence" of the union acknowledged that the union was in danger of being broken apart. It did not, however, admit that the dissolution had already occurred—because Lincoln could not and would not do so.

The "perpetuity of popular government" was something else again. Here Lincoln was referring not to the perpetuity of the union, but to the survival of the very notion of democracy itself. The concern that secession would doom democracy had increasingly figured in his thinking since secession. Lincoln was worried not merely that the union would fail, but that this failure would prove the impossibility of the framers' ambitious goal of creating, for the first time, a functioning form of democratic self-government. Addressing the New Jersey Senate in February 1861, on his way to Washington, D.C., to be inaugurated, Lincoln had put it this way:

> I am exceedingly anxious that that thing which they struggled for; that something even more than National Independence; that something that held out a great promise to all the people of the world to all time to come; I am exceedingly anxious that this Union, the Constitution, and the liberties of the people shall be perpetuated in accordance with the original idea for which that struggle was made.[66]

The particular vulnerability of self-government that worried Lincoln had to do with the minority's claim of the authority to secede, hence breaking majoritarian government. In his inaugural address, Lincoln had explained at greater length that "all our constitutional controversies" derive from the division of government "into majorities and minorities." Ordinarily, in a democracy, the majority was expected to prevail over the minority. But what if the minority held out? "If the minority will not acquiesce," Lincoln argued, "the majority must, or the government must cease. There is no other alternative; for continuing the government, is acquiescence on one side or the other."[67]

This was logically true—and it made sense coming from a long-time supporter of the compromise Constitution. Without agreement between majority and minority, government could not subsist. Lincoln then stated the problem with secession:

> If a minority . . . will secede rather than acquiesce, they
> make a precedent which, in turn, will divide and ruin them;
> for a minority of their own will secede from them, when-
> ever a majority refuses to be controlled by such minority.[68]

Lincoln was saying that secession had no logical stopping point. Any minority could decide no longer to be governed by any majority. The principle of a right to secession could be repeated ad infinitum. Lincoln warned the South to beware: "For instance, why may not any portion of a new confederacy, a year or two hence, arbitrarily secede again, precisely as portions of the present Union now claim to secede from it."[69] (In fact, the delegates to the Confederate constitutional convention actively debated whether to include a provision expressly allowing secession from the Confederacy. They voted it down as unnecessary, not least because its presence might have implied that the absence of such a provision in the U.S. Constitution meant secession was unlawful.)[70]

"Plainly, the central idea of secession," Lincoln reasoned, "is the essence of anarchy." This was a leap, but Lincoln made it. "A majority, held in restraint by constitutional checks, and limitations . . . ," he maintained, "is the only true sovereign of a free people." The moment "the majority principle" was rejected, what remained was either "anarchy, or despotism."[71]

Lincoln's definition of "sovereign" rule as residing in the majority was actually not the classical definition to which the framers' generation had subscribed. When they spoke of "sovereignty"—a word so fraught that it did not appear in the Declaration of Independence or the Constitution—the framers tended to place it in the people as a whole, not in a majority of them. Alternatively, the framers sometimes located sovereignty in the states—the logic on which the Confederacy rested the theory of secession. It was radical, and questionable, for Lincoln to make the majority sovereign. In practice, it took a part of the people out of the exercise of sovereignty.

The reason for Lincoln's innovation was that, through the lens of secession, he was identifying what he was coming to consider a flaw in majoritarian government. If a minority could secede at will, no majority could ever be stable. All majoritarian government would exist only at the mercy of the minorities who could threaten to walk away. The only thing that could hold such a government together was common interest, Lincoln assumed. And he asked, rhetorically, "Is there such perfect identity of interests among the States to compose a new Union, as to produce harmony only, and prevent renewed secession?"[72] The implicit answer was no.

As he called up the militia, Lincoln was saying that if majoritarian government was inherently unstable, the framers had gotten it wrong in designing the Constitution. There must be a structural solution to the threat of secession. That structural solution, Lincoln now proposed, was the power of the central government to coerce seceding states to remain in the union. That was why he invoked the "perpetuity of popular government" in his proclamation. Only military force from the federal government could prove that constitutional democracy was a viable form of government.

COERCION AND
THE BROKEN CONSTITUTION

Lincoln had not yet fully stated his theory. But there can be no doubt that he was approaching the profound, dark center of constitutional democracy. In its Madisonian form—which in turn went back to the English philosopher John Locke's idea of the social contract—the theory of the Constitution was a theory of consent. Just as Locke imagined individuals leaving the state of nature and consenting to enter into civil society by giving up some of their rights in exchange for the protection of government, so Madison pictured the people, organized into state ratifying conventions, consenting to the government created by the Constitution. The act of ratifying the Constitution was collective and consensual. Through it, the people consented to give up some of their rights—for example, the right to form independent countries—in exchange for the protection of the federal government.

The picture of consent that emerged from Locke and Madison had no place for coercion. A motivated, revolutionary people could at any time retake their fundamental right to determine their own government. When they did, they could (in theory) exit from the existing government just as they had entered by consent. The government would not have any right to coerce them to remain, against their withdrawal of consent.

This was also the theory of the Declaration of Independence. Jefferson had reduced it to his famous pithy formula:

1. All men are created equal [and] endowed by their Creator with certain unalienable rights, that among these are life, liberty and the pursuit of happiness.

2. That to secure these rights, governments are instituted among men, deriving their just powers from the consent of the governed.

3. Whenever any form of government becomes destructive of these ends, it is the right of the people to alter or to abolish it, and to institute new government.

When the people decided that the existing government to which they had consented no longer served the goals of government as they understood them, the people had the right to make a new government by revolution. Logically, then, the existing government was supposed to let them go, as the Declaration urged Britain to let the states become independent—and as the seceding states were urging the United States to do for them.

In Lincoln's emerging view, this classic consent formula had missed something absolutely essential. A permanent right to secede from constitutional government would render the majority constantly vulnerable to the minority's threat to leave. The solution—the only logically possible solution—was for the majority to be able to coerce the minority, effectively rejecting the minority's withdrawal of its consent.

This sort of coercion had less in common with the views of Locke and Madison than it did with those of Locke's predecessor, the philosopher Thomas Hobbes. In Hobbes's understanding of the structure of government, the sovereign state first of all exercised its coercive power to make all its citizens obey. Once their obedience to the state was in place, it could be argued that the citizens "consented" to it, on the grounds that they were much better off under the state's protection than they would have been under anarchy. Lincoln did not know Hobbes's work directly. But under the pressures of secession, he had intuited a part of Hobbes's view. It was not a pure coincidence that Hobbes had once written apropos of civil war that "*a Kingdome divided in it selfe cannot stand.*"[73]

By calling out the militia to coerce the seceding states into obedience, Lincoln was effectively proposing that the U.S. Constitution included a mechanism for counteracting the power of a minority to demand constant renegotiation of the terms of the original compromise. This version of the Constitution changed the basic terms under which the compromise Constitution had existed. It amounted to Lincoln's own revolution in constitutional thought.

The realities of the compromise Constitution had rested on a basic truth that Lincoln now refused to accept: constitutional government depended on the willingness of the majority to make concessions to the minority sufficient to keep them participating in the government. That is necessarily true of every constitutional government that has ever existed. Even guarantees of fundamental constitutional rights can be understood as concessions by the majority to the minority who will need to invoke and exercise those rights when the majority wants to silence or imprison them.

Put another way, in every constitutional government, the leverage that the minority possesses is ultimately neither more nor less than its willingness and capacity to secede from the government, thereby weakening the whole, potentially to the point of collapse. To preserve constitutional government, the majority must make concessions to the minority. Those concessions almost inevitably include granting to the minority a disproportionate share of government power.

The concessions made by the large states to the small states in the Philadelphia convention of 1787 are a perfect example. The delegates from the large states understood—and insisted repeatedly—that it was outrageous for the small states to demand equal representation in the Senate. That gave the citizens of the small states grossly disproportionate power relative to those of the larger states. But the majority population of the larger states made the concession to the small states because the smaller states credibly threatened that if they did not get what they wanted, they would refuse to enter the Constitution, even if that would threaten the dissolution of the union. Large state delegates went so far as to threaten that if no constitutional agreement could be reached, there would be civil war, and the small states would be swallowed up by the large states. The small states' response was, in essence, to call the large states' bluff.[74]

The compromise Constitution of the antebellum period reflected similar demands by a minority—white Southerners—for disproportionate power, and similar concessions made by a majority of white Northerners. Those concessions included the slavery-related provisions of the original Constitution (the three-fifths compromise, the fugitive slave clause, and the time-limited protection of the slave trade). They also included the Missouri Compromise of 1820, the compromise tariff that ended the nullification crisis of 1832, and the Compromise of 1850. In each instance, white Southerners' leverage came from the threat to leave the union.

The leverage of the majority in constitutional government is a more complicated matter. Under the compromise Constitution, the majority was traditionally *not* understood to possess the leverage to coerce the minority to remain in the government. It would simply not have been realistic for the federal government to field an army capable of forcing seceding states to remain. The federal government was minimal by today's standards. The army itself was tiny. A federal navy might have blockaded ports,* but such a blockade would probably not have been sufficient to force states not to secede. True, Andrew Jackson had threatened South Carolina during the nullification crisis, and had sent General Scott to show he meant business. But even Jackson was not contemplating a lengthy war of invasion and occupation. And in any case South Carolina was then claiming not a right to secede, but only a right to nullify a federal tariff.

In the absence of the threat of coercive force, the majority under the compromise Constitution still possessed leverage over the minority. The leverage consisted of the benefits that constitutional government gave to the minority. Those benefits included a military that could defend the United States and expand its borders, and membership in a national economic union that imposed no tariffs on goods moving between the

---

* In fact, when Madison, in the years before the Philadelphia convention, was trying to figure out how a national government could keep states in line, he had toyed with the idea that the only effective tool would be a national navy powerful enough to blockade the ports of resistant states. He abandoned the idea before the convention. Noah Feldman, *The Three Lives of James Madison: Genius, Partisan, President* (New York: Penguin Random House, 2017), 38–40, 105.

states. When the minority of Southern whites threatened to leave, the majority comprised of Northerners could always have refused to make concessions and said, "Go in peace."

These were the basic conditions of the compromise Constitution. Secession broke them. For the first time, some large proportion of white Southerners was no longer satisfied with the concessions being offered. Some Northerners were prepared to let those Southerners go. Suddenly, the conditions of the compromise Constitution were no longer adequate to preserve the union.

At precisely that moment, Lincoln sought to change the conditions of the compromise that had long existed. The basic change he sought was to assert the majority's right of coercion. The constitutional essence of calling out the militia was the assertion that the majority had another form of leverage at its disposal beyond the benefits conferred on the minority. That leverage was the threat of coercive war.

For the majority to be able to coerce the minority to remain represented a radically different balance of constitutional powers than had been understood to exist under the compromise Constitution. Secession broke the compromise Constitution. In reaction, Lincoln was asserting a new constitutional structure—one in which the majority would have vastly more leverage than it had ever possessed before.

COERCION AND NEGOTIATION

It was one thing for Lincoln to claim that the federal government had the constitutional authority to coerce the seceding states to remain in the Union. It was another thing entirely to achieve that coercion in practice. Calling up seventy-five thousand militiamen was a symbolic act that the president could accomplish with the stroke of a pen. Training them, organizing them, sending them into battle, and seeing them achieve success were concrete goals that could be accomplished only by money, complicated logistics, and the collective action of many thousands of people.

At the moment he issued his proclamation, Lincoln naturally hoped he would not have to send Union troops to invade the seceding states. Secession had been a political act that flowed from and was continuous with Southern negotiation. The new Confederacy had sent delegates to meet with Secretary of State Seward, although he had declined to receive them. Although seven states had seceded, the states of the Upper South had not yet done so—and perhaps they would not. Those states, especially Virginia, were themselves negotiating with Lincoln even as their secession conventions sat in session.

The upshot was that Lincoln hoped that calling out the militia would itself mark a step in an ongoing process of negotiation. If his ploy succeeded, the very act of assembling a force would strengthen his hand. The ultimate goal was the retraction of secession and subsequent reunification. Perhaps only the threat of military force would be necessary to achieve this goal. If some force was necessary, it might be limited in scope. Total war was a last resort, one that was still more or less unthinkable as of April 1861.

In furtherance of the goal of minimizing the use of force, Lincoln stated in his proclamation that "the first service assigned to the forces . . . will probably be to re-possess the forts, places, and property which have been seized from the Union."[75] The tentative word "probably" gave the president some room to maneuver. It meant the troops could do more than simply repossess federal property. But it also raised the possibility that the troops might not even have to do that.

"[I]n every event," Lincoln went on, "the utmost care will be observed, consistently with the objects aforesaid, to avoid any devastation, any destruction of, or interference with, property, or any disturbance of peaceful citizens in any part of the country."[76] This sounded almost like a repudiation of invasion, which would inevitably destroy property and disturb citizens. Only the phrase "consistently with the objects aforesaid" hinted vaguely that the militia force would be authorized to do what was necessary to succeed in its aims.

There was therefore a significant contradiction in Lincoln's proclamation. It lay between the radicalism of the president's claim of a right to coercion and his cautious limitation of what he said the troops were supposed to accomplish. A new, bold, and transformative constitutional vision was accompanied by a mild, almost apologetic half promise to operationalize it. On the one hand, Lincoln conveyed strength. On the other, he expressed a caution that could be taken for weakness.

The best explanation of this contradiction is that Lincoln saw his proclamation as a negotiating step, not as a decisive act of war. The strength and boldness were intended as projections of a probable course of action, but Lincoln also wanted to leave room for reversing course and pursuing a negotiated resolution of the crisis, with the Upper South and repentant Confederate states. The nature of such a negotiation necessarily entailed a tension. Changing the bargaining position of the Union demanded a projection of power. Remaining open to a solution demanded an openness that itself revealed a lack of single-minded commitment to coercive invasion.

Moreover, at the time Lincoln issued the proclamation, the union as yet had no capacity actually to carry out the threat of coercion. The seventy-five-thousand-member militia was notional. The states could raise that number, in principle. If Lincoln was successful politically and rhetorically, seventy-five thousand men might volunteer. But then they would have to be turned into an army and go to war in order to achieve the coercive threat that Lincoln was making. Never before in U.S. history had anyone seriously entertained the possibility of raising an army to coerce seven wayward states into submission. Whether it was possible to accomplish the goal was thoroughly uncertain. The speculative, probabilistic nature of these future events shaped the contradiction in Lincoln's formulation. He could confidently insist only on a right of coercion. He could not plausibly speak with confidence about its actual accomplishment—hence the caution, and the weakness.

The contradiction that could be felt in Lincoln's proclamation would persist for nearly eighteen months, until at least September 1862. Even after the conflict had become a war in earnest, with large armies in the field, Lincoln continued to seek a negotiated peace. Military necessity required it. His own long-term commitment to the idea of the union as a product of constitutional compromise had not been eliminated even by the war itself. That ongoing openness to eventual compromise is essential to understanding Lincoln's conduct throughout this period, starting with his April 1861 proclamation.

The crucial point is that, even by calling out troops and going to war, Lincoln was not abandoning the idea that the union could be preserved only through negotiated constitutional compromise. He was seeking to change the structure of the negotiation, enhancing the Union's leverage by asserting a right to coerce and then building the capacity actually to do so. The end state he envisioned did not change. In Lincoln's thinking, from the spring of 1861 until the fall of 1862, the way to end the conflict was for the Union to make some concessions in relation to the preservation of slavery, and for the Southern states to accept those concessions as superior to the grave costs of war.

For Lincoln, secession broke the compromise Constitution. But for the first year and a half of the war, he believed that the Constitution could be replaced only by some new version of the old compromise. The war was, to be sure, a function of the breakdown of the old Constitution. Yet Lincoln could see no alternative but to replace it with some mildly altered version of the original compromise that had lasted from 1787 until 1860. Slavery would be at the heart of that compromise—as it had always been.

REBELLION OR SECESSION?
(OR, CONGRESS AND THE PRESIDENT)

Lincoln ended his proclamation by calling for Congress to convene in a special session on the symbolic date of July 4, 1861.[77] He chose the day to invoke a unified nation. But July 4 was also a date associated closely with Thomas Jefferson's Declaration. Lincoln was fighting to own the legacy of the Declaration, focusing on its insistence that all men are created equal.

But July 4 was two and a half months away. Why did Lincoln choose to wait so long to convene Congress? The greatest crisis in the history of the republic was at hand. It would have seemed natural for him to convene the body that represented the people as soon as possible—which in any case would have been faster than eleven weeks.

The short answer is that Congress was a distraction. Lincoln wanted to be able to operate on his own before asking Congress for the tools he might need to fight the war—and before running the risk of being denied some or all of them. Lincoln, in other words, wanted to use the powers of the executive unfettered by constraints of congressional oversight and criticism. One of those executive powers was the de facto capacity to shape the narrative of the emerging conflict on his own.

By the time July 4 came, the need to define the conflict had grown immensely. On April 17, just two days after Lincoln's proclamation, the Virginia secession convention that had been sitting throughout the Fort Sumter crisis opted to secede. The next day, Virginia troops attempted to seize the federal arsenal at Harpers Ferry. Union troops burned the facility, but the Virginians were able to recover significant military supplies.[78] In May, Arkansas, Tennessee, and North Carolina adopted articles of secession. Kentucky declared itself neutral in the conflict.

Lincoln's response to this fast-declining situation was to offer Congress a more detailed constitutional theory of what was happening than he had previously done. The centerpiece of his July address was to describe what the South called "secession" as in fact "rebellion"—a word Lincoln had not used in his inaugural address or in the April proclamation. Those who perpetrated a rebellion were guilty of "treason."[79] Both "rebellion" and "treason" were words that appeared in the Constitution. Their invocation had consequences—consequences for the constitutional nature of the war that was starting.

Lincoln insisted that the word "secession" itself was a tool to facilitate secession. He hoped that naming secession as "rebellion" and "treason" would be a mechanism for facilitating its suppression. Lincoln then offered a whole series of arguments against the constitutionality of secession, all of which had been made before, by him and others. He was building to a basic depiction of the constitutional nature of the conflict:

> Our popular government has often been called an experiment. Two points in it, our people have already settled—the successful *establishing*, and the successful *administering* of it. One still remains—its successful *maintenance* against a formidable [internal] attempt to overthrow it. It is now for them to demonstrate to the world, that those who can fairly carry an election, can also suppress a rebellion.[80]

The framers had established a constitutional republic. The generations between them and Lincoln had run it. Secession now posed a new challenge: namely, "*maintenance*" of the republic in the face of armed rebellion. Secession was, according to this view, the final test facing the experiment of constitutional self-government.

Lincoln attempted to clarify the conflict with a complex metaphor contrasting ballots and bullets. According to the metaphor, war always comes first, and then bullets are succeeded by ballots: electoral democracy replaces violence. Once that happens, Lincoln argued, "when ballots have fairly, and constitutionally, decided, there can be no successful appeal, back to bullets." Constitutional democracy could legitimately proceed only through more voting: "[T]here can be no successful appeal, except to ballots themselves, at succeeding elections."[81]

The trouble with Lincoln's metaphor was, of course, that he had himself called up the militia, hence reverting back to bullets. In his address to Congress, he was asking for another 400,000 men to be signed up for terms of three years' service. He tried to claim that the point of force was to teach the lesson that force was itself illegitimate: "Such will be a great lesson of peace; teaching men that what they cannot take by an election, neither can they take it by a war—teaching all, the folly of being the beginners of a war."[82]

It mattered crucially for Lincoln to define secession as an act of rebellion—because there was no question that the Constitution authorized the government to put down rebellion. Defining secession as rebellion provided a solution to the question of whether the federal government had constitutional authority to invade a state and coerce it into submission. Buchanan and his attorney general had believed this power was lacking, and had a strong constitutional basis for thinking so. Lincoln had not fully resolved the issue in his inaugural address and April proclamation. Now he was finally offering an answer as to why the federal government had the constitutional authority to send its armies against the Confederacy: it was engaged in the suppression of rebellion.

Lincoln closed his address to Congress by offering a bigger-picture constitutional account of the course he was undertaking. At its core lay the notion that Lincoln had no choice but to proceed as he did: "It was with the deepest regret," Lincoln said, that he had "found the duty of employing the war-power, in defense of the government, forced upon him."[83] It would be left to Lincoln's supporters to play out the argument that the president's inherent war powers authorized him to use force against the seceding states.

One powerful advocate on his behalf was Anna Ella Carroll, a fascinating unionist pamphleteer and political activist who would become one of Lincoln's most effective proxies. Carroll came from a leading Maryland clan that had been among the Catholic founding families of the state; it boasted signers of the Declaration of Independence and the Constitution as well as the most famous American Catholic of the revolutionary era, Archbishop John Carroll. Yet she had been raised as a Protestant, and she made her first major foray into political writing with a 365-page anti-Catholic polemic she published during the 1856 presidential campaign in support of Millard Filmore, then the Know-Nothing candidate.[84] In 1857–58, Carroll had helped elect Thomas Holliday Hicks, the unionist, proslavery governor of Maryland. But in 1860 she freed her own slaves and turned her formidable writing skills to the support of Lincoln. A polarizing figure to later historians, Carroll has been alternately depicted as a feminist "military genius" who was "the great unrecognized member of Lincoln's cabinet" and as a bigoted, nativist self-promoter.[85]

In September 1861, Carroll wrote that because Lincoln was commander in chief, the president "needs, therefore, no statute law to enable him, in the absence of Congress, to defend the assault on the nation's life, because his right rests on the supreme or universal law of self-defense, common to nations as individuals—that everything that has life, every being that has existence, has the right to resist and slay the assailant when an attack is made upon that life."[86] Carroll reasoned, "Our fathers presumed not to foresee all the dangers which in time might beset the Constitution, or to prescribe the mode of its defense." By making the president commander in chief, she wrote, the framers "wisely left to him to resist the sword raised against the nation's heart by the sword. The express grant of the *war-conducting power* conferred upon the President carries with it the implied power to use every belligerent right known to the law of war."[87] Carroll was saying what Lincoln as yet would not: that secession triggered a self-defense power that was vested solely in the president, notwithstanding that the Constitution as written clearly gave Congress, not the president, the power to declare war.

As for Lincoln, he insisted that he could not have acted differently: "No compromise, by public servants, could, in this case, be a cure."[88] Anything other than the exercise of his war powers would have violated the will of the "people themselves" who had elected him—and therefore republicanism itself.

As a result, Lincoln declared (speaking of himself in the third person), "He felt that he had no moral right to shrink; nor even to count the chances of his own life, in what might follow."[89] As he had done in his inaugural address when he invoked his "oath registered in Heaven," Lincoln was saying that he was morally obligated to stand up for the preservation of government under the Constitution.

To be clear, Lincoln was not saying that the Constitution *itself* was moral. Nor could he, since he remained committed to the view that the Constitution protected slavery, which he believed to be immoral. "[A]fter the rebellion shall have been suppressed," he told Congress, he would still "be guided by the Constitution, and the laws." The Constitution and laws protected slavery. He added that, when the rebellion was over, "he probably will have no different understanding of the powers, and duties of the Federal government, relatively to the rights of the States, and the people, under the Constitution, than that expressed in the inaugural address."[90]

Lincoln's focus on his individual moral obligation to defend the government enabled him to duck the broader question of whether the Constitution was moral. He told Congress that he had done his duty and that the members should "according to your own judgment, perform yours." He expressed the hope that Congress would act, as he had done, "to assure all faithful citizens, who have been disturbed in their rights, of a certain, and speedy restoration to them, under the Constitution, and the laws."[91] The rights in question included the right to be governed by states under the authority of the federal government—precisely the right that most citizens of the seceded states did not want to exercise at all.

THE WAR OF REBELLION AND THE BROKEN CONSTITUTION

Ultimately, Lincoln's July 4 address to Congress inserted the idea of a broken Constitution into the constitutional paradigm for the war. According to Lincoln's paradigm, the seceding states had not dissolved their ties to the union under the Constitution, as they claimed to have done. Their act of secession was an act of rebellion. As rebellion, secession was unlawful under the Constitution. Furthermore, secession could not be considered an act of revolution justifiable under principles of universal, natural, or international law. In the face of rebellion, Lincoln argued, it was obligatory for him as president and for the federal government as a whole to respond by force. Lincoln had made the case that the seceding states had broken the Constitution, and that now he possessed not only the legal authority but also the constitutional duty to restore it by maintaining or reestablishing the government.

This narrative was intended to replace the narrative that the Buchanan administration had framed. That narrative treated secession as revolution, not rebellion. The Buchanan narrative denied the federal government the authority to invade and coerce the seceding states. It did not even contemplate Lincoln's view that such an invasion was a constitutional obligation.

Lincoln's paradigm faced three major challenges. The first was its novelty. No one, including Andrew Jackson, had ever explicitly argued before that the Constitution authorized or obligated full-scale invasion and coercive measures, not just to enforce federal law or restore federal property but also to force whole states to rejoin the union. The only possible solution to the newness of Lincoln's argument was time. In the crucible of war, Lincoln's argument would come to be accepted by the majority of the population of the Northern states—and as a result, it would gradually cease to seem new.

The second major challenge to Lincoln's paradigm was that it ran into a fundamental constitutional problem. From the founding, the basic idea of American constitutionalism had been the consent of the governed. No American since then had openly rejected that idea; nor could Lincoln. Now the seceding states had made it as clear as humanly possible that they no longer consented to be governed under the Constitution. They had seceded after gathering in conventions, the classic means of expressing popular consent that all the states had used to ratify the Constitution in the first place. They had joined together, drafted, and ratified a new constitution, again in conventions that represented the popular will. As far as they were concerned, they had demonstrated to an absolute certainty that the will of the people—that is, the will of the people within their states—had been exercised in favor of withdrawal from the union and entrance into the Confederacy. If they were to be forced to do otherwise, the government that did so would no longer be a government based on their consent and their popular will.

Lincoln's position required him to insist that the Constitution did not allow the withdrawal of consent by the people of the states—even when they had withdrawn consent through the same kinds of conventions they had used to consent to the Constitution in the first place. But that was not all. Lincoln also committed himself to the view that the Constitution *mandated* forcing people to be governed—against their will. Lincoln's only basis for justifying the coercion was to say that the people *as a whole* had not expressed the will for the seceding states to go. He claimed to represent the will of the people nationally, and to be coercing the seceding states in the name of that broader people, who had elected him.

This conflict between the consent of the governed and coercion by the government lay at the core of Lincoln's account of the broken Constitution theory. To overcome it, theory alone seemed unlikely ever to be adequate. For the consent of the governed to operate in practice as it was meant to in theory, the people being governed actually had to consent. Words and arguments were not going to reconcile real people in the seceding states to the idea that their withdrawal of consent had been illegitimate—that they were rebels, not loyal Americans or revolutionists in the tradition of 1776. Only military victory stood any chance of convincing the citizens of seceding states that they had been wrong. And even victory might not suffice. After victory, people and states could potentially be coerced into saying they had been wrong and swearing new oaths of allegiance to replace those they had broken. Making people believe what they were forced to say was something else again.

As formulated in July 1861, Lincoln's theory still did not include any obvious answer to the question of how to repair the contradiction of the broken Constitution, even after the war of rebellion was won. It would take many more months before an answer presented itself to Lincoln. That answer would involve remaking the prewar compromise Constitution, whose legitimacy depended entirely on consent, into a new kind of moral document whose legitimacy rested not so much on consent as on the moral truth of human equality.

The third challenge to Lincoln's paradigm was that its ultimate acceptance depended on successful military coercion in practice. While the war was being fought, it could be useful for Lincoln to say that the seceding states had broken the Constitution. If war failed, however, secession would come to be seen as legitimate and Lincoln's use of force would be treated as unjustified and unconstitutional. To make the states' secession definitively into an act of rebellion would require actually forcing them back into the union: that is, winning the war. And in July 1861, the prospect of such a victory seemed far off.

The challenges facing Lincoln's paradigm seemed almost insurmountable. Yet the idea of the broken Constitution also had strengths that help explain why Lincoln adopted it—and why doing so would make him the leading thinker in U.S. history on the meaning of the Constitution in crisis. The immediate advantage was that the idea of the broken Constitution made it possible to change the narrative of the conflict from being about slavery to being about the preservation of the union under the Constitution. Seward had recommended such a change to Lincoln in April, advising "that we must *Change the question before the Public from one upon Slavery, or about Slavery,* for a question upon *Union or Disunion.*" Seward's stated reason—at a moment when he was still desperately trying to head off war—was that he wanted to change the subject from what he considered a "Party" dispute to a question of "*Patriotism.*"[92]

For Lincoln, three months later, the benefit of focusing on the preservation of the Constitution and not on slavery was subtly different. A war fought over slavery would hardly leave room for the possibility of a negotiated, compromise reconciliation in which slavery was preserved. In contrast, a war fought to maintain the Constitution could be ended by a negotiated settlement that could be incorporated in the Constitution, by amendment or otherwise. At least in principle, the broken Constitution could be repaired by being restored—including by being restored to the status quo ante. Compromise over slavery had been at the center of the compromise Constitution, and perhaps could be again.

The greater, long-term virtue of Lincoln's broken Constitution paradigm was that it gave the president considerable latitude with respect to how he should interpret the Constitution while at war. If the seceding states had broken the Constitution, they could hardly be expected to insist on its enforcement down to the letter. Lincoln might have to break a few constitutional principles of his own. But he could do that most effectively if he did so while insisting that he was not breaking the Constitution so much as interpreting it to fit the circumstances.

Lincoln could make the argument that his constitutional interpretations were *necessary* to the preservation of the Constitution itself. No argument gave the president greater power and room for maneuver than an argument from constitutional necessity—as we shall see in the next chapter.

Finally, and above all, the idea of the broken Constitution allowed Lincoln to capture the tremendous benefits of constitutional continuity. Had he acknowledged even for a moment the possibility of the dissolution of the union, he would have squandered the prestige and authority that came with connecting the government he led directly to the tradition of the founders. The seceding states had plausibly argued that secession flowed from the founders' principles. Their state governments were, they argued, continuous with the state governments created in 1776. But they could not claim that the Confederacy itself actually was the direct descendent of the government of the United States created by the Constitution.

Lincoln, in contrast, was the president of the same republic that had existed under the Constitution, at least since ratification. His office derived from the Constitution. His oath was an oath to the Constitution itself. The maintenance and restoration of the broken Constitution gave a defining purpose to his role as president. Going to war to preserve the union did not fit neatly into the executive's traditional constitutional role. But in Lincoln's own brilliant reformulation, preserving the union was now the central constitutional duty of the president—and of the union itself.

Henry Clay. Lincoln's political idol, the founder of the Whig Party, and in an important sense the father of the compromise Constitution. His political life was devoted to preserving the Constitution through a series of compromises between North and South, all of which protected slavery. At the same time, the Great Compromiser insisted that slavery would someday disappear, and he championed efforts to free enslaved people—then send them to colonize Africa. In 1852, Lincoln eulogized Clay and praised "the SPIRIT of COMPROMISE" that he embodied.

Angelina Grimké. A South Carolina–born abolitionist and women's rights activist. Grimké argued in 1838 that slavery was inconsistent with the Preamble to the Constitution because it "subverts justice, promotes the welfare of the *few* to the manifest injury of the many, and robs thousands of the *posterity* of our forefathers of the blessings of liberty."

Charles Lenox Remond.
A Salem, Massachusetts–born free Black abolitionist, he attacked the Constitution as made for the benefit of whites, not African Americans. As he put it in 1844, "With all my knowledge of the origin and the progress, and my experience of the present practical workings of the American Constitution, shall I be found here advocating it as a glorious means to a glorious end? No! my fellow countrymen, I am here to register my testimony against it!"

William Howard Day.
A free African American, graduate of Oberlin College, newspaper editor, librarian, and later clergyman. He maintained in 1851 that although the federal government and Supreme Court were interpreting the Constitution as a proslavery document, he chose to read it differently: "Sir, coming up as I do, in the midst of three millions of men in chains, and five hundred thousands only half free, I consider every instrument precious which guarantees to me liberty."

Robert Purvis. An influential abolitionist who identified as Black. He said that "talk about the Constitution being anti-slavery seems to me so utterly at variance with common sense and what we know to be facts that ... I have no patience with it." He added that he had "no particular objection" when white people, "who have little to feel on this subject ... amuse themselves with such theories." But "when I see them imitated by colored men, I am disgusted! Sir, have we no self-respect?" In Purvis's view, "Washington and Jefferson were slave-drivers and thieves [whose] memory should be held in detestation."

Frederick Douglass. The best-known abolitionist, he was born in slavery in 1817 and escaped it in 1838. Douglass first condemned the Constitution as proslavery, then shifted to see the document as self-contradictory, then finally embraced the view that the Constitution should be read as antislavery. Douglass sharply criticized Lincoln's early rejection of emancipation as well as Lincoln's effort to blame the Civil War on African Americans. He met Lincoln twice, and ultimately praised the Emancipation Proclamation even as he worried it could be reversed.

James McCune Smith. A Glasgow-trained free Black physician in New York City. He sided with Douglass against Purvis, helping to convince the Colored National Convention of 1855 to vote that the Constitution should be interpreted as antislavery.

Stephen A. Douglas. An Illinois senator and Lincoln's debating counterpart who beat him in the 1858 Illinois Senate race and lost to him as the Democratic candidate for the presidency in 1860. His view that settlers of new territories should decide for themselves whether to permit slavery promised to enhance the Constitution's protection of the institution—and exacerbated tensions between North and South. Douglas died in 1861.

Dred Scott. An enslaved African American born in Virginia. After fleeing slavery and being recaptured, Scott sued for his freedom on the grounds that he had been held in a free state and free federal territory, nullifying his enslaved status. The Supreme Court's notorious decision in *Dred Scott v. Sanford* denied him the right to sue and also struck down the Missouri Compromise as unconstitutional. Chief Justice Roger Taney held that Black people "had no rights which the White man was bound to respect."

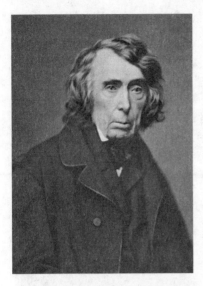

Roger Taney. The chief justice of the United States and Lincoln's constitutional nemesis. The author of the lead opinion in the repugnant *Dred Scott v. Sanford* decision, Taney also wrote the opinion in *Ex parte Merryman*, bravely condemning Lincoln's unconstitutional unilateral suspension of habeas corpus and condemning the declaration of martial law in Baltimore.

A Currier and Ives print, "**The Lexington of 1861**," produced rapidly to commemorate Baltimore's Pratt Street riot of April 19, 1861, in which a crowd tried to block Massachusetts troops from transiting through Baltimore to Washington, D.C. Twelve civilians and four soldiers died in the melee. The print reflected a strongly anti-Lincoln stance, implying equivalence between Southern resistance and the American Revolution.

John Merryman. A Maryland cattle farmer, minor politician, and state militia officer. He and his men allegedly burned railroad bridges in Maryland to stop federal troops from traveling south to Washington, D.C. Arrested and detained without trial by the U.S. Army, he was the subject of Taney's *Ex parte Merryman* opinion. Lincoln ignored Taney's order that he release Merryman from military detention.

Anna Ella Carroll. The brilliant and still-controversial pro-Lincoln popular writer and sophisticated theorist of Lincoln's expansive presidential power. Born into a famous Maryland Catholic family, she was also an anti-Catholic propagandist. Historians today are divided on whether she was a feminist "military genius" and "the great unrecognized member of Lincoln's cabinet" or a bigoted, nativist self-promoter. It is possible that she was all of the above.

Ambrose Burnside. A West Point graduate, Union general, and politician. As commander of the military department of Ohio, Burnside followed Lincoln's policy by suppressing newspapers and speech critical of the war effort, including closing the *Chicago Times* and arresting the congressman Clement Vallandigham. In April 1863, he issued an order stating, "The habit of declaring sympathies for the enemy will no longer be tolerated in the department." Yes, sideburns really are named after him.

Fort Lafayette. Dubbed the "American Bastille," the New York Harbor fort was built for the War of 1812. Hundreds of critics of Lincoln's administration were detained there without trial as political prisoners during the Civil War. *The New York Times* insisted in 1861 that the fort "is not a Bastile [*sic*] at all, in fact the fort is more like a hotel than anything else," where "the fare is excellent, and the view of the ocean extensive." The same article listed the names of ninety-two "political prisoners" then being held there. The fort survived until 1960, when it was destroyed to make room for the Brooklyn tower of the Verrazzano-Narrows Bridge.

Clement Vallandigham. An Ohio Democratic congressman, war critic, and aspiring 1864 presidential candidate. Arrested by Burnside and charged before a military commission with making speeches critical of the war, he was convicted and deported to the Confederacy. In response to criticism of the arrest, Lincoln made his most radical defense of suppressing free speech in wartime.

Emancipation Proclamation. The document that Lincoln used to effectively kill the compromise Constitution—and transform the meaning of the war from a defense of the union to a crusade against slavery. Karl Marx said its prose read like "an ordinary summons, sent by one lawyer to another." He also said it was "the most important document in American history since the establishment of the union, tantamount to the tearing up of the old American constitution."

Four

POLITICAL
PRISONERS

THE BALTIMORE CRISIS

When Lincoln called for seventy-five thousand militiamen on April 15, 1861, Massachusetts responded immediately. Volunteers had been organizing and training since January. On April 16, eight companies of the Sixth Regiment Massachusetts Volunteer Militia met in the city of Lowell and signed up for ninety-day terms of service. Many were textile workers in Lowell's vast mills, exemplars of free labor ready to fight for the Union. The next day, strengthened by three more companies, the Sixth Massachusetts left Boston by train after a ceremony at the state house, where the governor, John Albion Andrew, presented them with regimental colors.

Newspapers made sure the public knew the train was coming. As the Sixth Massachusetts steamed through Springfield, Hartford, New York City, Trenton, and Philadelphia, bells rang, bands played, and supportive onlookers set off fireworks and lit bonfires. The volunteers' destination was Washington, D.C.

The trouble started when the volunteers reached Baltimore on Friday, April 19—by coincidence, the anniversary of the Battles of Lexington and Concord. To pass through Baltimore, train cars had to be decoupled at the President Street Station, then pulled on rails by horses along Pratt Street and across a bridge to Camden Station, where they could be reattached and sent on their way south. As the train cars containing the volunteers crossed town, a hostile mob formed to stop them.

Maryland was a slaveholding state. It had not seceded, but many Maryland Democrats hoped it would join other Upper South states in doing so now that Fort Sumter had been attacked and war had begun. Not only was sympathy for the Confederacy high, but even many of those who opposed secession rejected Lincoln's idea that the federal government could invade and coerce the Southern states. To them—as to the welcoming crowds farther North—the Sixth Massachusetts was the visible proof of Lincoln's plan. For those who favored secession, the Massachusetts volunteers were the vanguard of the occupying troops of the enemy.

The mob, which soon numbered as many as ten thousand, attempted to block the volunteers from changing trains. The first seven companies made it through. But when the protesters covered the rails with sand and anchors from the docks, it became impossible for the train cars to be dragged from one station to the other. Four companies consisting of 220 men were stuck at President Street. The only way they could rejoin the rest of the regiment to catch the train to Washington was to march a mile across town—through the mob itself. The officer in charge ordered the volunteers to load their weapons but not to fire unless fired on.

As the men began to march, the situation deteriorated. The crowd began throwing bricks and cobblestones they pulled up from the street. As is common in such circumstances, it is not clear who fired the first shot. But an exchange of gunfire certainly occurred. Soldiers fired into the crowd, and civilians fired pistols at the soldiers. Only the intervention of the Baltimore police, whom the crowd did not want to harm, enabled the Massachusetts volunteers to reach the Camden Street station.

Crowds chased their trains along the tracks as they finally made it out of town for the short ride to Washington.

In the melee that came to be called the Pratt Street riot or the Baltimore riot, twelve civilians and four soldiers were killed. One, a seventeen-year-old Lowell factory worker named Luther C. Ladd, was identified as the first person to die in the Civil War. Thirty-six other militiamen were wounded. A hastily produced Currier and Ives lithograph echoed Paul Revere's famous print of the Boston Massacre, a worrisome parallel from the Union's perspective. Neighboring Virginia had seceded on April 17. It seemed conceivable that the provocation of the events would drive Maryland into secession, as the mob may well have intended.

If troops could not come through Baltimore by rail, they could not reach Washington from the north except by sea or by a circuitous march. The capital was vulnerable—a lesson learned the hard way in the War of 1812. Another Massachusetts Regiment, the Eighth, was traveling just behind the Sixth, accompanied by Benjamin Butler, a Lowell mill owner and Massachusetts state legislator with no military experience who had successfully lobbied to get himself appointed a brigadier general. On hearing that Baltimore was impassable, Butler got his troops onto a steamboat and headed to Annapolis, south of Baltimore and closer to Washington. When he got there, Butler occupied the Naval Academy in Annapolis and assumed control of the state capital.

On April 23, a Maryland farmer, state legislator, and part-time state militia officer named John Merryman led a group of local militiamen in burning six bridges of the Northern Central Railroad and destroying the telegraph wires running alongside them. Merryman would later claim to have been acting on orders from General George H. Steuart of the Maryland militia and local Baltimore officials. The governor of Maryland, Thomas Holliday Hicks, would deny having given the ultimate order—a denial that was plausible but not fully convincing. The burning of the bridges was a far more decisive step than the riots. It made it vastly more difficult to bring troops through Maryland to Washington, D.C., despite Butler's efforts to restore rail service.

Addressing the crisis, Governor Hicks called the state legislature into special session, not in occupied Annapolis or in pro-secession Baltimore, but in the town of Frederick. Writing to General Winfield Scott on April 25, Lincoln expressed his concern that, once convened, the legislature would, "not improbably, . . . take action to arm the people of that state against the United States." He considered the possibility of directing the army under Scott to "arrest, or disperse the members" of the legislature "upon the ground of necessary defence." He added, however, that it was not time for such drastic action—yet. At the moment, he said, "I think it would *not* be justifiable; nor, efficient for the desired object."[1]

As Lincoln reasoned it out, the Maryland legislature had "a clearly legal right to assemble." He could not "know in advance, that their action will not be lawful, and peaceful." To make matters more complicated still, Lincoln believed he could not "permanently prevent" the Maryland legislature from challenging federal authority: "If we arrest them, we can not long hold them as prisoners; and when liberated, they will immediately re-assemble, and take their action." If "we simply disperse them," the result would be that "they will immediately re-assemble in some other place."[2]

Lincoln's solution was to tell Scott to wait and see what the Maryland legislature would do. "[I]f it shall be to arm their people against the United States," he wrote, then Scott was "to adopt the most prompt, and efficient means to counteract, even, if necessary, . . . the bombardment of their cities—and in the extremest necessity, the suspension of the writ of habeas corpus."[3] Suspending habeas corpus meant arresting civilians without warrants, and holding them indefinitely without judicial review.

Lincoln had been contemplating suspension of the writ of habeas corpus at least since April 19, the day of the Baltimore riot, when he had asked the attorney general, Edward Bates, to give him a written opinion on the legality of suspending habeas corpus on his own. He had not yet received a response when he authorized Scott to suspend the writ in case the Maryland legislature resisted federal authority.

Suspending habeas corpus was an act of massive significance, for two separate yet related reasons. First, the writ of habeas corpus, also known as "the great writ," was widely understood as the most basic form of judicial oversight, fundamental to the rule of law. In a system where the writ could be requested and issued, the government could not detain citizens without having to prove in court that they had been seized pursuant to lawful arrest and would be put to trial. In a system where the writ did not exist or was suspended, the government could arrest anyone—and hold the person indefinitely, whether with a trial or without one. In essence, suspending the writ meant going outside the bounds of a rule-of-law system and imposing dictatorial control. Never in U.S. history had the federal government officially suspended the writ.*

The second reason it would be an epochal decision for Lincoln to suspend habeas corpus was that the president almost certainly lacked the constitutional authority to do so. Article I of the Constitution spec-

---

* General Andrew Jackson had done so when his army was occupying New Orleans at the end of the War of 1812, not only imposing martial law and making arrests but even jailing a judge who tried to stop him; but President James Madison had repudiated Jackson's actions as unlawful. Amanda L. Tyler, *Habeas Corpus in Wartime: From the Tower of London to Guantanamo Bay* (New York: Oxford University Press, 2017), 145. The Rhode Island state legislature had suspended habeas corpus in its state courts in 1842 when it was facing a revolutionary challenge in the form of an alternative state government headed by one Thomas Dorr; but that suspension had left the federal courts open and functioning, and did not rely on the U.S. Constitution. Brian McGinty, *The Body of John Merryman: Abraham Lincoln and the Suspension of Habeas Corpus* (Cambridge, Mass.: Harvard University Press, 2011), 112–13.

ified that "the privilege of the writ of habeas corpus shall not be suspended, unless when in cases of rebellion or invasion the public safety may require it." The provision appeared alongside the other powers of Congress, which strongly suggested that the power of suspension belonged to Congress, not to the president.

Lincoln hesitated before taking such a drastic step. Almost a decade later, Seward recalled that habeas "had not been suspended because of Mr. Lincoln's extreme reluctance at that period to assume such a responsibility." Seward also claimed that Lincoln's advisors "almost to a man, opposed this action." In his telling, Seward visited the White House himself and advised the president "that this step could no longer be delayed," and that "perdition was the sure penalty of further hesitation." Seward imagined his intervention as decisive: "He sat for some time in silence," Seward recounted, "then took up his pen and said: 'It shall be so.'"[4]

Seward's dramatic (and self-dramatizing) story may not be precisely accurate. Seward thought the events occurred on a Sunday, which does not seem to fit the chronology. In any case, on Saturday, April 27, still without a response from his attorney general on whether he possessed the authority to suspend the writ unilaterally, Lincoln wrote to Scott again. This time the communication took the form of a direct order. Lincoln began by telling Scott formally, "You are engaged in repressing an insurrection against the laws of the United States." This statement was meant to trigger the constitutional conditions of rebellion that were required for suspension. Lincoln went on:

> If at any point on or in the vicinity of any military line, which is now or which shall be used between the City of Philadelphia and the City of Washington . . . you find resistance which renders it necessary to suspend the writ of Habeas Corpus for the public safety, you personally, or through the officer in command at the point where the resistance occurs, are authorized to suspend that writ.[5]

Lincoln was telling Scott that he could suspend habeas corpus by summarily arresting anyone who interfered in the passage of troops between Philadelphia and Washington.

As it happened, the passage of troops from the North to Washington continued to be seriously hampered. The Maryland legislature met on April 29 and voted 53–13 against secession. But the members also voted not to reopen railroad connections to the North, thus attempting to ensure that no Union troops would come through Baltimore en route to Washington or points south. And they adopted a resolution demanding that Lincoln cease the federal "occupation" of their state. The Maryland legislature no doubt thought it was taking a middle ground. In effect, however, the state was trying to pursue a policy of neutrality. And if Maryland as a neutral state were to block the passage of federal troops to Washington, the capital would become indefensible and Lincoln's ability to gather an army of invasion would become logistically impossible.

For the moment, Lincoln continued to hold off on arresting the legislature.* But the Maryland crisis was only building. Butler, who already controlled the port and state capital at Annapolis, decided on his own initiative to take action. On May 13, 1861, in a thunderstorm, Butler brought the Sixth Massachusetts back to Baltimore by train from Washington. Avoiding Pratt Street, he took his force of 950—the Massachusetts men supplemented by some New York volunteers—up Federal Hill, where they spent the night digging in and establishing a basic earthwork fortification. From the hill, Butler pointed his artillery down at the city. He informed the commander at Fort McHenry that he had "taken possession of Baltimore." And he requested, "If I am attacked to-night, please open upon Monument Square with your mortars."[6]

The next morning, the residents of the city woke to see a large

---

* On September 17, a third of the Maryland legislature would be arrested.

American flag on the hill. Butler issued a proclamation announcing that he had "occupied the city of Baltimore for the purpose, among other things, of enforcing respect and obedience to the laws." In the same proclamation he declared martial law and ordered Maryland militia officers to report to him so that he could "know and distinguish the regularly commissioned and loyal troops of Maryland from armed bodies who may claim to be such."[7]

John Merryman's militia company was a prime example of an armed body not loyal to the Union. And Butler, who was focused on reestablishing transportation through Baltimore, had good reason to make an example of Merryman for burning the railroad bridges in the first place. At 2:00 a.m. on May 25, federal troops seized Merryman at his farm outside town and imprisoned him at Fort McHenry. This was a military arrest, not a civilian proceeding pursuant to a warrant issued by a federal court.

Merryman's lawyer, George Williams, responded swiftly and cleverly. He sought out the chief justice of the United States, Roger Taney, a pro-unionist Maryland native, now eighty-four years old. Under the federal court system as it then existed, the justices of the Supreme Court each had responsibilities to act as lower-court judges in specified areas of the country when the Supreme Court was not in session, a practice called "riding circuit." Taney was the justice assigned to the circuit that included Maryland. Although at the time he was in Washington, where he had moved some years before after the death of his wife from yellow fever, he had the authority to hear federal cases arising in Maryland, much in the way that the other, lower federal court judge who sat full-time in Maryland could.

Taney was not just any judge. He was Lincoln's legal nemesis, the justice who had written the controlling opinion in the *Dred Scott* case four years before. Because he was the chief justice, any decision he reached would have stature far greater than a decision by a lower court judge. Williams may even have hoped that the Supreme Court itself would act on the petition.

The petition filed on behalf of Merryman demanded a writ of habeas corpus. It stated straightforwardly that Merryman had been "imprisoned without any process or color of law whatsoever." There had been "no warrant from any court, magistrate or other person having legal authority . . . to justify such arrest." Thus, Merryman had been arrested "without color of law and in violation of the Constitution and laws of the United States, of which, he is a citizen."[8] In formal legal terms, the request for the writ meant that Merryman was asking Taney to order the commander of Fort McHenry, General George Cadwalader, to appear in court, to produce the living body of Merryman (the "corpus") and explain as a matter of law why he was justified in detaining him.

On receiving the petition, Taney must have felt a jolt of recognition. He had gone to college with Merryman's father many decades before, and he probably knew Merryman personally. When he received the petition in Washington, Taney duly sent an order to Cadwalader at Fort McHenry demanding that he produce Merryman in court in Baltimore the next day, May 27.

As a legal matter, Taney was being careful not to require Cadwalader to appear outside the geographic limits of the area under his military command, which did not include Washington, D.C. At the same time, he was leaving some room for ambiguity about the capacity in which he himself was acting: Was Taney sitting as a justice of the Supreme Court, and therefore issuing his ruling "in chambers" as a justice? Or was Taney sitting as a circuit judge in Maryland, issuing his ruling as a member of a lower court? The ambiguity would remain throughout the case, and has never been satisfactorily resolved. It is likely that Taney intended it.

At the appointed hour, Taney was on the bench in the federal courtroom in the Masonic Hall in Baltimore. Cadwalader did not appear. Instead, the commander sent an officer, Colonel R. M. Lee, carrying a letter to Taney explaining that Merryman would not be produced. Merryman had been charged with treason, the letter from Cadwalader said. It went on:

> He has further to inform you, that he is duly authorized by the president of the United States, in such cases, to suspend the writ of habeas corpus, for the public safety. This is a high and delicate trust, and it has been enjoined upon him that it should be executed with judgment and discretion, but he is nevertheless also instructed that in times of civil strife, errors, if any, should be on the side of the safety of the country. He most respectfully submits for your consideration, that those who should co-operate in the present trying and painful position in which our country is placed, should not, by any unnecessary want of confidence in each other, increase our embarrassments. He, therefore, respectfully requests that you will postpone further action upon this case, until he can receive instructions from the president of the United States, when you shall hear further from him.[9]

Taney responded sharply, asking Lee, "Have you brought with you the body of John Merryman?" Lee had not. Taney then announced that Cadwalader had "acted in disobedience" of the writ of habeas corpus. As a consequence, he directed "that an attachment to be at once issued against" Cadwalader, returnable the next day at noon. An attachment was a finding of contempt. Rather than demanding only that Cadwalader produce Merryman, Taney was now demanding that Cadwalader appear himself and submit to the court's contempt ruling.

News of Taney's confrontation spread fast. The next day, May 28, a scant two weeks after martial law had been declared in Baltimore, a crowd of two thousand people gathered outside the Masonic Hall in anticipation of the follow-up hearing.[10] Cadwalader did not come. Taney questioned the deputy U.S. marshal, who explained that he had gone to Fort McHenry to deliver the writ of attachment and had been denied entrance to the fort.

Taney then briefly explained the state of affairs. First, he stated bluntly, "The president, under the Constitution and laws of the United States, cannot suspend the privilege of the writ of habeas corpus, nor authorize any military officer to do so." Lincoln's order authorizing the suspension of habeas corpus was unconstitutional.

Second, Taney stated, a military officer could not lawfully arrest "a person not subject to the rules and articles of war" unless "in aid of the judicial authority." If the military did make such an arrest, "it is the duty of the officer to deliver him over immediately to the civil authority, to be dealt with according to law."[11] Taney was saying that martial law could not be applied to Merryman, and that therefore as a matter of law he had to be handed over to the court. More important still, Taney was now implicitly rejecting the very idea that Baltimore could be occupied and put under martial law. He was asserting that military authority could be used over civilians only in support of the jurisdiction of the civil courts.

Taney knew a longer statement of his position would be needed. He told the audience that he would put his opinion in writing and file it by the end of the week. He then announced that, while according to law the U.S. marshal could gather a posse and seek to arrest Cadwalader, because of the power of the army, "such a proceeding can result in no good, and is useless." However, he added, if Cadwalader "were before me, I should impose on him the punishment which it is my province to inflict—that of fine and imprisonment."[12]

When court was over, Taney, still sitting on the bench, was approached by Baltimore mayor George William Brown, who was himself implicated in the burning of the bridges and would be held for fourteen months without charge. Brown later recounted that Taney had said to him, "I am an old man, a very old man, but perhaps I was preserved for this occasion." Brown replied, "Sir, I thank God that you were." Taney then told Brown "that he knew that his own imprisonment had been a matter of consultation, but that the danger had passed." And according to Brown, Taney "warned me, from information he had received, that my time would come."[13] There is little other credible evidence that Chief Justice Taney was actually in danger of being arrested by the Lincoln administration.[14] But Taney thought so, according to an autobiographical memoir that he began but was finished by another writer. The memoir recounted that in the morning, "as he left the house of his son-in-law," Taney "remarked that it was likely he should be imprisoned in Fort McHenry before night, but that he was going to Court to do his duty."[15] In the atmosphere of Baltimore in the late spring of 1861, such a fear of arrest would have been understandable—even on the part of the chief justice of the United States.

EX PARTE MERRYMAN

Taney issued his written judgment, known as *Ex parte Merryman*, on June 4. It was and remains one of the great state documents in U.S. history.

After describing the facts of the case, Taney began by pointing out the embarrassing truth that Lincoln had never publicly announced that he was suspending the writ. "As the case comes before me," Taney wrote, "I understand that the president not only claims the right to suspend the writ of habeas corpus himself, at his discretion, but to delegate that discretionary power to a military officer, and to leave it to him to determine whether he will or will not obey judicial process that may be served upon him."[16] Taney was hinting that Lincoln was trying doubly to avoid taking direct public responsibility for the suspension. Not only had "no official notice . . . been given to the courts of justice, or to the public, by proclamation or otherwise, that the president claimed this power";[17] Lincoln had told Scott and his other generals that they could suspend the writ when they wanted, thus deflecting responsibility onto them.

Taney then spoke personally. On hearing in court that Lincoln claimed the right to suspend habeas, he noted, "I certainly listened to it with some surprise, for I had supposed it to be one of those points of constitutional law upon which there was no difference of opinion, and that it was admitted on all hands, that the privilege of the writ could not be suspended, except by act of Congress."[18] This was unusually strong language in an opinion by a Supreme Court justice. Taney was setting the stage by explaining that Lincoln's view was not only wrong but also unheard of.

As he had done in the *Dred Scott* case, Taney went back to the founders—specifically to the discussion about the possibility of suspending habeas that took place at the time of Aaron Burr's 1806 conspiracy to create a breakaway country out of territories owned by the United States and Mexico. At the time, Taney noted, Thomas Jefferson, then president, had not claimed the power to suspend the writ on his own, but had "communicated his opinion to Congress, with all the proofs in his possession, in order that Congress might exercise its discretion upon the subject." Congress had debated the suspension, Taney explained, adding, "And in the debate which took place upon the subject, no one suggested that Mr. Jefferson might exercise the power himself, if, in his opinion, the public safety demanded it."[19] This was historically correct. In the end, the Senate had voted to suspend habeas in order to detain suspects in Burr's conspiracy, but the House had voted the other way, and no suspension had occurred. Jefferson had not so much as hinted that he had the power to suspend on his own.

Taney then turned to the structure of the Constitution. Article I, where the suspension clause appeared, enumerated the powers of

Congress. A long list appeared in section 8, capped by the most general grant of power to Congress, its power to make all laws "necessary and proper" for the fulfillment of its other powers. In light of this broad grant, Taney reasoned, the framers wanted to make sure that Congress observed some basic limits to its rights. It was therefore "deemed necessary," he went on, "to guard more effectually certain great cardinal principles, essential to the liberty of the citizen . . . by denying to Congress, in express terms, any power of legislation over them." Those limitations appeared in section 9 of Article I, immediately after the grant of power. "First in the list of prohibited powers" was the suspension of habeas corpus, a power "denied, and its exercise prohibited, unless the public safety shall require it."[20]

The argument was so powerful that it was almost irrefutable in terms of traditional constitutional interpretation. True, Taney had tactfully omitted what was actually the first prohibition on Congress in Article I, section 9—the clause stating that Congress could not ban the slave trade for twenty years, until 1808. So the prohibition on the writ of suspension except when required by public safety in cases of rebellion or invasion was actually second on the list, not first. But that did not affect the structural logic of Taney's argument. The other prohibitions that followed in the list included bans on bills of attainder or ex post facto laws, bans on certain kinds of taxes that Congress could not impose, a ban on taking money from the Treasury without appropriation, a ban on the granting of titles of nobility, and a ban on accepting emoluments from foreign powers without permission from Congress. All had to do with Congress.

Taney then turned to Article II of the Constitution, which established the powers of the executive branch. He argued that if suspending habeas corpus, "the high power over the liberty of the citizen," had been "intended to be conferred on the president, it would undoubtedly be found in plain words in this article."[21] But Article II had nothing to say on the subject of suspension: "[T]here is not a word in it that can furnish the slightest ground to justify the exercise of the power." What was more, Taney hastened to add, the president of the United States was not a king. His short term of office and constrained powers "show the jealousy and apprehension of future danger which the framers of the constitution felt in relation to that department of the government." The framers had "withheld" from the president many powers of the English king that they considered "dangerous to the liberty of the subject; and conferred (and that in clear and specific terms) those powers only which were deemed essential to secure the successful operation of the government."[22]

Again, Taney's argument was extremely convincing as a matter of constitutional interpretation. The framers had been acutely aware of Parliament's enactment of the Habeas Corpus Act of 1679, long considered one of the hallmarks of individual liberty in England. That law ordered all the king's subjects to comply with a judicially issued writ of habeas corpus, thereby effectively blocking even the king from suspending the writ unless Parliament should change the law or make an exception. It was highly unlikely that the framers would have intentionally given the president a power to suspend individual liberties that the king of England lacked. "No one can believe," Taney put it, that the framers "would have conferred on the president a power which the history of England had proved to be dangerous and oppressive in the hands of the crown; and which the people of England had compelled it to surrender, after a long and obstinate struggle on the part of the English executive to usurp and retain it."[23]

In support of his position, Taney then invoked at length the great English legal commentator William Blackstone's account of the rise of habeas corpus in England. He cited a passage from the Supreme Court justice Joseph Story's influential *Commentaries on the Constitution*—a passage leaving no doubt that "the power is given to Congress to suspend the writ of habeas corpus."[24] Story had not even contemplated the possibility of presidential suspension. Taney also quoted the great chief justice John Marshall: "If at any time, the public safety should require the suspension of the powers vested by [the federal habeas corpus law] in the courts of the United States, it is for the legislature to say so."[25]

When Taney wrote his opinion, neither Lincoln nor any officer of the federal government had yet made a formal legal defense of presidential suspension of habeas corpus. Taney, however, could intuit the only line of argument available to the president: an argument from the inherent power of the government as sovereign to do what was necessary to save itself. He set out to demolish that argument before it could be made. "Nor can any argument be drawn," he insisted, "from the nature of sovereignty, or the necessity of government, for self-defense in times of tumult and danger."[26] The reason lay in the very nature of the government created by the U.S. Constitution. That government was "one of delegated and limited powers; it derives its existence and authority altogether from the Constitution." Consequently, there were no inherent powers of sovereignty contained in the Constitution. No part of the federal government could "exercise any of the powers of government beyond those specified and granted." The Tenth Amendment said so explicitly. Taney quoted it: "The powers not delegated to the United States by the Constitution, nor prohibited by it to the states, are reserved to the states, respectively, or to the people."[27]

Taney was arguing that the federal government created by the Constitution was different from other kinds of governments, including the state governments. Most governments could claim to exercise sovereignty, that nearly magical force of ultimate authority that might carry with it all sorts of justifications for action outside the bounds of ordinary limits. But as Taney presented it, the government of the United States was not like those other governments, because it did not possess ultimate sovereignty—that is, ultimate authority or control over its citizens. The federal government under the Constitution was something different: a government of limited powers, one that could act only pursuant to authority granted to it by the people via the Constitution. The Tenth Amendment was Taney's ultimate proof of this claim, because it made it clear that both the people and the states held back some of their inherent, sovereign powers from the federal government. Taney's exposition of the issue of sovereignty and necessity was brief but trenchant. Lincoln would have to answer it directly if he wanted to raise an even faintly plausible constitutional justification for suspending habeas.

Having made the constitutional argument that Lincoln could not suspend habeas corpus without Congress, Taney went further, expressing his view about what would happen if Congress did in fact suspend habeas corpus, an eventuality he thought possible and probably likely. As he had done in his brief statement in court, Taney explained that even if habeas were suspended by Congress, the government could not use martial law to arrest, hold, or try anyone "not subject to the rules and articles of war."[28] Although Taney did not go into the question of what kind of people were not so subject, the general principle he had in mind was that noncombatants were not subject to martial law unless they were living in a war zone.

With this analysis, Taney was not addressing Merryman's situation precisely. After all, Merryman was alleged to have belonged to a rogue wing of the Maryland militia that was acting against the United States. Burning down bridges to stop troops from passing through Baltimore was arguably an act of war by a combatant.

Taney's target was the idea that Baltimore counted as a war zone. Butler had announced that the city was under occupation and had declared martial law. But the situation in Baltimore was far different from that in, say, South Carolina. There had been no act of secession in Maryland. Taney did not mince words. "The military authority in this case has gone far beyond the mere suspension of the privilege of the writ of habeas corpus," he said. "It has, by force of arms, thrust aside the judicial authorities and officers to whom the Constitution has confided the power and duty of interpreting and administering the laws, and substituted a military government in its place, to be administered and executed by military officers."[29] Taney was stating that Butler's imposition of martial law violated the Constitution.

He explained why: The federal courts were open. Federal officials, including Taney, were doing their jobs. When Merryman was arrested, he pointed out, "the district judge of Maryland, the commissioner appointed under the act of Congress, the district attorney and the marshal, all resided in the city of Baltimore, a few miles only from the home of the prisoner." What was more, "up to that time" of Merryman's arrest, "there had never been the slightest resistance or obstruction to the process of any court or judicial officer of the United States, in Maryland." The only resistance to the courts, the chief justice noted pointedly, came from "the military authority"—the refusal to obey his writ. Taney explained what should have happened to Merryman under the Constitution: "If a military officer . . . had reason to believe that the prisoner had committed any offence against the laws of the United States, it was his duty to give information of the fact and the evidence to support it, to the district attorney." In turn the federal prosecutor would have sought a warrant, ordered an arrest pursuant to it, and presented Merryman for a bail hearing and a criminal trial in federal court. All this, Taney said, would and could have happened: "There was no danger of any obstruction or resistance to the action of the civil authorities, and therefore no reason whatever for the interposition of the military."[30]

Taney was impugning Butler's imposition of martial law in Baltimore. By doing so, Taney was also telling the world that even if Congress were to suspend habeas, he would be prepared to issue a legal judgment holding that the suspension had no legal effect in Baltimore. As he had done in the *Dred Scott* case, Taney was using the tool of obiter dicta—the judicial prerogative to make statements about a case

that might not be necessary to the holding—to make a broader political statement.

Taney's conclusion was one for the ages. He recited the due process clause of the Constitution: "No person shall be deprived of life,
liberty or property, without due process of law." He quoted the Fourth
Amendment protection against arrest without warrant. He invoked
the Fifth Amendment guarantee of a speedy, public trial in a court of
justice. And he intoned: "These great and fundamental laws, which
Congress itself could not suspend, have been disregarded and suspended, like the writ of habeas corpus, by a military order, supported
by force of arms."[31] The suspension of habeas corpus was not just the
suspension of one legal procedure. It amounted to the suspension of
the Constitution itself—and the rule-of-law principles contained in it.

Taney then delivered a devastating judgment. If the judicial authority under the Constitution "may thus, upon any pretext or under any
circumstances, be usurped by the military power, at its discretion, the
people of the United States are no longer living under a government
of laws." Instead of the rule of law, "every citizen holds life, liberty and
property at the will and pleasure of the army officer in whose military
district he may happen to be found."[32] The United States was no longer
being governed by law, Taney was asserting. If martial law could be applied in Baltimore, then the rule of law had been suspended nationwide.

What could Taney do? Even as chief justice of the United States,
Taney acknowledged, his powers were limited by the reality of the
military situation. "My duty was too plain to be mistaken," he stated.
"I have exercised all the power which the Constitution and laws confer
upon me, but that power has been resisted by a force too strong for me
to overcome"—the U.S. Army. Taney explained that he would order
that his opinion be sent "under seal, to the president of the United
States. It will then remain for that high officer, in fulfilment of his constitutional obligation to 'take care that the laws be faithfully executed,'

to determine what measures he will take to cause the civil process of the United States to be respected and enforced."[33]

This last sentence of Taney's opinion was the first time he had addressed himself directly to Lincoln in the entire opinion. As Taney and the whole country well knew, Lincoln had, from his inaugural address forward, cited his constitutional obligation to execute the laws as the basis for coercing the seceding states back into the union. Taney was turning the "take care" clause against Lincoln. He was saying that, under that clause, Lincoln must obey his judicial order to release Merryman.

Taney was the chief justice of the United States. He had made it as clear as language allowed that the president had no legal authority to arrest people within the loyal United States and hold them without a civil charge. Taney recognized that he had no troops to back up his constitutional position. His goal was necessarily political and rhetorical. He stated the law and announced that it was up to Lincoln to enforce it.

ALL THE LAWS BUT ONE

After Taney issued his opinion in *Ex parte Merryman*, Lincoln could have backed down and transferred Merryman to civilian custody for trial. He had been careful not to announce a general suspension of habeas corpus, preferring to direct his generals privately that they could suspend habeas if necessary for public safety. That in itself suggested that Lincoln was not fully committed to suspension—and it gave the president substantial leeway. He could, for example, have told the generals to stop the suspensions or to dial them down. Taney had intentionally left Lincoln some room to retreat gracefully, writing that "it is possible that the officer who has incurred this grave responsibility may have misunderstood his instructions, and exceeded the authority intended to be given him."[34] This was an invitation to Lincoln to disown the actions of the officers who had detained Merryman.

Before Taney's opinion, it would seem, Lincoln might possibly have been open to this option. On May 17, a week before Taney announced his opinion, Lincoln had received a letter from the U.S. attorney in Washington, D.C., protesting the fact that the military was making arrests on its own in the city, outside the sphere of civilian authority. In a memorandum that may have been directed only to himself, Lincoln had jotted down one sentence: "Unless the *necessity* for these arbitrary arrests is *manifest*, and *urgent*, I prefer they should cease."[35] The language suggests that Lincoln had not yet fully embraced the policy of military arrests he had set in motion.

Yet once Taney had personalized the attack on Lincoln, the president seems to have decided to double down. On May 30, he renewed his request to Edward Bates, the attorney general, to give him a formal opinion on his authority.

Lincoln did not have faith that Bates could do the job without help. He may have known that Bates had asked for assistance on the issue from one of his own sons, a lawyer, and from Titian J. Coffey, a Pennsylvania attorney. Coffey had concluded that only Congress could suspend habeas[36]—exactly the opposite of the conclusion that Lincoln wanted. Bates also knew, and Lincoln must have known, that the same conclusion had been reached in 1857 by Caleb Cushing, then Buchanan's attorney general.[37]

So this time Lincoln directed Bates to get input from Reverdy Johnson, a Maryland lawyer and politician who had been attorney general under Taylor and Fillmore and who had represented the slave owner in the *Dred Scott* case. The tone left no doubt that Lincoln expected his attorney general to authorize his actions. "Will you do the favor to confer with Mr. Johnson," Lincoln wrote, "and be preparing to present the argument for the suspension of the Habeas Corpus."[38] Lincoln must have been told that Johnson had different ideas on the subject, and wanted Johnson's views to appear in Bates's official opinion.[39]

Having tasked the attorney general with preparing a technical legal response to Taney's opinion, Lincoln decided to make an answer of his own, focusing on the deeper constitutional issues. He chose to include his answer in his address to the special session of Congress on July 4—the same speech in which he justified the use of force against the seceding states.

It made sense for the president to include the habeas issue in that address. The speech included an overall justification for the actions that Lincoln had taken unilaterally before Congress came into session. The suspension of habeas corpus was, like the calling up of the militia, an act that Lincoln had performed without awaiting congressional authorization. Furthermore, in the speech, Lincoln was asking Congress to take action validating what he had already done. Referring to his call for militia, Lincoln told Congress that his "measures, whether strictly legal or not, were ventured upon under what appeared to be a popular demand, and a public necessity; trusting, then as now, that Congress would readily ratify them."[40] Just as he was asking Congress to authorize the raising of another 300,000 volunteers, he was asking Congress to take steps to suspend habeas corpus. That would solve the constitutional problem that Lincoln had created and that Taney had targeted in his opinion.

Lincoln began his defense of his actions by explaining that "it was considered a duty to authorize the Commanding General." In his first draft he had written, "I felt it my duty."[41] The change from active to passive reflected the need to proceed cautiously around the topic of conduct that the Chief Justice of the United States had declared unconstitutional.

Lincoln defended the use of suspension as rare.[42] Yet by now the arrests included not only Merryman but also the Baltimore marshal of police (that is, the chief of police), George Proctor Kane, arrested June 27. (The entire Baltimore Board of Police Commissioners would be arrested a few days later.) And as Taney had explained in his opinion, the effect of any suspension of habeas under martial law was far-reaching. If anyone could be arrested and held without warning, then all it took was a handful of well-publicized arrests to put the fear of arrest into the entire population.

Now Lincoln turned to Taney: "[T]he legality and propriety of what has been done under it, are questioned; and the attention of the country has been called to the proposition that one who is sworn to 'take care that the laws be faithfully executed' should not himself violate them."[43] This time Lincoln used the passive voice to avoid referring not only to himself but also to Taney. In his draft, Lincoln had written, "I have been reminded from a high quarter."[44] That language would have echoed Taney's move to personalize the conflict between the two men and their respective roles as chief justice and president of the United States. Lincoln's final version sought to depersonalize the conflict to the extent possible.

Lincoln then made what would become his most famous argument in justification of suspending habeas corpus. "The whole of the laws which were required to be faithfully executed, were being resisted, and failing of execution, in nearly one-third of the States," he stated accurately. This was the general theory of his whole address: the laws were not being executed in the seceding states, and it was his constitutional duty to enforce them. But he went on to offer a notably different variant of the argument with respect to suspension:

> Must [the laws] be allowed to finally fail of execution, even had it been perfectly clear, that by the use of the means necessary to their execution, some single law, made in such extreme tenderness of the citizen's liberty, that practically, it relieves more of the guilty, than of the innocent, should, to a very limited extent, be violated?[45]

This was an extraordinarily convoluted sentence from an extremely clear speaker and writer—perhaps because it contained a genuinely radical idea. Flipped around, it expressed a rhetorical question: Wasn't it better to violate the single law governing habeas corpus than to allow the rest of the laws to go unenforced? The idea was radical because it strongly implied that Lincoln actually had broken the law by suspending habeas. Although Lincoln did not say so, the law he had broken was not just a federal statute but law contained in the Constitution. By his question, Lincoln was suggesting that he had broken the Constitution in order to save it.

Sandwiched in the parenthetical middle of the question was a dismissal of the importance of habeas corpus itself. Lincoln was saying that the writ of habeas manifested a "tenderness" in favor of liberty that mostly protected the guilty. Lincoln's choice to disparage the right of habeas went hand in hand with his treatment of the right as just another law—one whose breaking did not outweigh the enforcement of the rest of the laws. This, too, was radical to the point that it should still astonish today. The entire Anglo-American legal tradition, which Taney had invoked, treated habeas corpus not just as one law, but as the guarantor of the rule of law itself. By allowing suspension of habeas corpus, Lincoln had not merely violated a single law; he had authorized military rule over U.S. citizens, any one of whom could be arrested and detained indefinitely without judicial review.

Lincoln did not shrink from the argument. He leaned into it, rephrasing it more accessibly: "To state the question more directly, are all the laws, *but one*, to go unexecuted, and the government itself go to pieces, lest that one be violated?"[46] Again, Lincoln was insisting that habeas corpus was just one single law. Seen that way, he was arguing, it made sense to violate it in order to achieve the greater good of enforcing all the other laws. And he was adding that, had habeas been enforced, there would have been another consequence, greater even than nonenforcement of all the laws: If habeas were respected, "the government itself" would "go to pieces."

Now Lincoln was not simply comparing the weight of one law to the weight of all the other laws. He was directly invoking the idea that unless he suspended habeas, he could not maintain the government. This was an argument from necessity of the kind that Taney had tried to refute in advance. In essence, Lincoln was saying, he had to suspend habeas because he had to protect the federal government from dissolution.

To underscore the point, Lincoln asked a third rhetorical question: "Even in such a case [of violating the law], would not the official oath be broken if the government should be overthrown, when it was believed that disregarding the single law, would tend to preserve it?"[47] Again the radicalism of his idea was throwing Lincoln into an unaccustomed mode of obfuscation. Lincoln was suggesting that, if he had allowed the government to be overthrown by declining to suspend habeas, he would have been breaking his oath to take care to enforce the laws. By this logic, Lincoln had to break the Constitution in order to fulfill his oath to uphold it.

This was the most extreme position that Lincoln would ever take in expressing his theory of the broken Constitution. He was proposing that, since the seceding states had broken the Constitution, he had a constitutional duty to break it, too. The difference was that his act of breaking came in fulfillment of his oath to uphold the Constitution, the oath he had described his inaugural address as one "registered in Heaven." Lincoln needed to break the broken Constitution still further in order to repair it.

The structure of rhetorical questions that Lincoln used allowed him to stop just short of actually stating his theory in overt terms. He wanted to come as close to the edge of the radical argument as he could—without going over. In the sentences that followed, he pulled back from the brink. And he did so by the doubtful means of arguing that in fact he *did* possess the authority to suspend habeas. Reverting yet again to the passive voice, Lincoln said, "It was decided that we have a case of rebellion, and that the public safety does require the qualified suspension of the privilege of the writ which was authorized to be made."[48] He therefore had not truly broken the Constitution.

Of course, Taney had held that only Congress could decide that rebellion existed and suspend the writ, not Lincoln as president. That was also the obvious and natural reading of the Constitution. Lincoln rejected the argument: "[T]he Constitution itself, is silent as to which, or who, is to exercise the power," he pointed out artfully. And he gave a practical reason for his interpretation:

> [A]s the provision was plainly made for a dangerous emergency, it cannot be believed the framers of the instrument intended, that in every case, the danger should run its course, until Congress could be called together; the very assembling of which might be prevented, as was intended in this case, by the rebellion.[49]

Lincoln was asserting that, since the suspension clause described conditions of emergency, it should not be interpreted so that it would fail to meet the emergency. Congress was not in session when the events at Fort Sumter and the crisis in Baltimore had taken place. The Constitution should be interpreted to allow the president to have acted on his own—out of necessity under emergency conditions.

In the months and years that followed, Lincoln's supporters would try to devise further arguments to claim that the president did have the constitutional authority to suspend habeas. For example, Anna Ella Carroll, the pro-Lincoln Maryland writer, composed an extended essay, "The War Powers of the General Government," which was published in 1862 under the imprimatur of the State Department and, according to Carroll, "fully approved at the War Department and by President Lincoln."[50] In it, Carroll advanced the creative claim that since the suspension of habeas was, from an "analytic point," not legislation but action, it should rest with the president instead of the legislature.[51] Suspension fell "naturally under the class of military powers," she wrote. Hence, "by inevitable logic, it is the commander of the military force who ought to possess the power of setting aside the writ of *habeas corpus* when he finds it employed mischievously to defeat the operations of war."[52] Carroll modestly explained that she was not a lawyer (she could not have been a member of the bar, given the sexist prohibitions of the day), but her argument clearly reflected skilled constitutional analysis and suggested that she had studied law, possibly with her father, a former governor of Maryland. The intended effect of legalistic arguments like Carroll's was to naturalize the suspension of habeas corpus as at least quasi-legal. Lincoln was prepared to make an argument from necessity, but he preferred to be able to say that he had not in fact broken the Constitution by suspension.

THE FIRST WAVE

The president had spoken. Now, as hostilities continued, it fell to Congress to respond. The next day, July 5, the same day that the sitting governor of Missouri led 6,000 men into battle against 1,100 federal troops at Carthage, Missouri, Congress's first order of business was to consider a bill "to approve and confirm certain acts of the president of the United States, for suppressing insurrection and rebellion."[53] Had the bill passed, and had Congress then officially authorized the president to suspend habeas, Lincoln's unilateral suspension of habeas corpus would have become a footnote to the history of the Constitution in the Civil War. The suspension would still have told us something important about Lincoln's developing theory of the broken Constitution in the crucial days between his inauguration and the beginning of the special session of Congress. The confrontation between the chief justice and the president, the heads of two of the branches of government, would still have been high drama—but it would be a drama resolved without a clear victor, through the intervention of the third branch: namely, Congress.

Yet many in Congress, including not only Democrats but also some Republicans, objected to ratifying Lincoln's habeas decision. The language of "approve and confirm," several thought, would amount to a declaration that what Lincoln had done had been lawful, a view that was extraordinarily difficult to maintain in legal or constitutional terms.[54] The result was that on August 6, 1861, Congress enacted a joint resolution that never mentioned the suspension at all—and arguably excluded it. It said that "all the acts, proclamations, and orders of the President . . . respecting the army and navy of the United States, and calling out or relating to the militia or volunteers from the States, are hereby approved and in all respects legalized and made valid."[55] It was conceivable that the president's directive to Scott authorizing the suspension of habeas counted as an order "respecting the army." Yet it was also clear that Congress had balked at an explicit ratification of the suspension.

Even more important, Congress—unwilling to take action that would formally authorize Lincoln to do in the future what he had done already—very clearly declined to authorize the president to suspend habeas corpus going forward. A number of bills were subsequently proposed to authorize presidential suspension, but for two years none of them passed.

It was one thing for Lincoln to have acted unilaterally when Congress was not in session. Lincoln himself had argued in his address to Congress that the framers could not have intended "that in every case the danger should run its course until Congress could be called together." In other words, Lincoln had argued that unilateral suspension could be justified as an interim measure until Congress could convene and express its view.

But it was a far greater arrogation of constitutional authority for

Lincoln to continue to authorize arrest and detention without judicial review now that Congress had in fact convened—and had refused to authorize suspension. Unilateral executive suspension could no longer be justified as an emergency interim measure. It was now a policy of the president, based on an assertion of constitutional power that had been rejected explicitly by the chief justice of the United States and implicitly by Congress. Lincoln was now violating the Constitution—even according to his own hints in his address to Congress—on a quasi-permanent basis.

During the wave of detentions in 1861, all without congressional authorization, Lincoln did not exercise his power sparingly. The arrests, spearheaded by Allan Pinkerton, the private detective turned intelligence chief, focused on sites of crisis along the border, like Maryland and Missouri. And they quickly extended beyond alleged quasi-rebels like Merryman to include newspaper editors and elected officials. Francis (Frank) Key Howard, the editor of Baltimore's *Daily Exchange*, was arrested on September 13 for an editorial he had published that criticized the suspension of habeas corpus and the imposition of martial law; his publisher was arrested soon after. Thomas W. Hall, editor of *The South*, was similarly arrested, as were several of his reporters.[56] Both newspapers were prohibited from using the mail to send copies, as was a third paper, *The Daily Baltimore Republican*.[57]

Howard was held at first in Fort McHenry, the same fort that his grandfather, Francis Scott Key, had seen bombarded forty-seven years earlier to the day from a British prison ship in Baltimore Harbor—the event memorialized in "The Star-Spangled Banner." Howard later wrote, "As I stood upon the very scene of that conflict, I could not but contrast my position with his . . . The flag which he had then so proudly hailed, I saw waving, at the same place, over the victims of as vulgar and brutal a despotism as modern times have witnessed."[58] Howard would spend fourteen months in military detention in various forts.

The Maryland legislature, which had adjourned in early August, planned to reconvene in Frederick on September 17. When it did, federal troops appeared and arrested nearly a third of the members—all whom were suspected of pro-Confederate sympathies. The arrests prevented the legislature from forming a quorum. The next spring, federal troops arrested a Maryland state judge, Richard Bennett Carmichael (who was also a state legislator), beating him and dragging him unconscious from his courtroom. He would not be released for more than six months.[59] At least 116 Marylanders were subject to military arrest in 1861, and at least 509 across various military jurisdictions.[60]

One of the most consequential arrests in this wave, again authorized by Lincoln through Secretary of War Edwin Stanton and Pinkerton, was that of Henry May, a Democratic U.S. congressman from Maryland. May had gone to Richmond, Virginia, in July to meet with Jefferson Davis, apparently with explicit permission from Lincoln. While in Richmond, May had reportedly condemned Lincoln's military arrests in Maryland. After he returned to join the special session of Congress, May was criticized by House Republicans, who launched a Judiciary Committee investigation of his conduct. Defending himself on the floor of the House, May harshly criticized the occupation of Baltimore and the suspension of habeas corpus there. He proposed a resolution declaring that the military was violating the Constitution, then another calling for the appointment of peace commissioners to end the conflict, preserving the union if possible but recognizing the Confederacy if not.[61]

May was arrested by the army in September, just a few days before the members of the Maryland legislature were detained. He was imprisoned first in Fort McHenry, then ultimately in Fort Lafayette in New York, where he remained for several months. Unlike Merryman, who had been given access to lawyers, May was held incommunicado. His brother died in October, and May was released on parole to attend the funeral. He was able to rejoin Congress when it convened in December 1861.

Back in Congress, May, now a veteran of military arrest and detention, became the leading advocate for legislation that would block Lincoln from the course he was pursuing. In March 1862, May proposed a law that would require the secretaries of war and state periodically to inform the federal courts of the names of all "political prisoners" being held by the military. Those named would then have to be indicted by a grand jury and charged with treason in the civilian courts or else released upon swearing an oath of allegiance to the Union and promising not to support the Confederacy.

May's bill was at least in part meant to impugn an order on political prisoners that Stanton had issued under Lincoln's direction on February 14, 1862. The order directed that "all political prisoners or state prisoners now held in military custody be released" provided they promised not to give aid or comfort to the enemies of the United States. What was more, it guaranteed amnesty for any past acts of treason or disloyalty by anyone making the promise.[62] But the fine print told the secretary of war that "in his discretion" he might continue to hold "any persons detained as spies" and also, more pertinently, any "others whose release at the present moment may be deemed incompatible with the public safety."[63] The second clause of this exemption potentially vitiated much of the legal effect of the order. Lincoln was releasing "all" political prisoners—except for the ones he continued to deem dangerous. What was more, Lincoln's order said nothing about future arrests. May's proposed law drew attention to these limits.

When Stanton issued the order in mid-February 1862, Lincoln may well have believed that he would not need many future arrests. The border states of Maryland and Kentucky had been kept in the union, and he had just commanded the army and navy to commence an offensive against the Confederacy. But things did not go the way Lincoln thought they would. Instead, the days and months that followed saw the worst series of events in Lincoln's presidency. The disasters of the spring and summer of 1862 would both shake and galvanize

Lincoln—and lead him to new ground with respect to the broken Constitution and what he must do to remake it.

ARRESTING WAR CRITICS

The troubles of 1862 began with a personal one for Lincoln. On February 20, his son Willie, eleven years old, died of typhoid fever. Lincoln's wife, Mary, plunged into a serious depression. Lincoln himself was distraught, but with the war finally beginning in earnest, he could not afford to collapse.

The story of Lincoln's appointment of, and subsequent frustration with, General George McClellan has been often told. In brief, Lincoln had given McClellan command of the Army of the Potomac in July 1861 in the expectation that McClellan would drive south to Richmond—an expectation based on a plan that McClellan had drawn up and presented to Winfield Scott. But after the first Battle of Bull Run, McClellan balked. Napoleonic war doctrine demanded the concentration of vast forces on one objective, and McClellan did not have vast forces. In the months that followed, McClellan replaced Scott as commander of the army. Yet the Union squandered any first-mover advantage it might have had.

The Peninsula campaign, begun in March 1862, represented Lincoln's most serious effort to get McClellan to attack Richmond. McClellan's army of 121,500 men moved slowly, and ultimately failed even to lay siege to the Confederate capital. McClellan, out-generaled by Lee, also believed (with some justification) that Lincoln, who had no military knowledge whatever, was trying to direct his operations for him. The campaign failed, and McClellan was lucky to leave Virginia in June with most of the Army of the Potomac intact. Lincoln's initiative to take Richmond and end the war had been an abject failure.

That was just the beginning. In August, after winning the second Battle of Bull Run, Lee went on the attack, invading Maryland.

McClellan had to respond, and on September 17, the Confederate and Union armies fought the Battle of Antietam, the bloodiest of the war. In total, 22,717 men from both sides were killed or injured. Lee had to retreat back to Virginia. But it was also not a true victory for McClellan, who again squandered the initiative by failing to pursue Lee. Lincoln would relieve McClellan in November. The idea that the Union could defeat the Confederacy expeditiously had to be definitively abandoned.

A central consequence of Lincoln and McClellan's ineffectuality was that it negatively affected enthusiasm to volunteer for the Union's forces. On July 17, shortly after the failure of the Peninsula campaign, Congress passed the Militia Act of 1862. The law is mostly remembered today because it enabled the enlistment of African Americans as soldiers and laborers. At the same time, however, the law also authorized conscription by states that could not meet their militia quotas by using volunteers.

The state-level draft worked poorly from the start. That posed an existential challenge to Lincoln's war effort. Without men, the Union could not win the war. The Confederacy had instituted a universal draft for all adult men in March. Facing a new crisis, this time of manpower, Lincoln chose a remarkable course of action. Undeterred by May's proposals and the ongoing congressional debates around suspension of habeas corpus, Lincoln decided the best response to the manpower crisis was to shut down all criticism of the war.

The centerpiece of Lincoln's plan to support the draft by suppressing antiwar speech was a proclamation issued on September 24, 1862. The proclamation went far beyond Lincoln's action during the Baltimore crisis the year before, which had authorized Scott to suspend habeas when necessary to ensure public safety. The original authorization of suspension had been directed at potential Confederate collaborators—traitors, as Lincoln called them. Now the target was expanded to include critics of the failing war effort.

The new proclamation had two components. One authorized arrest and trial before military courts of anyone, including civilians, charged with "discouraging volunteer enlistments, resisting militia drafts, or guilty of any disloyal practice, affording aid and comfort to Rebels against the authority of the United States." The other went further still. It stated bluntly that "the Writ of Habeas Corpus is suspended" for anyone detained by the military currently or "hereafter during the rebellion."[64]

Lincoln justified this wide-reaching and unprecedented suspension of habeas with a brief introductory statement. He observed that it had "become necessary to call into service not only volunteers but also portions of the militia of the States by draft."[65] The volunteer enthusiasm of April 1861 had given way to the realities of a war that, everyone was realizing, could not be won quickly, if it could be won at all. The result was a military draft—itself a legislative mechanism for the involuntary impressment of otherwise free citizens into military service.

If a draft existed, a draft could be resisted. Lincoln asserted flatly that "disloyal persons are not adequately restrained by the ordinary process of law from hindering [the draft] and from giving aid and comfort in various ways to the insurrection."[66] Put simply, ordinary law did not prohibit or deter those opposed to the draft from speaking out against it and encouraging young men to refuse to serve. The point of the proclamation was to allow Lincoln to arrest people deemed to be encouraging draft resistance—and to hold them for the remainder of the war if he so chose, either with military trial or without.

The scope of the suspension of basic rights was broader even than it appeared on the surface. Resisting the draft was the nominal target. But the proclamation extended to "any disloyal practice" that tended to help the Confederacy. That authorized the military to arrest essentially anyone whose views Lincoln considered disloyal or dangerous. And because habeas was suspended for all military prisoners, there could be no review of the military's decisions, by the courts or by anyone else. The president of the United States was the final authority. A more total fulfillment of Taney's worst fears could hardly be conceived.

The idea of necessity had enabled Lincoln to extend the logic of his original suspension authorizations to an astonishing degree. He had begun with the view that because secession blocked the execution of the laws, he was justified in suspending a single law—habeas—because doing so was necessary to execute the rest. From there he had moved to the view that it was necessary to draft an army in order to defeat the Confederacy. By extension, he maintained, it was necessary to suspend the writ whenever anyone threatened to take action that would interfere with the draft. The final extension was the idea that any disloyalty threatened the draft; hence, military arrest of anyone expressing disloyalty was necessary to restoring the union—and justified suspension.

SUSPENSION, THE PRESS— AND THE "AMERICAN BASTILLE"

Perhaps it should not come as a surprise that, once habeas corpus was suspended in the name of fighting disloyalty, suppressing newspapers critical of the war effort and of the president became a major project for Lincoln's administration and his generals—and a tactic condoned and even embraced by Lincoln himself. Today, in the wake of the posthumous deification of Lincoln as the savior of the republic, it is disquieting to discover the extent of Lincoln's suppression of the free press and free expression in wartime. It simply does not fit our received narrative of an anguished, ethical Lincoln seeking to save the Constitution.

Attacks on press critical of the war and sympathetic to allowing the seceding states to go in peace had begun already in 1861. At first these were spontaneous local riots against individual Democratic-leaning newspapers, usually carried out by mobs and sometimes by volunteer soldiers—and mostly in the aftermath of the disastrous Union defeat at the first Battle of Bull Run.[67] In just two weeks of August of that first year of the war, crowds destroyed newspaper offices in Concord, New Hampshire; Bangor, Maine; Bridgeport, Connecticut; Easton, Pennsylvania; and West Chester, Pennsylvania. The editor of the *Essex County Democrat* was tarred and feathered and run through Haverhill, Massachusetts, on a rail.[68] The timing corresponded to the crisis brewing in Maryland that had led to the first major suspension of habeas corpus.

Soon federal government officials began to respond to the public mood. On August 16, a federal grand jury led by a prominent Republican had sent a note to the presiding judge of the Southern District of New York asking whether a group of named newspapers could be indicted for opposing the war.[69] The judge took no immediate action, but six days later, on August 22, the New York postmaster—a federal patronage appointee—ordered that those papers were not to be sent through the mail. The federal marshal in Philadelphia seized copies of the papers when they arrived by train.[70]

Missouri, like Maryland, was a slave state on the border, where sympathy to secession ran deep and some risk of actual secession then existed. General John C. Frémont declared martial law in St. Louis on August 14, 1861. The provost-marshal he appointed immediately ordered the closure of two newspapers, the *Missourian* and the *War Bulletin*, stating that they had been "shamelessly devoted to the publication of transparently false statements respecting military movements in Missouri."[71] When the editor of a Church of Christ paper wrote to the marshal asking if his paper would be next, the marshal replied that the paper "should abstain from publishing articles of a political character, calculated to inflame the passions of men, and evidently hostile to the Government of the country." So long as the newspaper stuck to religion, the marshal wrote, it would not "come under the discipline of this [military] department."[72] Newspapers were also shuttered in at least eight smaller Missouri cities and towns.[73]

In August and September, some half a dozen Baltimore newspaper editors were arrested as part of the sweep-up of suspected Southern sympathizers, and at least five newspapers were shut down.[74] James McMaster, the editor of the conservative, Catholic *New York Freeman's Journal*, one of the papers named by the New York grand jury, started a new paper, the *New York Freeman's Appeal*. Secretary of State William Seward ordered McMaster's arrest for "editing a disloyal newspaper." McMaster, a convert to Catholicism who was committed to states' rights, was held for as long as eleven weeks without trial, and released only after agreeing to take a loyalty oath. His paper did not return to being published until April 1862.[75]

By the fall of 1861, many of the newspaper editors arrested around the country had been moved to Fort Lafayette, a forbidding War of 1812 fortification just off Bay Ridge, Brooklyn. (The fort existed until 1960, when it was destroyed to make room for the Brooklyn tower of the Verrazzano-Narrows Bridge.) Critics dubbed Fort Lafayette "the American Bastille," a name that appeared in multiple memoirs by incarcerated editors and eventually became the title of a lengthy postwar book recounting many hundreds of arrests and detentions by the Lincoln administration. An article in the pro-Lincoln *New York Times* in September tried to minimize the criticism by insisting preposterously that the fort "is not a Bastile [*sic*] at all, in fact the fort is more like a hotel than anything else" where "the fare is excellent, and the view of the ocean extensive." But the same article also listed the names of ninety-two "political prisoners" being held in the fort.[76]

In all, two hundred newspaper editors and their offices were "identified, menaced, arrested, imprisoned, humiliated, bankrupted, mobbed or sacked" in 1861.[77] A full historical analysis of the Lincoln administration's attacks on the press remains challenging. One of the best and most-relied-upon sources is the yearbook associated with *The New American Cyclopædia* (later renamed the *American Cyclopædia*), published annually after 1858. The yearbooks from 1861 through 1864 contained regular, detailed entries on "Freedom of the Press" compiled from information gathered across the country. It is likely, however, that even those entries were underinclusive and did not cover the full extent of press suppression at any point during the war. What can be said with confidence is that the methods and the scope of the suppression were unprecedented in U.S. history. The Sedition Act of 1798 was used by the Federalist administration of John Adams to prosecute more than two dozen Republican newspaper editors, many of whom were convicted, served prison terms, and were required to pay hundreds of dollars in fines.[78] But this effort was the result of a duly enacted federal law and took place via jury trials, neither of which was the case for Lincoln's efforts. The Sedition Act targeted editors, not newspapers, and was backward looking, not forward looking. And its reach did not even come close to that of Lincoln's efforts.

Harold Holzer, the scholar who has written the most recent, definitive work on Lincoln and the press, argues that the efforts to suppress the free press during 1861 were "uncoordinated" and could have been more extreme. But as he acknowledges, press suppression was undertaken by the departments of war, state, interior, and treasury, not to mention the U.S. Post Office.[79] With this degree of participation across the Lincoln administration, the fact that Lincoln himself did not provide a unified strategic direction itself looks like a strategy, not an oversight. Lincoln was certainly aware of his administration's efforts—and it is a fair inference that he approved.

Holzer also argues that 1861 marked the high point of Lincoln's newspaper suppression.[80] Be that as it may, over the course of 1862, the banning of newspapers from being sent through the mail continued. Three newspapers from Louisiana and another eight published in California were banned from the mail during the year.[81] Four newspapers in Illinois were closed.[82] During 1862, military authorities arrested at least a dozen editors suspected of Copperhead (Peace Democrat) sympathies.[83] *The American Cyclopaedia* yearbook reported that in Paris, Ohio, the editor of the *Stark Country Democrat*, Archibald McGregor, was arrested by federal troops for criticizing the U.S. Army. Another, Dennis A. Mahony of the *Dubuque Herald*, was detained without charge or trial for four months. He ran unsuccessfully for Congress from the Old Capitol Prison in Washington, D.C., and wrote an account of his arrest and imprisonment published the next year under the evocative title *The Prisoner of State*.[84] The book was acerbically dedicated to Stanton, who had, Mahony explained, earned the "unenviable distinction" of being "connected imperishably to . . . acts of outrage, tyranny and despotism."[85]

Also in 1862, the Lincoln administration implemented a telegraph censorship regime aimed at the press in Washington, D.C. Ostensibly intended to prevent the publication of sensitive troop movements, the system was established in an order issued by the secretary of war, dated February 25, 1862. The order banned all "telegraphic communications in regard to military operations not expressly authorized by the War Department." And it stated that a newspaper that published any military news "not authorized" by the department would be barred from receiving any telegraph traffic and from sending its papers by railroad.[86]

The effect of the order was to subject essentially all war reporting to advance censorship. Most war-related reports traveled over the telegraph via the capital, and the secretary of war soon extended the rules to all telegraph lines anywhere in the country.[87] A House Judiciary Committee investigation, whose report ran to a thousand pages, found that the censorship went far beyond troop movements. "Despatches, almost numberless, of a political, personal, and general character have been suppressed by the censor," the committee reported. "Correspondents have been deterred from preparing others because they knew that they could not send them to their papers by telegraph." The Lincoln administration had exploited the new technology of the telegraph, "a most important auxiliary to the press in our country," to create an effective system of censorship.[88] The congressional committee was correct to note the deterrent effect of regulation. The primary goal and effect of press censorship and suppression is ordinarily to encourage self-censorship by newspapers that have not been targeted or shut down. Although the Democratic press may have affected the 1862 elections,[89] there can be little doubt that the Lincoln administration's policies of suppression significantly affected the press's ability and willingness to criticize the war effort.

To today's readers it may seem incomprehensible that all these efforts to suppress the free press were not met with an outpouring of objections based on the First Amendment, which states that "Congress shall make no law . . . abridging the freedom of speech, or of the press." To be sure, observers of the Lincoln administration understood that freedoms of speech and the press were being abridged. The fact that *The American Cyclopædia* yearbook collected instances of this suppression under the heading "Freedom of the Press" indicates as much. Yet it is also the case that the constitutional right to free speech and free press figured remarkably little in the discourse of the time. Holzer's prize-winning 733-page book mentions the First Amendment exactly once.[90]

The main reason for this absence is that the constitutional law of free speech and the free press as we know it was not invented by the Supreme Court until World War I, and not developed into its current form until the 1960s. The text of the First Amendment applies only to Congress, not to the president. Many, although not all, interpreters of the free-speech protections believed until 1919 that its language prohibited only "prior restraint"—what today we would call advance censorship—and not punishment for speech after the fact. Congress did not, during the Civil War, pass any laws that by their terms applied specifically to speech or the press. The suspension clause of the Constitution functioned as an exception to *all* constitutional rights, not just those protected by the First Amendment. Whether suspension was carried out by Lincoln or Congress, the opposition to it did not focus on the First Amendment, both because the tradition of free speech was not yet what it would later become and because the very purpose of suspension was to allow the suppression of basic rights.

The upshot is that our evaluation of Lincoln's conduct in suppressing free speech and the free press must be clear-eyed in the light of our own values and simultaneously nuanced in our understanding of what aspects seemed salient to his contemporaries, whether critics or supporters. During the war, Lincoln suppressed free speech and free expression to the greatest degree that they have ever been suppressed in U.S. history. By our standards today, the First Amendment was egregiously breached. By the standards of the time, the main constitutional violation lay in the unilateral suspension of habeas corpus by a president who was not authorized by Congress to do so until March 1863.

THE SUSPENSION ACT

Finally, on March 3, 1863, after nearly two years of debate, Congress passed the Habeas Corpus Suspension Act—its first formal action on habeas since Lincoln had unilaterally suspended the writ almost two years earlier. The law was a compromise measure. In its most basic provisions, the Suspension Act gave Lincoln a significant legislative victory. The law began with the declaration that "during the . . . rebellion, the President of the United States, whenever, in his judgment, the public safety may require it, is authorized to suspend the privilege of the writ of Habeas Corpus throughout the United States."[91] The language was intentionally ambiguous as to whether this was a statement oriented toward the future alone, and only authorizing future action by Lincoln, or alternatively was meant as a congressional declaration that under the Constitution, the president had always been authorized to suspend habeas, as Lincoln had all along insisted. Regardless of the proper interpretation, Lincoln would be able to rely on congressional authorization if and when he suspended habeas corpus in the future.

And he would also be able to claim that Congress had validated his repeated decisions to suspend habeas unilaterally.

The law went on to indemnify all military officials against civil damages for anything they had done or might do to suspend habeas. This, too, could plausibly be seen as a vindication of Lincoln's policies. Although technically this provision of the law was simply protecting military officers against civil suit, its broader symbolic meaning was surely to indemnify Lincoln himself against the charge that he had violated the Constitution.

At the same time, the law gave hints that Congress believed Lincoln had overreached. The Suspension Act incorporated the proposals made the year before by Henry May, the Maryland congressman who had himself been detained. Following May's suggestion, the act required the secretaries of war and state to provide the federal courts with lists of all detainees designated as "state or political prisoners." Those designated either had to be indicted by a grand jury and charged in the federal courts, or else released. This part of the law was designed to put an end to long-term detention without trial.

The law thus denied the legality of trying civilians before military tribunals where the courts were open—as Taney had urged in his *Ex parte Merryman* opinion. The requirement to try civilians in federal court, not before military tribunals, implied a rejection of Lincoln's insistence on using military tribunals. In combination, these provisions could be read as a congressional rejection of many of the elements of Lincoln's suspension policy.

The Suspension Act gave Lincoln cover to continue the suppression of dissent and criticism of the war. General Milo Hascall, who took charge of the military department of Indiana in March, issued orders that effectively silenced every Democratic newspaper in the state. His approach was so blatant that Lincoln himself questioned whether Hascall had gone too far.[92] On May 11, 1863, the federal general in charge in St. Louis barred the sale of five national papers.

And on June 1, General Ambrose Burnside, commander of the military department of Ohio, issued an order blocking distribution of New York's *World* and directly closing the *Chicago Times*, which fell within his military jurisdiction.[93]

The order to close the *Chicago Times* was especially dramatic and significant. The paper had criticized Lincoln unstintingly, and after Lincoln released his first draft of the Emancipation Proclamation in September 1862, the *Times* had condemned it as a "monstrous usurpation, a criminal wrong, and an act of national suicide."[94] Burnside's order was a direct military command to cease publication—censorship at its most blatant. It was not the first direct shutdown of a newspaper, but it was the first targeted at such a major paper, one published in Lincoln's home state.

Unlike many of the other newspapers that had been previously subject to the Lincoln administration's suppression efforts, the *Chicago Times* fought back. Wilbur Fisk Storey, the paper's editor, sought an injunction from a federal judge, Thomas Drummond, to counteract Burnside's order. Judge Drummond issued a temporary midnight injunction directing the military not to act until he could hold a hearing. Burnside seems to have ignored it. On June 3, 1863, federal troops occupied the *Times'* offices and stopped the printing presses. The *Chicago Tribune* reported that Storey had been on the brink of publishing that day's paper when the troops arrived.[95]

Burnside had gone too far. The Illinois public responded with outrage. The state legislature voted 47–13 to condemn the closure as "in direct violation of the Constitution of the United States . . . and destructive to those God-given principles whose existence and recognition for centuries before a written Constitution was made." The "revolutionary" order, the legislature declared, was "equivalent to the overthrow of our form of government, and the establishment of a military despotism in its stead."[96] From Springfield, Lincoln's former law partner, William Herndon, sent Lincoln a telegram that was co-signed by David Davis, an Illinois friend and colleague of Lincoln's whom the president had appointed to the U.S. Supreme Court the previous year. "We deem it of the highest importance that you revoke the order," the message read.[97] In addition, several prominent Chicago Republicans signed a petition urging Lincoln to revoke the order, and sent it to Lincoln by telegram.[98]

On the night of June 3, a crowd gathered in front of the *Times'* Chicago offices, then grew as it moved into Court House Square. The people in the square adopted a resolution: "Twenty thousand loyal citizens of Illinois, assembled this evening to consult upon their interests, do resolve . . . [that] the constitution guarantees the freedom of speech and of the press" and that "an abrogation of these rights is the overthrow of the Constitution." The courts, not the military, they said, should decide whether the press had broken the law. And they called on Lincoln personally to rescind Burnside's order.[99]

Informed of the protest, Lincoln initially gave in, directing Burnside by telegram on June 4 to revoke the order. When he got the message, Burnside sent a two-sentence message to Storey revoking the order and telling him he was "at liberty to resume" publication.[100] Lincoln's reaction reflected not a principled commitment to the free press, but a political judgment made in the heat of the moment. Later the same day, Lincoln received further information in the form of a telegram to the effect that the closure was not actually being condemned by all the Illinois Republicans who signed the petition. He telegraphed Burnside a second time to countermand his own directive and leave the closure in place. This telegram told Burnside, "[I]f you have not acted" on the earlier message, "you need not do so but may let the matter stand as it is until you receive a letter by mail forwarded yesterday." Burnside got the message only after he had already reopened the *Times*—and he did not shut it down again.[101]

This evidence of Lincoln's willingness to embrace press closures is important because it undermines the apologetic myth that Burnside was acting entirely on his own, against Lincoln's wishes. The truth is that on June 1, before he got word of criticism of the closure, Lincoln was perfectly happy for the closure to remain in place for some time. That day, Stanton wrote Burnside a letter describing Lincoln's priorities in general terms and offering the president's measured criticism of Hascall's censorship in Indiana. In a postscript to the letter, Stanton told Burnside that he had just heard that Burnside had closed the *Times* and that the president had asked him to convey that "in his judgment, it would be better for you to take an early occasion to revoke that order." And he added that in the future, Burnside should consult Lincoln before "the arrest of civilians and the suppression of newspapers not requiring immediate action."[102]

Does this letter indicate that Lincoln opposed Burnside's newspaper closures before the public outcry began? In fact, both Stanton and Lincoln knew the letter would not arrive for days or even weeks— during which the *Times* would have remained closed. (In fact, the letter reached Burnside on June 12.) Lincoln could have telegraphed Burnside on June 1 to order him to reopen the paper, as he actually did on June 4, after learning of the first wave of public criticism.[103] The fact that he did not indicates his willingness to allow the *Times* to stay closed until some "early occasion" to be chosen by Burnside.

Press suppression did not end with Lincoln's reversal of Burnside's closing of the *Times*. It remained in place throughout the duration of the war. On September 15, 1863, Lincoln invoked the Suspension Act in issuing yet another suspension proclamation.[104] This one straightforwardly suspended the writ "throughout the United States" for "prisoners of war, spies, or aiders or abettors of the enemy"; anyone who was in or who had deserted from the U.S. military; and anyone "otherwise amenable to military law, or the Rules and Articles of War." It extended to draft resisters and to anyone accused of "any other offence against the military or naval service."[105] This suspension did not specifically mention civilians who opposed the draft or criticized the war, but its language was broad enough to include them in the light of Lincoln's theory that anyone who weakened the Union's war efforts was aiding the enemy. The suspension would continue, the proclamation said, "throughout the duration" of the rebellion, unless Lincoln revoked it.[106]

More surprising, perhaps, was Lincoln's conduct when it came to the provisions of the Suspension Act that could have been interpreted as condemning the detention of critics: he simply ignored them. Historians of the period have not found any evidence that either the secretaries of war or state ever sent lists of detainees to the federal courts, as required by the law.[107] So far as is possible to determine, no political or state prisoners were ever handed over to the federal courts for trial.[108] In July 1864, Lincoln declared martial law in Kentucky, in apparent defiance of the Suspension Act's requirement that civilians be tried by civilian courts where no insurrection existed.[109]

In sum, the provisions of the Suspension Act designed to restrain Lincoln seem to have had little effect on him. Once acclimated to acting unilaterally, without congressional authorization, Lincoln acted as though Congress lacked the authority to limit his conduct. Certainly, Congress lacked the real-world power or will to do anything about it.

In another strange and intriguing episode in 1864, Lincoln personally ordered the closure of two New York newspapers, *The World* and the *Journal of Commerce*, and the arrest of their editors, after they published a spurious presidential declaration calling out 400,000 more troops and declaring a national day of "fasting, humiliation, and prayer." The forged order turned out to have been delivered to the city's papers via an Associated Press messenger by one Joseph Howard, Jr., an anti-Lincoln journalist who hoped to profit by driving up the price of gold and driving down the stock market on the fake news that Lincoln thought the war was going badly. Other papers caught the deceptions before publishing, in one case apparently after printing twenty thousand copies of a morning edition that had to be pulped.[110] It was perhaps not a pure coincidence that *The World* took a virulently anti-Lincoln editorial line.

The New York press reacted negatively to the shutdown and arrest orders. The two editors were freed and the newspapers allowed to re-open just a few days after Lincoln had ordered them closed. Howard was sent to Fort Lafayette. Manton Marble, the editor of *The World*, went back to pursuing his criticism of Lincoln, this time with the added legitimacy of the near martyr. The episode led to a legal battle over whether the civilian courts could proceed against the military officers who had performed the closure. In court, the officers' defense was that habeas corpus had been suspended pursuant to the Suspension Act, and that the closure was therefore entirely lawful. The judge ruled that the case could go forward, but no prosecution was ultimately brought.[111] In a telling postscript, the secretary of war initiated an investigation and takeover of the Independent Telegraph Company, even though it had nothing to do with the hoax. Its employees in both New York and Washington were interrogated and imprisoned without charge as the army looked for a scapegoat for the embarrassment Lincoln had suffered.[112]

In total, over the course of 1864, at least thirty-four newspapers were shut down or destroyed across the United States, according to *The American Cyclopaedia* yearbook. All Democratic papers were banned in Kentucky. All Democratic newspapers were excluded from Memphis, Tennessee.[113] These statistics, alongside the New York episode, strongly indicate that the Lincoln administration never systematically stopped suppressing the press while the war continued.

The nature of government efforts to shut down press freedoms is to change the terms of public discourse. Acting without congressional authorization from 1861 until March 1863, and with that authority afterward, Lincoln suppressed critical newspapers and arrested and imprisoned editors without trial. A number of these political prisoners may have been Confederate sympathizers. Yet that possibility should not distract us from the reality of Lincoln's undertaking—and the extent to which the basic freedoms of speech and press were suspended along with the suspension of habeas corpus. The idea that in suspending habeas, Lincoln preserved "all the laws but one," should be recognized as essentially a myth.

DICTATORSHIP?

Under the proclamation of September 24, 1862, Lincoln could order the arrest of anyone he wished, and his decisions were formally and legally final. Did this transform Lincoln into a dictator? And if so, was this dictatorship justified under the Constitution or only outside it? The German constitutional thinker Carl Schmitt, who joined the Nazi Party in 1933 and was Adolf Hitler's favorite constitutional lawyer (for as long as Hitler needed a constitutional lawyer), certainly thought so—and he approved thoroughly. It is worth considering Schmitt's analysis of Lincoln seriously. Schmitt was a morally repugnant person. But he was also a strange kind of a genius—the kind who reflected more deeply than any other constitutional thinker of the modern age about dictatorial power, how to seize it, and what it meant for the constitutional order.

Schmitt believed that sovereignty must exist somewhere in every functioning political system, and that the ultimate definition of the sovereign was the one who had the concrete ability to declare an exception to otherwise existing laws.[114] Suspending habeas corpus is a perfect example of the exception that Schmitt made central to his view. The Constitution as written appeared to give the power to declare the exception to Congress, the delegate of the people's sovereignty. But in practice, it was Lincoln, the president, who exercised that power without Congress until the Suspension Act was passed.

This made Lincoln the "decider," to use a term that goes back to Schmitt and was popularized in the United States during the presidency of George W. Bush. In Schmitt's terms, Lincoln was the archetype of the "sovereign dictator." As Schmitt put it, the "dictatorship suspends the constitution in order to protect it . . . in its concrete form." Schmitt thought that Lincoln had set a precedent for every subsequent dictator:

> The argument has been repeated ever since—first and foremost by Abraham Lincoln: when the body of the constitution is under threat, it must be safeguarded through a temporary suspension of the constitution. Dictatorship protects the specific constitution against an attack that threatens to abolish this constitution.[115]

Schmitt believed there was a difference between a dictator who seized power without any reference to the existing constitution or laws, and a dictator like Lincoln who appealed, as he put it, not "to an existing constitution, but to one that is still to come." He thought that Lincoln was appealing to a power that was not "itself constitutionally established," but that was "nevertheless . . . associated with [the] existing constitution in such a way that it appears to be foundational to it."[116]

Schmitt meant that Lincoln could not convincingly rely on the existing Constitution to suspend habeas, but that he was nonetheless appealing to the Constitution in another sense—to the Constitution as the people would ultimately agree to accept it. According to this account, Lincoln was changing the Constitution as he went. He was breaking the Constitution in order to remake it as something new.

Writing in 1948, in the wake of World War II, the American political scientist Clinton Rossiter, best known today as the modern editor of the *Federalist Papers*, partially agreed with Schmitt—but only partially. Rossiter conceded that Lincoln had been a dictator in "the eleven weeks between the fall of Sumter and July 4, 1861." But he considered that period "the paragon of all democratic, constitutional dictatorships," because "if Lincoln was a great dictator, he was a greater democrat."[117] After Congress convened, Rossiter argued, "the normal organization of the government began to function again, and continued to do so for the remainder of the war."[118] In other words, Rossiter thought that Lincoln's dictatorship was over long before Congress authorized suspension in March 1863.

Rossiter had to acknowledge that Lincoln's suspension of habeas before this time "was effected without even a reference to Congress." Rossiter did admit that Lincoln was in this period "exercising dictatorial power." But he maintained that, in suspending civil liberties, Lincoln "had the acquiescence of Congress and the overwhelming support of the loyal population."[119] Acting with the support of the people and Congress, Lincoln was merely a "constitutional dictator," acting pursuant to power authorized by the Constitution.*

Rossiter's position depended on the idea that Lincoln's constitutional claim to the power of suspension could be validated, at least to some extent, by the reality of popular support. And Rossiter considered the eventual passage by Congress of the Suspension Act as having "ratified" Lincoln's actions. Where Rossiter differed most basically from Schmitt was that Rossiter did not want to see Lincoln as a sovereign, the ultimate decider, but as a tool of the sovereign, democratic people, acting in fulfillment of their wishes and ultimately being validated by them. For Schmitt, any dictator was ultimately outside the democratic constitutional order as it exists. For Rossiter, a constitutional dictator remained within that order, and was authorized by it.

Did Lincoln believe he was a dictator of either sort? The short answer is that, even at his most extreme moments of invoking powers we might call dictatorial, Lincoln always insisted that he was acting within the authority of the Constitution and at the behest of the people. That

---

* Rossiter also tried to downplay the degree of Lincoln's exercise of the power of arrest. "In the entire course of the war there were not more than 25,000 arrests of this nature," he wrote (!). "It is certain that no government in mortal struggle ever dealt less severely with traitors."

is, Lincoln always spoke as a constitutional actor. The longer, more complex answer is that, despite making this claim in each instance, Lincoln also repeatedly acknowledged the possibility that his constitutional arguments were wrong and went too far. In those moments, he offered justifications based on necessity. And those justifications passed beyond the territory of the Constitution, into the possibility of the dictatorship described by Schmitt: one based on the Constitution not as it had existed up to the time, but as it would exist when transformed in the future.

VALLANDIGHAM, OR THE EXILED WOULD-BE PRESIDENT

Over the course of the Civil War, at least 14,400 and conceivably as many as 38,000 military arrests of civilians within the Union were made under Lincoln's suspension of habeas corpus in its various iterations.[120] One in particular came to exemplify the extreme powers that Lincoln claimed at the end of his chain of necessity. The arrest itself and Lincoln's response illuminate in rich detail the question of whether Lincoln was a dictator.

On April 13, 1863, a month after the Suspension Act passed, General Burnside, commander of the Department of the Ohio, an administrative military district that consolidated troops from Ohio, Indiana, and Illinois—the same man who would close the *Chicago Times* two months later—issued a general order prohibiting any public or private statement of sympathy for the Confederacy:

> The habit of declaring sympathies for the enemy will no longer be tolerated in the department. Persons committing such offences will be at once arrested, with a view to being tried . . . or sent beyond our lines into the lines of their friends.

The same order also specified that "all persons found within our lines who commit acts for the benefit of the enemies of our country, will be tried as spies or traitors, and, if convicted, will suffer death."[121] The stated legal basis for Burnside's order was Lincoln's proclamation of September 24, 1862, authorizing military arrest and trial of anyone impeding the war effort and unilaterally suspending habeas corpus without congressional authorization.*

The structure of the Civil War was and remained that the Union was fighting to coerce the seceding states to return. Burnside could therefore maintain, following Lincoln's chain of reasoning, that any opposition to continued prosecution of the war amounted to supporting the Confederacy, since all the Confederacy wanted was for the war to end. Burnside chose to interpret criticism of the war as a declaration of sympathy for the enemy. Under his order, criticizing the war was an act of treason that could result in imprisonment, exile to the Confederacy, or death.

Clement Vallandigham was an Ohio Democrat who had served two terms as a member of Congress, leaving office in early 1863 after losing in a district gerrymandered to beat him. Along with Henry May, he had led the House inquiry into Lincoln's use of censorship and arbitrary arrests. Despite losing his seat, Vallandigham still had national political stature. His pro-compromise, antiwar stance made him a potential Democratic presidential candidate in 1864. In his final speech in the House, delivered on January 14, 1863, Vallandigham had condemned Lincoln's constitutional violations, including the suspension of habeas corpus and the Emancipation Proclamation. He left no doubt that he sought peace with the Confederacy and reunion under the terms of the Constitution as it had existed before the war.

---

* Congress had passed the Habeas Corpus Act in March 1863. But Lincoln did not invoke the powers conferred by Congress until September 15, 1863, when he issued a fresh proclamation. Hence Burnside had to, and did, rely on Lincoln's September 1862, unilateral suspension.

On May 1, 1863, Vallandigham, back in Ohio, gave another speech reiterating these themes. He denounced the president as "King Lincoln" and declared that the war had been transformed into an effort to free the slaves—not a popular objective in Ohio, which was next to the slave state of Kentucky. The speech was a direct challenge to Burnside's order.

On May 5, in a show of force aimed at antiwar speech, Burnside sent 150 Union soldiers to arrest Vallandigham at his home in Dayton. In short order, a military commission convicted the ex-congressman of "expressing . . . sympathy for those in arms against the United States" and "declaring disloyal sentiments and opinions."[122] For this crime, the commission sentenced Vallandigham to military detention for the remainder of the war. Vallandigham's lawyers sought a writ of habeas and were denied. Lincoln commuted the sentence to banishment to the Confederacy, a sentence that was immediately carried out.* A potential challenger to Lincoln in the next year's election was now barred from entering the Union, much less the presidential race.

Reaction to the Vallandigham affair was rapid, and mostly negative. A typical response came in Albany, New York, on May 16. A public meeting adopted several resolutions. One declared support for the Union and for all constitutional and lawful actions taken to preserve it. The obvious inference to be drawn was that the Albany meeting did *not* support unconstitutional and unlawful action taken in the name of the war. The second resolution made that implication explicit: it condemned the Lincoln administration for its unconstitutional suspension of habeas and its military arrests of civilians. A third resolved to take steps to maintain the government and the country despite the "folly" or "wickedness" of Lincoln's administration.

---

* It was particularly strange for Lincoln to exile a U.S. citizen to territory that, according to him, was still part of the United States. The action all but admitted the hypocrisy of insisting that secession had been constitutionally unsuccessful.

The Albany men were Democrats, but they were not radicals, or radically antiwar. They simply believed Lincoln had gone too far, violating the Constitution by suppressing freedom of speech through the suspension of the writ. They backed up their beliefs by detailing the Constitution's strict requirements of a public trial for any treason prosecution, and indeed for any criminal prosecution whatever. They asserted that "these safeguards of the rights of the citizen against the pretentions of arbitrary power, were intended more *especially* for his protection in times of civil commotion." And they pointed out that the same safeguards had "stood the test of seventy-six years of trial, under our republican system, under circumstances which show that while they constitute the foundation of all free government, they are the elements of the enduring stability of the Republic."[123]

Lincoln replied to this criticism in a public letter to the Albany men, dated June 12, 1863. He began by sharply repudiating the resolutions' premise that the constitutional safeguards were designed to operate during "civil commotion." The safeguards did not apply in a rebellion, Lincoln said, quoting the suspension clause.[124] What was more, Lincoln argued, the arrests were not criminal prosecutions for treason, but something else entirely. To explain what the arrests were, Lincoln launched a stunning revisionist account of how the rebellious Confederacy had manipulated the laws, engaging in what today would be called "lawfare"—the conduct of hostilities by peaceful legal means. He insisted that "the insurgents had been preparing for [the war] more than thirty years," while during that time, "the government had taken no steps to resist them."[125]

It was a wild oversimplification, indeed a distortion, to project the war backward and date secession to the nullification crisis of 1828–1832. Southerners, even those contemplating disunion, had not been consciously relying on constitutional protections to plot a rebellion. They had believed they lived in a constitutional republic in which their right to self-expression allowed them to discuss the right of the states to secede. Lincoln went on to suggest that objecting to the suspension of habeas corpus was itself a form of aiding the enemy:

> [U]nder cover of "Liberty of speech" "Liberty of the press" and "*Habeas corpus*" they hoped to keep on foot amongst us a most efficient corps of spies, informers, supplyers, and aiders and abettors of their cause in a thousand ways. They knew that in times such as they were inaugurating, by the constitution itself, the "Habeas corpus" might be suspended; but they also knew they had friends who would make a question as to *who* was to suspend it; meanwhile their spies and others might remain at large to help on their cause. Or if, as has happened, the executive should suspend the writ, without ruinous waste of time, instances of arresting innocent persons might occur, as are always likely to occur in such cases; and then a clamor could be raised in regard to this, which might be, at least, of some service to the insurgent cause.[126]

Never in his presidency did Lincoln sound more paranoid—even unhinged. His paranoia focused on the invocation of constitutional rights. Lincoln was claiming that the basic rights to free speech and habeas corpus were nothing but "cover" for undermining the Union. More astonishing, he was claiming that standing up for those rights was itself proof of motive to help the Confederacy. Even raising the issue of whether the president had the right to suspend habeas, as Taney had done, proved friendship to the "insurgent cause."

There was more to follow. Lincoln complained that, out of respect for individual rights, he had been "slow to adopt the strong measures, which by degrees" he had been "forced to regard as being within the exceptions of the constitution, and as indispensable to the public Safety."[127] This was essentially an admission that Lincoln had started interpreting the Constitution to fit what he perceived as the needs of the moment.

The moment, in turn, proved to Lincoln that the rule of law itself must be put on hold in wartime: "Nothing is better known to history than that courts of justice are utterly incompetent to such cases," he said. Courts existed to try individuals for "crimes well defined in the law." But large bands of thieves could overwhelm the courts even in peacetime—and "the insurgent sympathizers even in many of the loyal states" outnumbered such bands. Not only were the courts insufficient to take on the Confederate sympathizers, who were now seamlessly equated to dangerous criminals, but trial by jury could not work, because most juries "have at least one member, more ready to hang the panel than to hang the traitor."[128] This was the argument from necessity run amok. Lincoln was insisting that trial by jury was inadequate because sometimes it might not produce a conviction.

Lincoln was building to the central claim of his letter: that free speech itself was inapplicable in wartime. "[H]e who dissuades one man from volunteering, or induces one soldier to desert," he argued, "weakens the Union cause as much as he who kills a union soldier in battle." If speaking against the war robbed the army of one man, it was equivalent to a battlefield shooting by a rebel soldier. "Yet this dissuasion, or inducement," performed through speech, "may be so conducted as to be no defined crime of which any civil court would take cognizance."[129] By this reasoning, speech had to be suppressed by military arrests precisely *because* it was ordinarily a protected right.

Later in the letter, Lincoln sought to underscore this argument by an appeal to pathos. The penalty for desertion was death, but the president was always asked to commute the sentence. His experience of executions for desertion was personal. "Must I shoot a simple-minded soldier boy who deserts," Lincoln asked, "while I must not touch a hair of a wiley agitator who induces him to desert?"[130]

It was just possible to glimpse here how Lincoln had talked himself into the position that criticizing the war was treason. The personal agony of ordering young men to be executed seems to have made him furious at those who might encourage desertion. The problem was that, whatever his emotions, Lincoln extended the chain of causation more and more tenuously. Agitation against the war, he claimed, was "none the less injurious when effected by getting a father, or brother, or friend, into a public meeting, and there working upon his feeling, till he is persuaded to write the soldier boy, that he is fighting in a bad cause, for a wicked administration of a contemptible government, too weak to arrest and punish him if he shall desert." The conclusion, to Lincoln, was that suppressing criticism of the government was necessary to preserve the life of the would-be deserter: "I think that in such a case, to silence the agitator, and save the boy, is not only constitutional, but, withal, a great mercy." Necessity—of an extremely remote type—made suppression of criticism "constitutional."[131]

Just before making his argument from necessity, Lincoln had turned to the purposes of military arrest compared to ordinary criminal arrest. Military arrests, he explained, "are made, not so much for what has been done, as for what probably would be done." Such arrests were "preventive." This was certainly an honest description of what arrests like Vallandigham's were designed to do: not to punish criminal conduct but to suppress opposition. Lincoln then offered what can only be called a chilling justification for preventive arrests. "In such cases," he claimed, "the purposes of men"—that is, their underlying motives— "are much more easily understood, than in cases of ordinary crime." How so?

> The man who stands by and says nothing, when the peril of his government is discussed, can not be misunderstood. If not hindered, he is sure to help the enemy. Much more, if he talks ambiguously—talks for his country with "buts" and "ifs" and "ands."[132]

In terms that would sound familiar in any dictatorial regime, the president of the United States was saying that anyone who remained silent in the face of discussion of the war was "sure to help the enemy." Ambiguity of expression was worse—certain proof of disloyalty. No other presidential statement made at any moment in the country's history comes close to this sort of insistence that silence itself was traitorous. And Lincoln made it in a public letter devoted to justifying the detention and arrest of political opponents on only the thinnest constitutional justification.

To support his claim, Lincoln named half a dozen senior Confederate generals, including Robert E. Lee. All, he said, had been "within the power of the government" at some point after Fort Sumter. None had been arrested, because "no one of them had then committed any crime defined in the law." Had they been detained, they "would have been discharged on Habeas Corpus, were the writ allowed to operate." Lincoln's point was that "if we had seized and held them, the insurgent cause would be much weaker." He concluded acidly: "I think the time not unlikely to come when I shall be blamed for having made too few arrests rather than too many."[133]

Lincoln was drawing to the end of his remarkable letter. He had to address two final counterarguments, both connected to the constitutional provision that allowed suspension. One was that, in Ohio, where Vallandigham had been arrested, as in Baltimore, where Merryman had been detained, no rebellion or insurrection was under way. The courts were open and operating. Taney had made it clear in his *Ex parte Merryman* opinion that suspension could not apply under such circumstances, even if Congress had exercised it.

Lincoln dismissed the distinction between places where rebellion actually existed and those where it did not: "the constitution itself makes no such distinction." Military arrests were therefore "constitutional *wherever* the public safety does require them." And by "*wher-*

ever," Lincoln meant anywhere in the country where there was a war effort, including the draft.[134]

Lincoln was interpreting the Constitution to give himself the power of military arrest in every part of the Union, without exception. This was the high-water mark of declared presidential power in Lincoln's administration—and indeed in the history of the United States. Lincoln claimed—and exercised—the authority to arrest and detain anyone whose conduct or inclinations detracted from the war effort, anywhere in the country. It was no longer plausible for him to say that he had suspended a single law so that "all the laws but one" could be enforced. Lincoln had suspended the basic constitutional right to free speech and the core element of the rule of law.

This was the final and most essential point Lincoln had to address— the concern that, by suppressing constitutional rights, he was breaking the Constitution, and hence destroying the legacy of fundamental rights it was built to protect. "If I be wrong on this question of constitutional power," Lincoln wrote, "my error lies in believing that certain proceedings are constitutional when, in cases of rebellion or invasion, the public Safety requires them, which would not be constitutional when, in absence of rebellion or invasion, the public Safety does not require them."[135]

Here was Lincoln's most basic constitutional claim of necessity, stripped to its essentials: If the suspension clause was in the Constitution, then the Constitution itself authorized its violation in times of rebellion. "The constitution itself makes the distinction" between ordinary times and rebellion, he pointed out. The country was sick, Lincoln said, and it must be treated with strong medicine:

> I can no more be persuaded that the government can con-
> stitutionally take no strong measure in time of rebellion,
> because it can be shown that the same could not be lawfully

taken in time of peace, than I can be persuaded that a particular drug is not good medicine for a sick man, because it
can be shown to not be good food for a well one.[136]

The language was plain, but the metaphor of the statesman as a physician who must heal the state by carefully chosen medical treatment
went back to Aristotle.[137] Lincoln was suggesting that the suspension
clause of the Constitution embodied an ancient truth about statecraft.
He, not Congress, was the healer.

From the medical metaphor, it followed, Lincoln said, that the
suspension of rights was not dangerous to the long-run health of
constitutional democracy:

> Nor am I able to appreciate the danger . . . that the Amer-
> ican people will, by means of military arrests during the
> rebellion, lose the right of public discussion, the liberty of
> speech and the press, the law of evidence, trial by jury, and
> Habeas corpus, throughout the indefinite peaceful future
> which I trust lies before them, any more than I am able to
> believe that a man could contract so strong an appetite for
> emetics during temporary illness, as to persist in feeding
> upon them through the remainder of his healthful life.[138]

Lincoln was saying that painful temporary remedies would not outlast the circumstances that required them. The violation of basic constitutional rights would not extend beyond the end of the rebellion.
Just as the Constitution contained a provision authorizing its own
violation, it also carried within it the seeds of its own eventual repair.
The body politic—the people—would not develop a taste for living
without civil liberties.

Thus, Lincoln was still offering an ultimately democratic justification for suspending constitutional rights. The rights belonged to

the people. The people would want them back. By implication, Lincoln's decision to suspend those rights served the people themselves. It therefore could not endanger them.

This formulation came very close to a dictator's claim to be authorized by the people to break ordinary constitutional restraints. Yet it also resonated with Lincoln's claim all along to be acting constitutionally. Referring to the people's ultimate preferences further suggested that if Lincoln was indeed breaking the Constitution, he was doing so in a way that the people would ultimately vindicate. If that was so, Lincoln was not only breaking the Constitution to preserve it: he was transforming the Constitution into something new, something that would in turn have to be ratified afresh by the people.

CONGRESSIONAL AUTHORIZATION— AND AFTER

The final acts of the suspension drama played out throughout the end of the war—and beyond. The emblematic centerpiece was the detention and trial of antiwar Indiana Democrat Lambdin P. Milligan in August–September 1864—all in apparent violation of the restrictions created by the Suspension Act passed the year before. Milligan, a pro-peace Copperhead Democrat and a staunch Lincoln critic, was associated with a secret organization of pro-Confederate activists, some of whom actually attempted to attack a prisoner-of-war camp in Indiana to free Confederate soldiers held there. Milligan and several other prominent Indiana Democrats were arrested by the military and tried by military tribunal for conspiring against the government, offering aid and comfort to the Confederacy, and inciting insurrection. They were swiftly convicted. Milligan and some of his co-conspirators were sentenced to death.

Milligan was a civilian. The federal courts in Indiana were open. Under the Suspension Act, Milligan should have been tried not by a military commission, but by a federal civilian court. The only conceivable argument for the military trial was that Milligan was in fact a combatant, not a civilian. To prove that, it would have been necessary to prove that he had actively associated himself with the Confederate Army, a charge that the evidence apparently would not sustain, even before a deferential military tribunal. The detention and military trial of Milligan violated both federal law and, if Taney had been right, the Constitution as well.

Milligan's case did not make it to the Supreme Court until 1866, after the war was over. But when the court did consider it, the justices ruled that it had been both unlawful and unconstitutional to detain and try Milligan in the military courts when the federal courts of Indiana were open and there was no rebellion there. The court held that the Suspension Act did not authorize the military trial of civilians. Taney's constitutional position was vindicated, although neither he nor Lincoln lived to see the judicial resolution of their interbranch conflict.

Unlike Taney's opinion in *Ex parte Merryman*, which despite its importance cannot be cited as Supreme Court precedent, *Ex parte Milligan* stands as a landmark judgment on the right of habeas corpus. It was cited (and debated) by the Supreme Court justices in considering the detention of suspected al-Qaeda combatants after the September 11, 2001, attacks. The case is understood to stand for the proposition that civilians may not be denied habeas corpus or tried in military courts so long as the courts remain open. The official judgment of U.S. constitutional law is that Lincoln's suspension of habeas corpus exceeded the bounds set by the Constitution.

When it came to suspension, then, Lincoln failed to transform the broken Constitution into a new constitutional ideal or principle that would come to be broadly accepted by the public. The leading defenders of Lincoln's conduct—at least, those who are not Schmittian lovers of dictatorship—tend to depict the suspension of habeas corpus as a temporary, stopgap measure, justifiable only under conditions of emergency. They tend to pass quickly over the two central elements of Lincoln's justification: that suspending habeas was necessary to the survival of the Union, and that the Constitution should be understood to authorize the president to do whatever he deems necessary to preserve the government and enforce the laws. (They also tend to downplay Lincoln's efforts to suppress free speech and the free press.)

The reason to shortchange Lincoln's own repeatedly expressed justification is that neither part is entirely convincing or satisfactory. It is, in fact, extremely difficult to argue in retrospect that suspension of habeas corpus was necessary to success in the Civil War, as Lincoln believed. The Baltimore crisis certainly needed to be addressed, and Union troops had to be able to travel uninterruptedly from the north to Washington, D.C. It may well have been necessary for the U.S. Army to take Federal Hill and emplace artillery to send the message to the citizens of Baltimore that they must stop interfering with troop transportation. Yet the declaration of martial law in Baltimore seems not to have been necessary to accomplish the goal.

The initial arrest of John Merryman may well have been necessary, given the allegation that he had burned railroad bridges and that the militia company he commanded was acting against the interests of the United States. But it is hard to argue convincingly that it was necessary for Lincoln to defy the chief justice of the United States when Taney ordered Merryman released from military custody. Lincoln did not have to free Merryman. He could simply have ordered Merryman to be prosecuted in federal court. Merryman could have been put on trial in Maryland—and there is little reason to believe he would have been acquitted. If the atmosphere in Baltimore was too contentious and pro-secession to find an impartial jury, the trial could have been moved elsewhere.

Lincoln perceived Taney's insistence on habeas corpus and condemnation of martial law in Baltimore as a fundamental challenge to his authority. Seen from the distance of history, it seems clear that this was not so. Whatever Lincoln may have believed, Taney was not seeking to repeat his *Dred Scott* decision by asserting judicial power in a way meant to block another branch of government and save the Union. He was trying to preserve the Constitution's protection of individual liberties during wartime.

By defying Taney, and getting away with it, Lincoln prepared the way for a much greater distortion of the constitutional structure. It was perhaps constitutionally defensible (if only barely) for Lincoln to assert that when Congress was not in session, the Constitution must be interpreted to allow the president to suspend habeas under emergency conditions. But Lincoln went much further than that.

His unilateral suspension of habeas continued even after Congress returned and conspicuously failed to authorize what he had done. It ran from July 1861, when Congress convened, until September 1863, when Lincoln finally issued a new suspension relying on what Congress had authorized the previous March. His actions reflected his ongoing belief that the Constitution made him the ultimate judge of necessity. During this period, suspension was in fact *not* necessary. Lincoln extended the reasoning of necessity to an outrageous degree, until it incorporated any criticism of the war effort, which was construed by him to interfere with the draft and thus with the conduct of the war. Ultimately, the freedom of political speech was suppressed in this period more extensively than in any other era in U.S. history—no matter what apologetic frame some commentators would like to put around it.

The evidence that suspension of habeas and the suppression of political speech were not truly necessary reveals what was wrong with Lincoln's constitutional theory of necessity. He reasoned that, in an ongoing emergency like the Civil War, the president must have the power to determine whether necessity existed. Yet a president exercising his constitutional power did so effectively unsupervised by the other branches of government, the Supreme Court and Congress. Lincoln could have taken account of the input from the other branches, but mostly he did not. Having ignored Taney, he went on to ignore Congress. When Congress did pass the Habeas Corpus Suspension Act, Lincoln paid no mind to the provisions designed to end the detention of political prisoners. Habeas corpus remained suspended until the end of the war, and free speech was its main casualty.

This ongoing suspension strongly supports the conclusion that the Constitution should not have been interpreted to enable the president alone to decide on the necessity of suspension. It is certainly sensible to maintain, as Lincoln did, that the Constitution contains in itself the provisions necessary for its own survival. Yet the responsibility for implementing the necessary means to make the Constitution survive must be spread across all three branches of government, not restricted to the presidency. Nothing in the Constitution so much as hints that the separation of powers should disappear in wartime. True, the suspension clause itself contemplates sidelining the judiciary when public safety requires it. But constitutional suspension is an act of Congress, inevitably implemented by the president. It therefore requires at least two branches of government to participate. Lincoln's suspension was held in the hands of just one branch—and, hence, of just one man.

Lincoln did not ultimately transform the Constitution with respect to the protection of civil liberties in wartime. The Espionage Act convictions of World War I and the Smith Act prosecutions of Communists during the Cold War came after the passage of laws by Congress and ordinary criminal trials, not unilateral suspension of habeas corpus or the application of military law to civilians. That these later wartime efforts to limit speech did not follow Lincoln's paradigm may say something about the uniqueness of the Civil War. Certainly, Lincoln would have argued that the unique circumstances of the laws being violated justified a unique response, whereas other wartime conditions were, by definition, not as grave, because they did not represent existential threats to the Constitution. According to this argument, Lincoln might in fact have succeeded—but we would not know it until faced by another civil war, in which the future president might well follow Lincoln's precedent.

But it is more likely that Lincoln was unable to remake the Constitution's protection of civil liberties because he could offer no compelling moral case for doing so. Necessity itself is an argument that can operate free of moral constraints or limits. Every state, whether morally constituted or otherwise, sees its own survival as the ultimate necessity. The idea of raison d'état—reason of state—transcends the type of government or regime.

Breaking the Constitution in order to preserve the Constitution is ultimately morally justifiable only if the Constitution itself proves to be morally worthy. In breaking the Constitution by suspending habeas, Lincoln was struggling with a central problem: the compromise Constitution that he had set out to defend as the war began was not itself inherently morally defensible—even in Lincoln's own mind. It is difficult to make a moral case that it is desirable to break civil liberties in order to protect civil liberties—unless civil liberty is itself under threat. But secession did not threaten civil liberty in the North. Had the Confederacy survived, civil liberties in the Union would presumably have remained unchanged. Lincoln's argument from necessity therefore lacked a powerful moral basis of the kind that would have enabled it to anchor permanently in American public consciousness.

As the war proceeded, Lincoln came to understand the limits implicit in defining the war as a struggle to save the Union as formed by the compromise Constitution. In April 1861, Seward had urged him to redefine the struggle as a war over the union, not a war over slavery—and at the time, Lincoln took his advice. But in the summer of 1862, as it became clear that the war could not be won quickly or easily, Lincoln slowly changed direction. He would have to find a moral basis for the war beyond preserving the union under the Constitution that was itself immoral. To do so, he would have to change the war into a battle over the moral rightness of slavery. And that would require radically remaking the Constitution—into a moral compact based not on a compromise over slavery, but on liberty for all.

Five

EMANCIPATION
AND MORALS

Abraham Lincoln came into office promising to protect slavery. He had hopes of reversing secession, which would have required restoring the compromise Constitution—a compromise based on preserving the institution. Just as important, even after Southern secession, the Union that Lincoln was trying to preserve included four slave states. Maryland, Missouri, Delaware, and Kentucky all enshrined slavery in their state laws. These border states were pivotal to Lincoln's notion of how to win the war. As long as they remained loyal, they formed a frontline bulwark against the Confederacy. If they were to switch sides and secede, it was possible the war could not be won. Keeping slave states in the Union, Lincoln thought, required maintenance of the slavery compromise for their sake, even after most of the other slave states had seceded.

Alongside these strategic calculations, there was a more basic reason why Lincoln promised to preserve slavery in his inaugural address: he was totally committed to upholding the Constitution as it then existed. The entire purpose of the war as he described it was to restore and implement constitutional government. He had taken an "oath registered in Heaven" to uphold the Constitution, Lincoln said in his first inaugural speech. He had a constitutional duty to take care that the laws be executed, he explained in his address to Congress on July 4, 1861. To perform that duty under the Constitution, Lincoln argued, he must call up militia and use force to coerce the seceding states back into the Union.

The upshot is that, while Lincoln was willing and even eager to deploy unilateral executive power to go to war and suspend habeas corpus—conduct that critics said made him a dictator—he had at the time no similar inclination to use the power of the presidency to end slavery. If Lincoln's basic theory of why he had to fight depended on the Constitution, then there could be no question of violating the Constitution with respect to slavery. Lincoln's instinct to protect slavery was put to the test almost immediately. The challenge came from Major General John C. Frémont, the picaresque adventurer who had been the Republican nominee for the presidency in 1856. Frémont's political base was in the West, especially in California and Oregon, where he had made his reputation as an explorer and occasional military occupier. His career had begun in earnest when he married the daughter of the Missouri senator Thomas Hart Benton. When the war began, Lincoln appointed Frémont commander of the Western Department based in St. Louis.[1]

Frémont faced challenges in Missouri analogous to those General Benjamin Butler was facing around the same time in Maryland. He reacted similarly, declaring martial law on August 30, 1861. Frémont's declaration formally confiscated all "real and personal" property belonging to anyone in Missouri proved to have taken up arms against the United States. And it stated that "their slaves, if any they have, are hereby declared free."[2] Frémont was ordering the emancipation of slaves belonging to rebels in the military district under his command.

Lincoln immediately wrote to Frémont telling him to retract the emancipation order. "I think there is great danger," he wrote, that "liberating slaves of traitorous owners, will alarm our Southern Union friends, and turn them against us." Exercising caution and politeness in addressing his Republican rival, Lincoln added that his letter was "written in a spirit of caution and not of censure."[3] To Lincoln's irritation, Frémont balked, replying, "If . . . your better judgment still decides that I am wrong . . . respecting the liberation of slaves, I have to ask that you will openly direct me to make the correction."[4] Lincoln then directly ordered the emancipation order to be reversed. In October, he replaced Frémont.

On September 22, 1861, Lincoln explained his logic at greater length in a letter to his longtime colleague Illinois Republican Orville Browning, who had supported Frémont's proposed emancipation order. The letter captures a snapshot of Lincoln's thinking about the legality of military emancipation exactly a year before he would issue a preliminary emancipation proclamation of his own.

The bottom line was clear: emancipating slaves was "not within the range of *military* law, or necessity," Lincoln explained. "If a commanding General finds a necessity to seize the farm of a private owner, for a pasture, an encampment, or a fortification, he has the right to do so, and to so hold it, as long as the necessity lasts; and this is within military law, because within military necessity." The seizure was, however, temporary, lasting only as long as the necessity remained, and no longer. "But to say the farm shall no longer belong to the owner, or his heirs forever; and this as well when the farm is not needed for military purposes as when it is, is purely political, without the savor of military law about it."[5]

Lincoln then clarified that "the same is true of slaves." Under the laws of war, seizure of slaves could only be temporary. Permanent emancipation was not lawful: "If the General needs [slaves], he can seize them, and use them; but when the need is past, it is not for him to fix their permanent future condition." The permanent legal status of slaves "must be settled according to laws made by law-makers, and not by military proclamations."[6] (It was this view on which Lincoln must have relied in May 1861, when his cabinet approved without comment General Butler's decision in Maryland to treat slaves who escaped from their masters in seceded Virginia as "contraband" of war who would not be freed but also would not be returned to their owners.[7])

To bring home the point that emancipation would be unlawful and unconstitutional, Lincoln condemned Frémont's declaration in the harshest possible terms: "The proclamation in the point in question," he wrote, "is simply 'dictatorship.' It assumes that the general may do *anything* he pleases—confiscate the lands and free the slaves of *loyal* people, as well as of disloyal ones." In fact, Frémont had not gone quite that far, purporting only to free the slaves of rebels. But because doing even that violated the customary law of war as Lincoln saw it, Lincoln reasoned that the proclamation logically entailed the view that the military commander's power was unbounded. Emancipating all slaves might be "popular with some thoughtless people," he commented. "But," he asserted, "I cannot assume this reckless position; nor allow others to assume it on my responsibility."[8]

Emancipating slaves outside the law, Lincoln concluded, would subvert the very purpose of the war: namely, preserving the rule of law itself. Lincoln told Browning:

> You speak of it as being the only means of *saving* the government. On the contrary it is itself the surrender of the government. Can it be pretended that it is any longer the government of the U.S.—any government of Constitution and laws,—wherein a General, or a President, may make permanent rules of property by proclamation?[9]

Congress might have the authority to order military emancipation as Frémont had done, Lincoln said, and he might even vote for it if he were a member of Congress. "What I object to, is, that I as President, shall expressly or impliedly seize and exercise the permanent legislative functions of the government."[10]

As the historian John Witt has shown, Lincoln's view rested on a distinctively American theory of a commanding general's wartime powers under the international law of war.[11] In both the Revolutionary War and the War of 1812, British commanders had announced that they would free slaves who came to their lines and joined their forces. The British claimed the right to do so under the customary international law of war as recorded by European scholars, who more or less unanimously took the view it was permissible to seize an enemy's property. In response, Americans—especially slaveholders, but non-slaveholders as well—developed the counterview that private property in land, as well as slaves, could not lawfully be taken in wartime. This became very nearly the universal view among American legal authorities. The only prominent American to have taken a different perspective was John Quincy Adams, who at the time of the Mexican-American War had said in Congress that he believed a general could abrogate slavery in wartime. But even Adams's position was undermined by the fact that he had made exactly the opposite argument during the War of 1812 and beyond while advocating for the rights of American slaveholders.[12]

Following the standard American view, Lincoln believed in September 1861 that it would be illegal and unconstitutional for him as commander in chief to emancipate slaves in the seceding states—states that Lincoln insisted still officially belonged to the union. Freeing the slaves would be an act of "dictatorship," a term he wholeheartedly rejected even as he had rejected emancipation by "an Alexander, a Caesar or a Napoleon" in his 1838 Lyceum address. Emancipation would amount to a repudiation of the rule of law and the Constitution—exactly what he was fighting the Civil War to preserve.

Anna Ella Carroll, in her quasi-official essay justifying a broad use of the president's war powers, reasoned, like Lincoln, that "the war must be waged to restore the Constitution, and hence the war power itself must not trample that institution into the dust."[13] Emancipation would be "a clear infraction of the Federal compact" and "an enormity against the practice of civilized nations."[14] Following Lincoln's lead, Carroll was prepared to confer near absolute powers on the president when it came to suspending habeas corpus. But as of December 1861, she flatly denied Lincoln's power to emancipate even the slaves of Southern rebels. The war was "intended not to destroy the Constitution but to preserve it."[15]

Contemporary critics believed that Lincoln meant what he said. From the floor of the House of Representatives, Republican Thaddeus Stevens publicly advised Lincoln that instead of eschewing the role of dictator, he should embrace it in order to emancipate Southern slaves. "If any unforeseen and uncontrollable emergency should arise endangering the existence of the Republic," he reasoned, the take-care clause of the Constitution "creates [the president], for the time being, as much a dictator as a decree of the Roman Senate . . . whether the means were inscribed on their tables or not."[16]

Frederick Douglass also interpreted Lincoln as believing genuinely that he lacked the constitutional authority to emancipate enslaved people. He noted the contrast between the president and Frémont, the Republican candidate of 1856. Douglass thought that Frémont's proclamation was a "memorable document" that "had found the true path out of our national troubles" in words "few and simple, but strong enough to vibrate the heart of a continent." In contrast, Douglass denounced the "weakness and imbecility of the letter of the President, condemning that proclamation." The same weakness and imbecility had "thus far characterized the whole war," he wrote. Lincoln, his administration, and the U.S. Army "stand paralyzed in the presence of slavery," Douglass convincingly argued. "They are determined only to save the Union so far as they can save slavery."[17] The abolitionist was condemning the president on the basis of his own words.

Lincoln suspended habeas corpus within weeks of the fall of Fort Sumter, and without leaving any record of uncertainty or hesitation. When it came to emancipation, his course was altogether different. It would take until September 1862 for his thinking to undergo a process of transformation. He would come to embrace the very position he had condemned as dictatorship—and to believe that breaking the compromise Constitution was not fatal to the union, but necessary to remake it in a new form.

STATES' RIGHTS AND COMPENSATION

When the war began, many moderate Northerners agreed with Lincoln's policy of protecting slavery. They, too, were committed to the Constitution, which committed them in turn to the constitutional protection of slavery in those states that maintained it. Secretary of State William Seward had his finger on the pulse of those moderates when he advised Lincoln to define the war not in terms of slavery—a partisan issue, he said—but in terms of loyalty to the Union—an issue of patriotism.[18]

As the war proceeded, however, moderate Republican public opinion in free states began to shift on the question of slavery. Abolitionist sentiment, previously considered a sign of radicalism, became increasingly mainstream among Republicans.[19] This development can best be explained as the hydraulic effect of secession itself. Moderate Northerners had long become accustomed to treating the Constitution as a framework for compromise with Southern slaveholders. Whatever moral compunctions they had about slavery were overcome by the pragmatic need to maintain the constitutional compromise on which the union depended. Now that the overwhelming majority of those Southerners had seceded, they were no longer participating in the compromise. With the imperative of compromise in decline, the moral case against slavery became more prominent. It is not so much that the immorality of slavery became clearer as that the countervailing self-interest that held back the argument was fading.

Lincoln responded to that gradual development in Republican

opinion with a series of modest antislavery initiatives from the fall of 1861 until the summer of 1862. All had in common a single overarching feature: respect for the constitutional order that protected slavery. All respected states' constitutional authority to make their own decisions about slavery within their borders. And all treated slaveowners' property rights as constitutionally protected by the Fifth Amendment, which specified that the federal government could not take private property without just compensation.

Lincoln's first move came in November 1861. Quietly and privately, Lincoln drafted legislation that he hoped Delaware would adopt to introduce gradual emancipation of slaves there, with compensation to be paid to slaveowners. The idea was for the state legislature to enact the measure, entirely in keeping with the states' constitutional right to make their own decisions about slavery.[20]

Addressing Congress in his annual State of the Union message on December 3, 1861, Lincoln cautiously proposed that Congress should find a way to fund the resettlement of slaves who might be freed during the war.[21] In August, Congress had passed the Confiscation Act, which specified that if Southerners used property for Confederate military purposes, that property would be taken by the federal government.[22] Such property included slaves. Addressing Congress, Lincoln suggested that slaves confiscated under the act would become free and should be sent to a new territory to be created for the purpose. This suggestion went beyond what Lincoln had written to Browning, but it conformed with the Constitution insofar as it was generally agreed in the North that the confiscation of enemy property used for military purposes was permissible. It also reflected Lincoln's continued interest in the old, unrealistic Whig project of colonization—sending freed Blacks to Liberia or Haiti or some other unspecified territory, thus "solving" the problem of how whites and Blacks could live together after emancipation.

On February 20, 1862, the day Willie Lincoln died, Lincoln publicly proposed that the border states, where slavery remained lawful, all

adopt state laws allowing for gradual emancipation, as he had confiden-
tially proposed for Delaware. He asked Congress to allocate the money
to compensate slaveholders.[23] The proposal reasserted Lincoln's basic
position that under the Constitution, the federal government could not
interfere with slavery in the states. Any action states would take pursuant to his proposal would be entirely voluntary, he explained.

On April 16, 1862, Lincoln signed into law the Compensated
Emancipation Act, which ended slavery in Washington, D.C. As
the name implied, the law set aside federal funds to pay slaveholders
deemed loyal to the union. A commission was set up to evaluate the
slaves' monetary worth and the owners' loyalty. Slaveholders eventually
received compensation for some three thousand slaves.[24] Again, the
law respected constitutional norms fully. The District of Columbia was
a federal enclave, governed by federal law. No one doubted that Congress had the authority to end slavery there, provided compensation
was paid to slaveholders for the taking of their "property." (Lincoln
had actually proposed compensated emancipation for the District of
Columbia while serving in Congress in 1849.) The provision of compensation in the law was a further recognition of a constitutional right
to hold slaves. Paying fair compensation to slaveholders signaled that
Lincoln and the federal government were recognizing the constitutionally protected property rights of the slaveholders, even as they
barred slavery in Washington.

Finally, on June 19, 1862, Lincoln signed a one-paragraph bill titled
"An Act to secure Freedom to All Persons within the Territories of
the United States."[25] The law stated that "there shall be neither slavery nor involuntary servitude in any of the Territories of the United
States now existing, or which may at any time hereafter be formed or
acquired by the United States." The law affected only a tiny number
of enslaved persons held in the Nebraska and Utah territories.[26] Its
importance lay in its repudiation of the idea that Congress lacked the
authority to pass it.

The law conformed to the Constitution as Republicans understood it—but not as it had been interpreted by the Supreme Court in the *Dred Scott* decision. The second part of the holding of the *Dred Scott* case, declaring the Missouri Compromise unconstitutional, had found that Congress lacked the authority to prohibit slavery in the territories. By ignoring that holding, Congress was adopting the position that Lincoln had articulated earlier: Taney's controversial Supreme Court decision did not count as legitimate precedent but must be restricted to the individual case of Dred Scott and his family.

It was certainly noteworthy that Lincoln was prepared to sign legislation that defied the Supreme Court's interpretation of the Constitution. The new law reasserted the power over slavery in the territories that Congress had exercised uninterruptedly from before the ratification of the Constitution until 1857. Yet, like Lincoln's other modest antislavery efforts in the winter and spring of 1862, the law prohibiting slavery in the territories did not challenge the principle that the Constitution protected slavery. It affected not states but federal territories, which had always been understood to be under federal control. And it did not deny the principle of compensation, because as written, the law did not actively emancipate slaves living in U.S. territories—it simply stated that slavery could not exist within the territories. Slaveowners in the territories could, in principle, leave with their slaves for border states, or could sell their slaves to residents of those states.

PUSHING CONSTITUTIONAL BOUNDARIES

Long before Lincoln took any formal steps affecting slavery, thousands of enslaved people in the Confederacy sought to self-emancipate by fleeing in the direction of the Union Army.[27] This reality, affected by the changing war on the ground, raised a fundamental question about the legal status of slaves from the Confederacy who made it to

Union lines or found themselves in Union-controlled territory. As of the summer of 1862, neither Lincoln nor Congress had established a uniform policy. Even though the cabinet had approved the keeping of slaves as contraband when General Butler did it, some Union generals nevertheless continued to return escaped slaves to their Southern masters. Some sought to use slaves for labor on a paid basis, or even to enlist them in the Union Army.[28] In July 1862, Congress passed two bills that addressed the issue. One, the Militia Act, permitted the enlistment of African Americans in state militias (although it was silent about the U.S. Army). Lincoln signed it.

The other bill, the Second Confiscation Act, prohibited the army from sending escaped slaves back to their Confederate owners. It formally declared that any rebel-owned slaves who reached Union lines or lived in territory occupied by the Union Army would become "forever free of their servitude." The bill also gave Lincoln the authority to tell Southerners that if they did not cease to rebel, their property could be seized and sold by the federal courts.[29]

The Second Confiscation Act gave Lincoln pause. Almost all the Republicans in Congress had voted in favor of the enactment, which combined disparate proposals that had been floating around Congress for months.[30] Yet the law pushed the boundaries of the Constitution— and Lincoln knew it. Secretary of War Edwin Stanton advised the president that the bill was frankly unconstitutional. Congress had no constitutional authority to legislate regarding slavery in the states, he pointed out. This had been a bedrock constitutional principle that Lincoln had always acknowledged. Furthermore, Stanton thought there was a constitutional problem with the way the bill seized the rebels' property permanently. Traitors' property could lawfully be seized, Stanton admitted. But it could be seized only for the lifetime of the owner, not permanently, so as to deprive his heirs of its value.[31] The reason was Article III, section 3, clause 2, of the Constitution, which said that "no Attainder of Treason shall work Corruption of Blood, or Forfeiture, except during the Life of the Person attainted." The proposed law, Stanton claimed, was in effect a bill of attainder—a law punishing a class of persons without trial. It constituted a seizure beyond the lifetime of the traitors.

The Illinois senator Orville Browning, another Republican who considered the bill unconstitutional, wanted Lincoln to understand the enormous political risks associated with signing a bill that violated the constitutional guarantee protecting slavery in the states. He warned Lincoln on July 14 that "he had reached the culminating point in his administration." Whether Lincoln signed the bill would "determine whether he was to control the abolitionists and radicals, or whether they were to control him." At stake was the future of the border states, Browning argued. If Lincoln vetoed the bill, "he would raise a storm of enthusiasm in support of the Administration in the border states which would be worth to us 100,000 muskets." If he signed it, however "our friends" in the border states "could no longer sustain themselves there." Lincoln told Browning that "he would give . . . his profound consideration" to the question.[32]

The border states were very much on Lincoln's mind. Two days earlier, on July 12, he had met with border-state congressmen, urging them to endorse the gradual emancipation plan that he had announced in March. The twenty-nine congressmen met that night to debate the proposal among themselves. Twenty-one of them refused to have anything to do with it. Just eight were willing to recommend Lincoln's plan to their constituents.[33] In response, on July 14, Lincoln proposed a new bill that would have compensated states that adopted emancipation by giving them federal bonds that could be canceled if the states changed their minds and brought back slavery. He had not given up on his idea of compensated emancipation in the border states, and in fact would cling to it for at least six months more.

Faced with the concern that, as Browning had told him, his decision on whether to sign the Second Compensation Act would be seen as a defining moment in his presidency, Lincoln tried to hedge his bets. He drafted a veto message, the document that presidents traditionally send Congress when refusing to sign a law. Then he tried to figure out what to do with it.

In the message, Lincoln split the difference, rejecting one of Stanton's objections to the law's unconstitutionality while embracing the other.[34] First, Lincoln offered a somewhat labored constitutional defense addressing Stanton's objection to the provision freeing slaves. "It is startling to say that congress can free a slave within a state," Lincoln admitted. This was a considerable understatement. The Constitution had been almost universally interpreted to prohibit Congress from interfering with slavery in the states since it was drafted and ratified. "[Y]et," Lincoln went on, "if it were said the ownership of the slave had first been transferred to the nation, and that congress had then liberated, him, the difficulty would at once vanish." Lincoln's theory was that a "traitor against the general government forfeits his slave." Title in the slave thus passed to the federal government. The question was what Congress would do with those slaves, Lincoln said. He concluded, "I perceive no objection to Congress deciding in advance that they shall be free."[35]

Having stated a theory of how Congress could constitutionally emancipate slaves, Lincoln reported that the state government of Kentucky had once done something similar: "To the high honor of Kentucky, as I am informed, she has been the owner of some slaves by *escheat*, and that she sold none, but liberated all." Kentucky had not seized slaves by decree in wartime. "Escheat" meant that the slaves had passed to the ownership of the state when their owners died intestate. But Lincoln was trying to establish some precedent for the idea of a government freeing slaves. "I hope the same is true of some other states," he said, without offering evidence.[36]

Then, for good measure, Lincoln added a practical argument for freeing confiscated slaves: "I do not believe it would be physically possible," he wrote, "for the General government, to return persons . . . to actual slavery. I believe there would be physical resistance to it, which could neither be turned aside by argument, nor driven away by force."[37] Lincoln did not make it clear whether he thought that slaves themselves would resist being returned to slavery or that someone else—say, abolitionists—would put up a fight. In any case, the claim was a bit doubtful. Union military commanders had already returned at least some slaves to their Southern owners, and there is little reason to think they could not have continued to do so unless the numbers of slaves became very large. Lincoln was using the draft veto message to try out arguments for freeing slaves.

Lincoln went on to admit that the Second Confiscation Act included no provision for a judicial process to determine "whether a particular individual slave does or does not fall" within the category of being owned by a rebel, in which case he could be made forfeit and Congress could free him; or whether he might be, for example, owned by a loyal unionist living in a border state—in which case the Constitution protected his owner. Lincoln said, however, that such a legal process "could be easily supplied."[38]

Lincoln wrote in the draft veto message that his real barrier to signing the act was the provision permanently seizing the property of rebels, to which Stanton had also objected. This, he claimed, constituted a bill of attainder prohibited by the Constitution, because it took property permanently, beyond the lifetime of the rebels. This concern, if Lincoln meant it seriously, might have interfered with any past or future decision to free rebels' slaves. "I may remark," Lincoln wrote, "that this provision of the constitution, put in language borrowed from Great Britain, applies only in this country, as I understand, to real, or landed estate."[39] If it was true that the ban on bills of attainder in the Constitution applied only to real property in land, it left the possibility that slaves, defined as movable chattel, could be permanently taken.

Having drafted the veto message, Lincoln then found a way to sign the act anyway. He went to Congress and asked for a congressional resolution stating that under the law, no punishment would be "so construed as to work a forfeiture of the real estate of the offender beyond his natural life."[40] Congress agreed. Lincoln was seeking a fig leaf to cover the constitutional objection he had identified in his message. On July 17, Lincoln signed the bill—and sent Congress his veto message anyway. This was highly irregular. The non-veto veto message had no formal legal effect, and both the House and the Senate condemned it. The message suggested that Lincoln was not quite ready to take full public responsibility for potentially unconstitutional action against slavery.

PRELUDE TO EMANCIPATION

Lincoln's convoluted non-veto veto message for the Second Confiscation Act showed how tangled his thinking still was about slavery itself—the single most important issue in a war that had been going on for more than fifteen months. Yet in the process of writing the message, Lincoln began to find his way to a possible resolution. The message, as drafted and delivered, marked a major change in his thinking about the constitutional protection of slavery. For the first time, he had articulated a theory of how slaves could be emancipated by the federal government. It was a two-step theory. First, the slaves of rebels were made forfeit to the government as punishment for rebellion. Second, the government would free them.

On July 13, as he was considering the veto message, Lincoln attended a funeral for the infant son of Edwin Stanton, the secretary of war. In a carriage with Secretary of State William Seward and Secretary of the Navy Gideon Welles on the way to the funeral, Lincoln spoke for the first time of which we have any record about the possibility of issuing a proclamation of his own to emancipate slaves in the Confederacy. According to Welles's diary, Lincoln "dwelt earnestly on the gravity, importance, and delicacy of the movement," and said that such a proclamation was "with the military necessity absolutely essential for the salvation of the Union."[41]

Welles believed that Lincoln had been affected by the failure of General McClellan's Peninsula campaign, which had just concluded. It was time to end a "forbearing policy" with regard to the Confederacy. Lincoln needed leverage to motivate the fight against the South—and a threat of the complete emancipation of all slaves in the Confederacy might do it. Welles also thought that Lincoln was taking into account the rejection by the majority of border-state congressmen of his plan for compensated emancipation, a rejection that had occurred the night before. The failure of the plan had led Lincoln to conclude "that emancipation in rebel areas must precede that in the border, not the other way around."[42]

No doubt these immediate factors were in Lincoln's mind when he was speaking to Seward and Welles. Neither, however, was as significant as Lincoln's broader shift in thinking about the nature of constitutional limits on his authority, which was in the course of being transformed in the summer and fall of 1862. The failure of the Peninsula campaign meant that the war would not be won quickly. If the war was entering a new phase, Lincoln needed constitutional powers to match it.

On July 22, Lincoln read his cabinet a draft order that he proposed to issue. It began by citing the Second Confiscation Act, which Lincoln had signed five days earlier. On the basis of the authority granted to the president by the law, the order then warned Confederates "to cease participating in, aiding, countenancing, or abetting the existing rebellion" within sixty days or else they would be subject to the "forfeitures and seizures" in the law. Those forfeitures included the seizure of Confederates' real property—as well as their slaves.[43]

Lincoln's proposed text then shifted from the tone of command to the language of politics. It expressed Lincoln's intention to go back to Congress to ask for funds to compensate states that might "voluntarily" adopt "gradual abolishment of slavery"—presumably, the border states. The document then explained "that the object"—the goal of the order—was "to practically restore, thenceforward to be maintain[ed], the constitutional relation between the general government, and each, and all the states, wherein that relation is now suspended, or disturbed." Lincoln insisted that "for this object, the war, as it has been, will be, prosecuted."[44] The object was the restoration of the old constitutional order, not emancipation. Lincoln was struggling with the constitutionality of the order. He was attempting to reassure the border states that the whole point of the war was to reestablish "the constitutional relation" between the federal government and the states. That relation included the protection of the states' right to make their own decisions about slavery. In his draft, Lincoln was insisting that he had no intention of denying the constitutional protection of slavery.

Then came the order's main thrust:

> And, as a fit and necessary military measure for effecting this object, I, as Commander-in-Chief of the Army and Navy of the United States, do order and declare that on the first day of January in the year of Our Lord one thousand, eight hundred and sixty-three, all persons held as slaves within any state or states, wherein the constitutional authority of the United States shall not then be practically recognized, submitted to, and maintained, shall then, thenceforward, and forever, be free.[45]

In embryo, this was the text that would eventually become the Emancipation Proclamation. It declared that, as of January 1, 1863, all slaves in Confederate states would be free. The draft offered no detailed constitutional justification for the action. But in the draft, Lincoln based his authority on the Second Confiscation Act. As he had written in the veto message that he had sent despite not vetoing the bill, he believed that Congress could seize Confederates' slaves as punishment for treason and then free them.

Where Lincoln's draft order differed drastically from the Second Confiscation Act was in its scope. The act freed only those slaves who reached Union lines. Lincoln's draft order purported to free all slaves everywhere in the Confederacy. In practical terms, slaves held within the Confederacy would not actually be released by Lincoln's order, he well knew. By its very terms, it applied only in states where the "constitutional authority of the United States" was not being recognized—in other words, exactly the places where Lincoln's order was sure to be rejected. Yet the order was still a direct threat to Confederates because it purported to free their slaves "forever." That meant emancipation would outlast the end of the war. It meant that, if the Civil War ended in victory for the Union, slavery would be abolished in the states of the former Confederacy.

Seen from the standpoint of the Constitution as it had existed until then, Lincoln's proposed order was a fundamental violation—and pointed toward a fundamental restructuring. The Constitution had been born as a compromise. That compromise had been repeatedly updated and reaffirmed until the Civil War began. As it had evolved, the compromise Constitution protected slavery in order to preserve a union capable of extending across the entire North American continent. The war reflected the failure of that compromise—the failure of the Constitution.

Until he proposed emancipation, Lincoln had remained publicly committed to the idea that, when the war ended, the Constitution could be remade. That would, he assumed, require a new compromise. To bear any resemblance to the compromise of the past, the compromise would still have to include slavery. That was why Lincoln had affirmed his commitment to the constitutional protection of slavery in his first inaugural address.

Now Lincoln was telling his cabinet that the old compromise Constitution would not be reestablished. If Confederate slaves were freed "forever," there would be no slavery in the former Confederate states when and if they rejoined the Union. Once that occurred, the abolition of slavery in the border states would become inevitable. Lincoln still hoped for that to take place through compensated emancipation, but in any case it would have to happen. It would make no sense for slavery to exist in the border states but not in those of the former Confederacy.

If there would be no slavery in the former Confederate states, it followed that there would be no compromise with them, either to end the war or in its aftermath. The Confederate states would be coerced not only to rejoin the Union but also to do so on Lincoln's new terms—without slavery. The moment Lincoln's proposed proclamation took effect, on New Year's Day, 1863, the compromise Constitution would be officially and permanently dead. Whatever would replace it would no longer contain the key feature of the compromise: it would no longer countenance slavery.

In principle, at least, Lincoln's proposed order took the form of a threat that could still be averted. By giving the Confederacy sixty days to cease the rebellion and avoid confiscation, it held out the theoretical possibility that the South could still maintain slavery if it would only stop the rebellion. In practice, however, as Lincoln fully understood, the proclamation would have the opposite effect. It would not encourage Southerners to rethink secession. Threatening to end slavery permanently made the Civil War into an existential threat to the Southern slaveholding way of life. The proclamation, if issued, would force slaveholding Southerners to fight to the bitter end.

The reaction from Lincoln's cabinet to his proposal shows just how radical it was. We know what happened in the meeting from the notes of Edwin Stanton and from a conversation that Lincoln had in February 1864 with Francis Bicknell Carpenter, the artist who painted the well-known picture of the meeting that now hangs in the U.S.

Capitol over the west staircase to the Senate wing.[46] Secretary of State Seward, the most influential member of the cabinet, immediately told Lincoln that announcing emancipation would give the United Kingdom an incentive to intervene in the war on behalf of the Confederacy in order to protect the supply of Southern cotton it needed for its manufacturing. Seward's worry depended on the premise that, without slavery, Southern cotton could never again be exported at a profit. The argument was counterintuitive to the point of being strange. Far from alienating Great Britain, an announcement of emancipation would ally the Union with the British policy of global abolition of slavery. Embracing abolition would make it less likely, not more, that Britain would intervene on behalf of the Confederacy, because it would create a stark difference between the slavery policies of North and South.[47] Seward seems to have simply been overwhelmed by the idea of unilateral emancipation, and instinctively objected.

Montgomery Blair, the postmaster general from Maryland, also opposed the proposal at the cabinet meeting, on the ground that it would hurt the Republicans in the upcoming 1862 election.[48] He must have had Maryland and the other border states particularly in mind. Blair's reaction showed the deepest political problem with Lincoln's proposal: namely, that it would surely alienate the border states. The second serious problem was that it might look like weakness to "emancipate" slaves who in practice remained in bondage. This was particularly true when the Lincoln administration had just tried and failed to invade Virginia and take Richmond. Several other cabinet members remained silent in the meeting but later expressed their deep concerns about emancipation.

Without any notable sign of approval from his cabinet, Lincoln decided not to announce the policy, at least not right away. But either he or another cabinet member leaked the idea of the proposal to the press. One newspaper reported the rumor that the cabinet had agreed to an abolition order. Others wrote more accurately that Lincoln had proposed emancipation but was holding off because of opposition within the cabinet.

Lincoln's conduct in the two months that followed suggests that he understood his cabinet's opposition to emancipation to stem from the radicalism of the idea—and that he would need to acclimate the public to the possibility of emancipation. Lincoln had made a great moral stride by proposing emancipation, yet he immediately had to enter on a course of political maneuvering and equivocation to gain support for the measure. To do so, one crucial element was to provide some comfort to whites in the Union, especially those in border states, who feared living alongside free African Americans. The concern derived from racial prejudice, Lincoln knew. In a simultaneous display of his far-reaching vision and his limitations as a politician of his times, Lincoln chose to engage that prejudice, not challenge it.

Lincoln believed he could assuage white concerns about abolition by making it clear that he shared the belief that whites and free Blacks could not live side by side, and by emphasizing the solution that he had always embraced in the past: sending free African Americans abroad to colonies specially created for them. The core problem with the idea, however, was that almost no African Americans showed any enthusiasm for colonization. In the hopes of addressing the issue, Lincoln created the Commission on Emigration. On August 4, he named the Methodist minister James Mitchell as the commissioner—and asked Mitchell to put together a White House meeting with a representative group of leading African Americans to discuss the issue.

As a religious figure, Mitchell naturally convened a preliminary meeting at an African American church. Those present made it clear that if Black leaders were going to meet with the president, they would do so only without a mandate for colonization. The African Americans at the meeting voted to adopt a resolution that, while it did not denounce colonization directly, flatly declared any discussion of colonization to be "inexpedient, inauspicious, and impolitic"[49]—that is, ill-timed. But they did agree to send five representatives to meet Lincoln.[50]

The five-member delegation that met with Lincoln on August 14, 1862, at the White House consisted of educated and sophisticated men who represented the capital's Black elite. Edward Thomas, the chairman of the delegation, was a member of one of the city's African American debating societies. He collected fine art and rare coins, and boasted a library of six hundred volumes, enormous for the era. John F. Cook, Jr., and Benjamin McCoy were each founders of important Methodist churches. Cornelius Clark was, like Cook and McCoy, a member of the Social Civil and Statistical Association, a civic group founded to "improve our condition by use of all proper means calculated to exalt our people" and headed by William Slade, who worked for Lincoln in the White House as his confidential messenger and valet. John T. Costin was a Freemason, as were Thomas and Cook.[51]

Rather than listening to what the delegates could have told him about colonization or African American attitudes to the war or any other subject, Lincoln talked at them. What he said was intended to reach a national audience—especially white Northerners. Lincoln began by asking rhetorically, "[W]hy . . . should the people of your race be colonized, and where?" More bluntly, "Why should they leave this country?" His answer was that Blacks and whites were racially incompatible:

> You and we are different races. We have between us a broader difference than exists between almost any other two races. Whether it is right or wrong I need not discuss, but this physical difference is a great disadvantage to us both, as I think your race suffer very greatly, many of them by living among us, while ours suffer from your presence. In a word we suffer on each side. If this is admitted, it affords a reason at least why we should be separated.[52]

Lincoln did not explicitly repeat to the African Americans in the White House what he had said when debating Stephen Douglas: namely, that the races were not only separate but that whites were superior to Blacks. But his meaning was nevertheless implicit.

Slavery was wrong, Lincoln went on to say, "in my judgment, the greatest wrong inflicted on any people." But the alternative was not racial equality: "[E]ven when you cease to be slaves, you are yet far removed from being placed on an equality with the white race." Lincoln then argued that although the "aspiration of men is to enjoy equality with the best when free," African Americans could never be equal in North America: "[O]n this broad continent, not a single man of your race is made the equal of a single man of ours. Go where you are treated the best, and the ban is still upon you."[53]

Lincoln understood that the delegation did not want to hear him directly urge emigration to Africa. But Lincoln was nonetheless trying to make a rational argument to free African Americans that emigration was in their own interests, because white racism would always block them from achieving equality in the United States. As to that racism, Lincoln said, it could not be changed: "I do not propose to discuss this, but to present it as a fact with which we have to deal." He could not "alter it," he said, even if he wanted to do so.[54]

Lincoln's main aim was less to convince African Americans to embrace colonization than to communicate to white Americans that the emigration of African Americans was the solution to the problem of race in the United States. The real victims of slavery, Lincoln argued astonishingly, were not Blacks but whites. "I need not recount to you," he told the delegation, "the effects upon white men, growing out of the institution of Slavery." Slavery had "general evil effects on the white race." The worst of these effects was the Civil War itself: "See our present condition—the country engaged in war!—our white men cutting one another's throats, none knowing how far it will extend; and then consider what we know to be the truth."[55]

The "truth" Lincoln had in mind was that the presence of African Americans in the United States was the but-for cause of the war:

> But for your race among us there could not be war, although many men engaged on either side do not care for you one way or the other. Nevertheless, I repeat, without the institution of Slavery and the colored race as a basis, the war could not have an existence.

If the presence of African Americans had caused the war, "it is better for us both, therefore, to be separated."[56]

Frederick Douglass reacted with outrage and horror to reports of Lincoln's words, which have the power to shock even today. Lincoln was "showing all his inconsistencies," Douglass wrote, "his pride of race and blood, his contempt for Negroes and his canting hypocrisy. How an honest man could creep into such a character as that implied by this address we are not required to show."[57]

Lincoln was blaming the Civil War on African Americans themselves, not on the white men who had enslaved Black people, nor on the compromise Constitution that had enshrined and protected that slavery throughout the history of the United States.[58] Douglass compared Lincoln to a "horse thief" or a "highway robber" blaming his crime on the horse or the traveler's purse. "No, Mr. President," Douglass rejoined, "it is not the innocent horse that makes the horse thief, not the traveler's purse that makes the highway robber, and it is not the presence of the Negro that causes this foul and unnatural war, but the cruel and brutal cupidity of those who wish to possess horses, money and Negroes by means of theft, robbery, and rebellion."[59]

It is hard to question Douglass's conclusion that blaming African Americans for the war was in fact Lincoln's intent. In his initial attempt to build a defense of emancipation, Lincoln sought a theory that would link the freeing of slaves to ending the war. If the war was caused by the presence of African Americans, the way to end the war was to induce African Americans to leave the country.

If this was an extreme instance of wishful thinking on Lincoln's behalf, it was wishful thinking that followed from the way he was trying to reimagine the constitutional order. The old constitutional order was based on the compromise over slavery. Any new order would have to take account of African Americans—provided they still lived in the United States. Lincoln had no idea how a new constitutional order could address or incorporate African Americans. (As we shall see, he never came up with an adequate answer to the question.) Consequently, he preferred to envision a future in which African Americans would not have to be taken into account at all. Such a future required colonization—on an enormous scale.

Less than a week after meeting with the delegation of African Americans, Lincoln made another very public statement intended again to assuage white Northern concerns about emancipation. This time, too, he sought to emphasize that his goal was not to save African Americans from slavery, but to re-create the union. The occasion was an open letter to Lincoln that Horace Greeley, the editor of the *New-York Tribune*, published on August 20. In the letter, Greeley urged Lincoln to declare emancipation of Southern slaves immediately, and to stop dragging his feet. He and other Northerners, he told the president, were "sorely disappointed and deeply pained by the policy you seem to be pursuing with regard to the slaves of the Rebels . . . We think you are strangely and disastrously remiss in the discharge of your official and imperative duty with regard to the emancipating provisions of the new Confiscation Act."[60]

Lincoln responded that he had "not meant to leave any one in doubt" with respect to his policy. He had only one overarching goal: "I would save the Union. I would save it the shortest way under the Constitution." The way to do that was to defeat the Confederacy: "The sooner the national authority can be restored; the nearer the Union will be 'the Union as it was.'"[61]

As for the future of slavery, it was entirely subordinate to saving the union. "My paramount object in this struggle," he wrote, "*is* to save the Union, and is *not* either to save or to destroy slavery." He went on:

> If I could save the Union without freeing *any* slave I would do it, and if I could save it by freeing *all* the slaves I would do it; and if I could save it by freeing some and leaving others alone I would also do that. What I do about slavery, and the colored race, I do because I believe it helps to save the Union; and what I forbear, I forbear because I do *not* believe it would help to save the Union.[62]

In the hopes of preparing the white public for emancipation, Lincoln wanted to be as clear as he could that his objective was to serve the interests of white Americans by restoring the union—not to liberate African Americans on moral grounds.

This instrumental attitude toward "slavery, and the colored race" was not an accident of Lincoln's time or attitudes, or the result of political constraint on his moral commitments. Lincoln consciously intended to insist that the aims of the union must come first. He explained the relationship in constitutional terms: "I have here stated my purpose according to my view of *official* duty." His view of official duty, which went back to his first inaugural address and ran through all his subsequent pronouncements, was that he was constitutionally obligated to do whatever necessary to execute the laws throughout the union. Lincoln added: "I intend no modification of my oft-expressed *personal* wish that all men everywhere could be free."[63] But this personal, moral wish was not part of the constitutional calculus of official duty that Lincoln wanted to emphasize.

The upshot of Lincoln's letter to Greeley is that, writing on August 22, 1862, a month after proposing emancipation to his cabinet, and a month before announcing his emancipation plan to the public, Lincoln wanted white Americans to hear him say that constitutional duty and morality were not the same thing. Although emancipation would put an end to the model of the compromise Constitution, Lincoln still had not fully understood or embraced the consequences of that change—or at least he was not prepared to say so publicly. By saying that he would gladly "save the Union without freeing any slave," he was repeating the basic premise of the compromise Constitution, the compromise over slavery to preserve the union.

Beyond the old formulation, Lincoln was newly saying that if he could save the union "by freeing all the slaves," he would do it. This assertion, which captured the essence of emancipation, repudiated the idea of compromise. It pictured the restoration of the union by coercion, without compromise over slavery and without the consent of the seceding states. What Lincoln was not yet prepared to say was that this alternative way to save the union incorporated the moral demands of human equality. With emancipation in view, Lincoln still wanted to insist that the immorality of slavery played no part in his thinking.

EMANCIPATION AND ITS DISCONTENTS

When Lincoln presented his draft emancipation order to the cabinet in July, the Peninsula campaign had just failed, guaranteeing the Union would not win the war in one fell swoop and raising the concern that emancipation would be seen as an act of desperation. In August, as Lincoln tried to prepare the ground to make such an order public, Robert E. Lee was making preparations of his own. In a stroke of military genius, he maneuvered his Army of Northern Virginia to take the fight to the North. On August 30, 1862, Lee's forces defeated General John Pope's Army of Virginia at the second Battle of Bull Run.

On September 3, Lee's troops entered Maryland. McClellan, now on the defensive, pursued Lee. The key battle of the Maryland campaign took place on September 17 at Antietam, where McClellan stopped Lee's advance. Although not a genuine victory for the Union, Antietam at least gave Lincoln the opportunity he believed he needed to announce his plan of emancipation.

On September 22, 1862, the same day that he ordered the suspension of habeas corpus, Lincoln issued the preliminary Emancipation Proclamation. The proclamation generally followed his proposed order of July 22, although its sequence was different and some elements were added. By now, the cabinet had accepted Lincoln's plans—albeit with trepidation.

Lincoln began by stating the aim of the war in the same terms he had done in the proposed order. The object of the war, he said, was "restoring the constitutional relation between the United States" and the seceding states. As he had done in the earlier proposal, Lincoln expressed his plan to ask Congress for money to fund compensated emancipation in the border states. This time he added that "the effort to colonize persons of African descent, with their consent, upon this continent, or elsewhere . . . will be continued."[64] The addition reflected Lincoln's efforts over the previous two months to promote colonization as a supposed solution to the problem of what should happen to freed African Americans.

The heart of the preliminary proclamation was the assertion that on January 1, 1863, "all persons held as slaves within any state, or designated part of a state, the people whereof shall then be in rebellion against the United States shall be then, thenceforward, and forever free."[65] This language differed from the July proposal only in that it spoke of states "in rebellion," whereas the earlier text had spoken of "the constitutional authority of the United States" not being "practically recognized." The new language was more fitted to the task of expropriating the slave property of rebels. And it was drafted broadly enough to include enslaved people in areas under Union occupation.

Lincoln now added to the earlier proposal the promise that the government and military would "recognize and maintain the freedom" of emancipated slaves and would "do no act or acts to repress" them "in any efforts they may make for their actual freedom." This provision told Lincoln's generals to treat slaves who came under their authority as genuinely free. Since not all Union generals had done so, this provision was an important statement of the new policy. The preliminary proclamation included a corresponding order to the armed forces "to observe, obey, and enforce" the provisions of the proclamation.[66]

When it came to the question of legal authority, Lincoln trod carefully. In his proposed order in July, Lincoln had asserted that he was acting "in pursuance of" the Second Confiscation Act, passed on July 17. Now he took a different tack. Using the passive voice, he wrote that "attention is hereby called" both to the Second Confiscation Act and also to an earlier act passed on March 13, 1862, which had prohibited the armed forces from returning fugitive slaves to their masters.[67]

The difference between relying exclusively on congressional authority and merely drawing attention to acts of Congress was subtle. Yet it mattered for the all-important question of whether the preliminary emancipation was in fact legal under the Constitution. Ordinarily, when the president takes an official act, he either says he is acting pursuant to congressional authority, says he is acting according to independent executive authority granted by the Constitution, or claims to rely on both. It was, and remains, highly unusual for a president to leave the whole question of the source of his authority ambiguous. Yet that was what the words "attention is hereby called" were certainly intended to do. Lincoln was announcing the single most consequential presidential action in the history of United States—and trying to avoid taking a clear position on what made it lawful.

The problem facing Lincoln was that it was at best an open question whether the president or Congress—or both, or perhaps neither—possessed the authority under the Constitution to emancipate slaves in wartime. If Lincoln had relied totally on congressional authority, as he had done in his proposed order, then he would have necessarily been asserting that Congress had the constitutional power to emancipate the slaves. There were at least two difficulties with that view. First, under the Constitution, everyone knew that Congress lacked the authority to interfere with slavery in the states. According to official Union legal policy, the seceding states were still states, because their secession had been unconstitutional. Second, if Congress was seizing slaves from the Confederacy "forever" as punishment for rebellion, then the seizure of slaves might count as an unconstitutional bill of attainder by Congress. Lincoln had himself raised this problem in his draft veto message to the Second Confiscation Act. And although he had tried to get around it by claiming that the constitutional provision prohibiting bills of attainder only applied to real estate, not chattel property like slaves, this distinction was too lawyerly to be entirely convincing.

Lincoln's alternative legal basis for the preliminary proclamation was to rely solely on his wartime authority as commander in chief. As his simultaneous order suspending habeas corpus demonstrated, Lincoln had an extremely strong conception of the powers that the executive could exercise under conditions of necessity during a rebellion. Lincoln could simply have asserted that, as commander in chief, he could expropriate property of the enemy as a war measure.

But again, there were at least two difficulties with such a claim. The first was that the seizure of enemy property in wartime was not considered an absolute right of governments at war—at least not by Americans. At the time, international law on the subject was in the form of custom, not treaty. But according to American authorities, on whom Lincoln himself had relied in reversing Frémont's emancipation order in Missouri, the customary law among nations that considered themselves "civilized" was that private property could not be seized from the enemy unless it was being used by the enemy to pursue war aims. Property being used to pursue war objectives could be seized, but even that property was by custom supposed to be returned to the enemy at the end of the war.[68]

From these principles of customary international law, it followed that slaves could be seized only if they were being put to war aims—which was what the first Confiscation Act had said. Even if it were presumed that all slaves were serving the Confederate aim of maintaining independence, it still did not follow that their seizure could be permanent. Thus, customary international law did not provide a sound basis for emancipation.[69]

To be sure, it was not absolutely certain that the customary international law of war applied in conditions of rebellion. Civil wars and wars between nations are not always treated the same under international law. But Lincoln had to get his authority to seize from *somewhere*. His constitutional powers as commander in chief were presumably derived from the customary international law of war. If that source of authority did not justify seizure, that left only the more abstract principle of necessity. Necessity, however, was not an established source of constitutional authority.

And even if the necessity of preserving the union did justify Lincoln's seizure of Confederate slaves, that left the second major difficulty with the theory of presidential authority: How did Lincoln have the power to free the slaves he had seized? In his draft veto message, Lincoln had written that if Congress seized ownership of slaves, Congress must have the authority to free them. But if the commander in chief seized slaves, surely they became the property of the U.S. government, not of the military or the executive branch. Freeing those slaves would thus appear to require congressional action. It was not within the president's ordinary constitutional powers to give away the property of the U.S. government. That led back to congressional authorization.

These serious and complicated problems of legality were the reason Lincoln wanted to have it both ways in the preliminary proclamation, stating neither that he was relying on congressional authority nor that he was acting solely in his capacity as commander in chief. The ambiguity therefore was full of meaning. Stripped of technicalities, the ambiguity about his source of legal authority meant that Lincoln could not come up with a clear explanation of why emancipation was constitutional.

As if to underscore this fundamental legal problem, the preliminary proclamation concluded with a remarkable paragraph. In it, Lincoln stated that "in due time," when the war was over, he would "recommend that all citizens of the United States who shall have remained loyal thereto throughout the rebellion, shall . . . be compensated for all losses by acts of the United States, including the loss of slaves."[70] The idea here was that any slaveholder loyal to the United States deserved compensation for the taking of his slave property—and would get it when the war was over. The only slaveholders whom the preliminary proclamation would reach were those who had proven disloyal by supporting the Confederacy.

Lincoln cannot have chosen this language accidentally, given his years of commitment to the idea of compensated emancipation and his months of careful thought about how emancipation could be lawfully achieved. The strong implication of the passage was that loyal slaveholders who happened to live in the Confederacy still possessed the constitutional right not to have their property seized by the government without just compensation. If that was the case, then it meant Lincoln was taking a position that the seceding states were still part of the union, and that the people who lived there still had constitutional rights—including the right to hold slaves. But if that was true, how could the federal government take their slaves permanently at all, even with compensation provided? Why wouldn't those loyal slaveholders be entitled to get their slaves back when the war was over, instead of receiving payment for them?

In practice, of course, Lincoln certainly knew and assumed that few if any Southern slaveholders were genuinely loyal or would be able to prove in retrospect that they had been. And he had already committed himself to the idea that any slaves who became free would not be returned to their former masters. The point of the provision was to offer a distinction between hypothetical innocent slaveholders, entitled to constitutional protection, and the guilty slaveholders who were having their property seized. The trouble with this distinction was that customary international law considered the seizure of enemy property not a form of punishment, but a form of military necessity authorized during the duration of war.

Lincoln, in contrast, was struggling to define emancipation as a punishment for slaveholders. That punishment was supposed to function as leverage that would help the Union win the war. This, however, was a radically new theory of necessity in wartime, one essentially unknown to international law and certainly unheard of in domestic constitutional law. According to Lincoln's implicit theory, the president could punish rebels in any way he wished if he deemed doing so to be necessary to winning the war.

EMANCIPATION IN THE DOCK

The extraordinary reach of Lincoln's claims of executive power did not go unnoticed—or unchallenged. Opponents of emancipation focused on the unconstitutionality of Lincoln's unilateral action, which the Democratic *Cincinnati Enquirer* called a "usurpation," the act of a "dictator," and "the complete overthrow of the Constitution he swore to protect and defend."[71] The highest-profile rebuff of the preliminary proclamation came from the retired Supreme Court justice Benjamin Curtis, who published a pamphlet titled *Executive Power*

almost immediately after Lincoln issued the preliminary proclamation and the habeas suspension order.[72] Curtis could not be dismissed as a Southern sympathizer. He was a Massachusetts man, a
graduate of Harvard College and the Harvard Law School, who had
distinguished himself on the bench by dissenting from Taney's *Dred
Scott* opinion. Shortly after clashing with Taney, Curtis had resigned
from the Supreme Court, an action sometimes characterized as the
only time a Supreme Court justice has ever resigned over a point of
principle.

In the pamphlet, Curtis described the preliminary proclamation
and the habeas suspension as twin exercises of a newly asserted presidential power to break any law or constitutional principle in order
to win the war. Curtis pointed out that Lincoln had not offered any
formal constitutional or legal explanation for this power. He quoted
the only statement of Lincoln's that seemed to him relevant, made on
September 13, 1862, to a delegation of Chicago ministers who had
come to Washington to urge the president to issue an emancipation
proclamation. Lincoln had told the ministers a bit offhandedly that he
had "no objections" to such a proclamation "on legal or constitutional
grounds" because "as commander-in-chief of the army and navy, in
time of war, I suppose I have a right to take any measure which may
best subdue the enemy."[73]

Curtis calmly and systematically set out to demolish this argument.
He demonstrated that the Constitution conferred no such absolute
power on the president in wartime. Discussing emancipation, Curtis
argued that the preliminary proclamation purported to "repeal and annul valid state laws" that had created the institution of slavery. Yet the
president obviously lacked such a power under the Constitution. What
was more, Curtis showed, the preliminary proclamation claimed to
emancipate the slaves as a "penalty." That meant the president "hereby
assumes to himself the power to denounce it as a punishment against

the entire people of the state, that the valid laws of that state . . . shall become null and void . . . by reason of the criminal conduct of a governing majority of its people."[74] The intent of the preliminary proclamation, according to Curtis, was that "by virtue of some power which [the president] possesses, he proposes to annul [state] laws, so that they no longer have any operation."[75] Yet the president had no such power to abrogate state laws under the Constitution.

When taken together with the habeas suspension, Curtis argued, Lincoln's preliminary proclamation stood for a single proposition:

> In time of war, the president has any and all power, which
> he may deem it necessary to exercise, to subdue the en-
> emy; and that every private and personal right of indi-
> vidual security against mere executive control, and every
> right reserved to the states or the people, rests merely
> upon executive discretion.[76]

This proposition could not be sustained as a matter of constitutional law, argued the former Supreme Court justice. The president as commander in chief could exercise control over the military. But he could not constitutionally use his powers as commander in chief to command the citizens of the nation. "Can a general-in-chief *disobey any law of his own country?*" Curtis asked rhetorically. His answer was devastating: "When he can, he super-adds to his *rights* as commander the *powers* of a usurper; and that is military despotism."[77]

Curtis's arguments demanded a response. Charles P. Kirkland, a New York lawyer, published a pamphlet in reply, emphasizing that the Confederate states were in rebellion, and that their laws therefore should not be treated as valid.[78] Kirkland also claimed that the military commander always had the legal authority to free slaves in enemy territory that came under his control, a proposition for which he quoted John

Quincy Adams, speaking in Congress in 1842.* Yet Lincoln remained quiet as to the subject of his legal authority—and would until the next spring.

Did the constitutionality of the preliminary proclamation matter? Some observers thought it did not. Curtis quoted a "respectable and widely circulated" Republican newspaper that was dismissive of the whole issue. "The Democrats talk about 'unconstitutional acts,'" the newspaper had written. "Nobody pretends this act is constitutional, and nobody cares whether it is or not."[79] This view, if taken seriously, stood for a significantly new perspective on the consequences of the broken Constitution. When it came to slavery, ran the argument, it was perfectly acceptable for Lincoln to break the Constitution in order to achieve a morally requisite result. The Confederacy had broken the Constitution. Now Lincoln could break it—and "nobody cares."

Curtis was deeply troubled by the possibility that nobody cared if Lincoln was violating the Constitution. The people "do *care*, and the president *cares*, that he and all other public servants should obey the Constitution," Curtis insisted. In the final paragraph of his pamphlet, Curtis wrote that it was up to the people to "take care, by legitimate means . . . that their will, embodied in the Constitution, shall be obeyed."[80] Curtis's language was meant to undermine Lincoln's claim that it was his duty as president to "take care" that the laws be executed—a claim that ultimately Lincoln was using to break the Constitution. Curtis was certainly expressing the hope that public opinion

---

* Speaking on April 14–15, 1842, in the context of the Mexican-American war, Adams had invoked the abolition of slavery in Colombia by Simón Bolívar. He had indeed said that under "the law of nations," military authority under occupation "takes for the time the place of all municipal institutions." It followed, Adams maintained, that if the Southern states were to seek federal troops to help put down a slave rebellion, the president of the United States would then have "the power to order the emancipation of the slaves." Excerpts from Adams's speech were published under the title *The Abolition of Slavery: The Right of the Government under the War Power* (Boston: R. F. Avallcut, 1862).

would lead Lincoln to reconsider his preliminary proclamation. The problem was that, except for voting Lincoln out of office in elections that were still two years away, there was no apparent constitutional mechanism for "the people" to stand up in favor of the Constitution and against either emancipation or the suspension of habeas corpus.

Congress, the people's branch of government, lacked the will or the capacity to block Lincoln. He had now leapfrogged Congress when it came to slavery by adopting a measure far more radical than the Second Confiscation Act, which had semi-emancipated slaves who reached Union lines. True, Congress had tried to constrain Lincoln mildly by declining to suspend habeas at his request. Some months later, it would take steps to limit the detention of political prisoners, steps Lincoln would largely ignore. Yet although Congress lacked the votes to go beyond the Second Confiscation Act, it also was not going to take any active legislative steps to reverse emancipation.

That left the Supreme Court as the only branch of government that might stand in Lincoln's way. Lincoln understood that there was some finite risk that, if a suitable case presented itself, the Supreme Court might actually refuse to enforce the proclamation or expressly hold it unconstitutional. Roger Taney was still the chief justice. Curtis's pamphlet would have given him, and the court as a whole, political cover to reject the proclamation. And in strictly legal and constitutional terms, it would have been much easier for the justices to strike down the preliminary proclamation than to uphold it.

Yet Lincoln also knew that the court would want to avoid a direct confrontation with him over slavery. He had ignored Taney's judgment in *Ex parte Merryman*. He had signed legislation effectively ignoring Taney's *Dred Scott* decision, fulfilling his campaign promise not to treat the ruling as binding precedent. These actions considerably weakened the authority of the court. If the justices challenged Lincoln over emancipation and failed, the court's authority would be weakened further still.

Perhaps most significant, Lincoln realized that for the Supreme Court to overturn his preliminary emancipation proclamation, it would have to take an action that would fly in the face of common-sense morality. By signing the primary proclamation, Lincoln positioned himself to take the historic role he would assume on January 1, 1863: the Great Emancipator, a Moses who had freed the slaves. If Lincoln could assume the moral high ground by declaring emancipation, the Supreme Court would have to take on the role of enslaver to reverse his judgment. That was a role that even Roger Taney would not embrace lightly.

EMANCIPATION AND MORALITY

The preliminary proclamation set the stage for a fundamental transformation in the constitutional structure of the United States. T. J. Barnett, a Hoosier by birth who worked in Lincoln's Department of the Interior, reported on the situation in Washington on October 6, 1862:

> No one here talks conservatism any longer, or speaks of the old Constitution, or of anything but a renewed and desperate raid for subjugation of the Rebels, and for a determined police system now organizing (to take effect under the second proclamation).[81]

The "old Constitution" was the Constitution of compromise over slavery. Emancipation under the "second proclamation" would make any return to such a compromise impossible. That was why no one in Washington was speaking of the old Constitution anymore. The only option that emancipation logically allowed was to defeat the Confederacy and impose new norms on Southern society by force—a "determined police system."

Frederick Douglass hastened to argue that the draft proclamation was effectively irreversible—even as he criticized Lincoln for taking so long to issue it:

> Abraham Lincoln may be slow. Abraham Lincoln may desire peace even at the price of leaving our terrible national sore untouched, to fester on for generations, but Abraham Lincoln is not the man to reconsider, retract and contradict words and purposes solemnly proclaimed over his official signature. The careful, and we think, the slothful deliberation which he has observed in reaching this obvious policy, is a guarantee against retraction.[82]

For Douglass, the "righteous decree" was "the most important of any to which the President of the United States has ever signed his name." It changed the moral calculus of the war, he explained. The proclamation "recognizes and declares the real nature of the contest, and places the North on the side of justice and civilization, and the rebels on the side of robbery and barbarism."[83]

On January 1, 1863, as promised in the preliminary proclamation, Lincoln signed the official Emancipation Proclamation. In broad outline, it followed the preliminary proclamation of September, the same way that document followed Lincoln's proposed order of July. But as was true of the preliminary proclamation, the details reflected changes in Lincoln's thinking.

The first significant difference between the preliminary and final proclamations was that Lincoln now entirely jettisoned any claim to rely on Congress. The September document had already moved away from the July proposed order's invocation of congressional authorization. Now Lincoln dropped any mention of Congress at all. The operative clause of the Emancipation Proclamation was announced on the authority of "I, Abraham Lincoln, President of the United States, by virtue of the power in me vested as Commander-in-Chief, of the Army and Navy of the United States in time of actual armed rebellion against the authority and government of the United States, and as a fit and necessary war measure for suppressing said rebellion."[84]

The decision to drop any claim to congressional authority must have been partially legal. The debate over the constitutionality of the preliminary proclamation had made it clear that no one thought Congress had the right to interfere with slavery. Lincoln's strongest claim to emancipate legally was to rely on his war power. That would alleviate any confusion about whether Congress was imputing treason to rebellious Southerners and thereby enacting an unconstitutional bill of attainder.

Yet the autumn's debate about emancipation must also have made it clear to Lincoln that, by owning the decision and excluding Congress, he would catapult himself into the position of sole emancipator. His decision to put his own name into the proclamation supports the idea that he was making a bid for historical significance based on his own personal agency.

A further change from the preliminary proclamation was that Lincoln abandoned the paragraph that promised to compensate loyal slaveholders for their losses after the war. The idea behind the original promise had been that emancipation was a penalty aimed at disloyal rebels, while loyal Southern slaveholders deserved and retained the constitutional right to compensation for the taking of their property. The abandonment of the compensation promise signaled that Lincoln was no longer necessarily treating emancipation as a penalty aimed specifically at rebels. It was a war measure that would affect all slaveholders in the Confederacy.

The final reason to avoid mentioning compensation was that it would disrupt a new moral narrative that Lincoln was gradually beginning to explore—a narrative that treated slavery not as a constitutional right but as a moral wrong. The political purpose of the compensation promise had initially been to reassure slaveholders in border states that Lincoln still respected their constitutional right to own slaves. Yet now, in the final version of the proclamation, Lincoln was taking account of a much broader audience—a global audience that considered slavery immoral. And to that audience, it would have seemed self-contradictory and even bizarre to offer to pay off slaveholders in the same document that emancipated slaves.

Lincoln addressed this global audience directly in the proclamation's final paragraph:

> And upon this act, sincerely believed to be an act of justice, warranted by the Constitution, upon military necessity, I invoke the considerate judgment of mankind, and the gracious favor of Almighty God.[85]

This passage reflected the complex, two-faced nature of the proclamation. Looking inward, Lincoln still wanted to describe the act as "warranted by the Constitution." But for the global audience of "mankind," Lincoln spoke of emancipation as "an act of justice." The "justice" in question could only have been justice for the enslaved. Lincoln was highlighting the immorality of slavery, which he had ignored in the preliminary declaration.

Karl Marx, who described the Emancipation Proclamation as "the most important document in American history since the establishment of the union, tantamount to the tearing up of the old American constitution," nevertheless suggested that Lincoln had intentionally drafted it to sound like "an ordinary summons, sent by one lawyer to another."[86] Marx's aperçu about Lincoln's rhetoric may have been true of the body of the proclamation, but it did not apply to the final paragraph.

Only morality, not the domestic U.S. Constitution, could explain Lincoln's invocation of "the considerate judgment of mankind" and the "gracious favor of God Almighty." The judgment of mankind was that slavery was morally wrong. And Lincoln was strongly hinting that

God shared the same point of view. The compromise Constitution was a domestic-facing document that had protected slavery. To appeal to God and to mankind was to reject that compromise—and to embrace a global-facing moral vision.

In referring to mankind and to God, Lincoln was also consciously harking back to the Declaration of Independence. The Declaration appealed to the "opinions of mankind" and referred to a Creator who endowed men with inalienable rights, including liberty. The Declaration had similarly been aimed at a global audience beyond the domestic one.[87] In its essence, it was a document grounded in morality, not British constitutional law—which it more or less shattered and rejected. By connecting the Emancipation Proclamation to the Declaration of Independence, Lincoln was trying to add it to the canon of foundational documents that the United States would give the world.

FREED MEN—AND THEIR INTERESTS

Not only did Lincoln address the world in his final version of the Emancipation Proclamation, as he had not done in his earlier versions, but he also addressed the African Americans who would be freed by the proclamation. Remarkably, the first thought Lincoln had with respect to former slaves was to "enjoin upon the people so declared to be free to abstain from all violence, unless in necessary self-defence."[88] The U.S. military was engaged in violent war against Confederates whom Lincoln himself had branded as traitors. Yet Lincoln urged people who had been enslaved to forgo violence. Presumably, his language was intended to salve the worry that former slaves might massacre their former masters. It certainly seems to reflect greater concern for slaveholders than for African Americans held in slavery.

Lincoln then wrote, "I recommend to them that, in all cases when allowed, they labor faithfully for reasonable wages."[89] This formulation was directed at freed slaves in Union-controlled territory. It showed that Lincoln wanted to take advantage of freed slaves' manpower, albeit with pay. This plan supported Lincoln's claim to be emancipating Confederate slaves as a war measure.

In further support of that goal, Lincoln declared "that such persons of suitable condition, will be received into the armed service of the United States to garrison forts, positions, stations, and other places, and to man vessels of all sorts in said service."[90] Enlisting freed African Americans in the U.S. Army and Navy had been a controversial idea until this point in the war. Congress had permitted state militias to enlist African Americans the previous March, but including African Americans in the regular U.S. military went a step further. Whatever Lincoln may have originally thought about this policy, the decision to frame emancipation as a war measure made it more or less necessary for him to announce that freed slaves could serve in the armed forces.

All the changes just described between the preliminary proclamation and the official proclamation of January 1 tend to show Lincoln as having gathered greater personal resolve over the course of the autumn. Only one change hinted at doubt—and that change, though subtle, was worrisome. The operative clause of the proposed order in July and the preliminary proclamation in September had declared that from January 1, the slaves "shall be then, thenceforward, and forever free." But when January 1 came around, Lincoln wrote, "I do order and declare that all persons held as slaves within said designated States, and parts of States, are, and henceforward shall be free."[91] Between September and January, Lincoln dropped the word "forever."

The distinction is not much noticed today, and has never been properly explained. But in context, it was significant. The preliminary proclamation of September, like the proposed order of July, purported to effect a permanent change in the legal status of slaves held in the Confederacy. The Emancipation Proclamation still declared their freedom. But by leaving out "forever," it implied the legal possibility that some or all enslaved people emancipated by the document could be returned to the state of slavery.

The change reflected Lincoln's desire to forestall legal objections— and by implication, his concern that the Emancipation Proclamation might eventually be reversed. Under the customary international law of war as long interpreted by Americans, it was not permitted to seize the enemy's property permanently, but only for the duration of hostilities. Lincoln knew that the eyes of the world would be on the Emancipation Proclamation, as his appeal to "mankind" indicated. He was trying to avoid the charge that, in emancipating Confederate slaves, he had broken the bonds of international legality.*

The simple fact is that, even after the Emancipation Proclamation was issued and hailed throughout the world as an act of transcendent morality, the belief persisted in the United States that it was unconstitutional—and unjustified under the customary international law of war. Lincoln offered no public constitutional justification for a stunning eight months. Finally, near the end of August 1863, he used a public letter to his friend and ally James Conkling to explain the basis for the proclamation. The explanation he offered was now squarely focused on constitutional authority and the law of war—with no hint of the moral justification hinted at in the proclamation itself.

Lincoln began by addressing a hypothetical critic: "You dislike the emancipation proclamation; and, perhaps, would have it retracted. You say it is unconstitutional—I think differently."[92] Lincoln was acknowl-

---

* In drafting his veto message for the Second Confiscation Act, Lincoln had addressed the concern that under the Constitution, punishment for treason could take place only during the life of the offender, not beyond. This domestic legal concern was not precisely the same as the concern about the customary law of war. And Lincoln, acting as commander in chief, did not have to address it, because unlike Congress he was not condemning the Confederate slaveholders as treasonous. Yet thinking about the permanence of the seizure for domestic constitutional law purposes is probably what put Lincoln in mind of the question of permanent freedom under international law.

edging the reality that some of his opponents even within the Union continued to think not only that the Emancipation Proclamation was unconstitutional but also that he should take it back.

Lincoln then began his argument: "I think the Constitution invests its commander-in-chief, with the law of war, in time of war."[93] His argument would rely on the idea that the Constitution conferred on the president in wartime those powers that belonged to a nation under the customary international law of war. The Constitution, in other words, incorporated the law of war by reference.

Framing a possible counterargument, Lincoln asserted that "the most that can be said, if so much, is, that slaves are property."[94] Lincoln equivocated in order to avoid committing himself fully to the idea that slaves were property. But he was saying that this was the view of opponents of emancipation—so he could take it as his premise.

He then turned to what the international law of war said about property. "Is there," he asked, "has there ever been—any question that by the law of war, property, both of enemies and friends, may be taken when needed?"[95] Certainly the customary law of war authorized seizure of property "when needed." But the circumstances had traditionally been limited (in the United States, at least) to property being used by the enemy for war aims, and needed for war aims by the side doing the seizing. And the seizure was only supposed to last as long as the war continued, not beyond.

Lincoln addressed these problems with a claim about when property was "needed." He asked, "And is it not needed whenever taking it, helps us, or hurts the enemy?"[96] This definition of necessity notably overstated the extent of the traditional doctrine of wartime seizure. In Lincoln's formulation, not only could the military seize specific property that would help its war effort, but it could also make any seizure of property that it judged useful to achieve victory. That could include, for example, taking any property belonging to the enemy as a threat or a penalty or in order to reduce the enemy to poverty.

Lincoln tried to support the argument by an appeal to real-world practice, which was, after all, supposed to be the source of customary law. "Armies, the world over," he wrote, "destroy enemies' property when they can not use it; and even destroy their own to keep it from the enemy." As a matter of customary practice, this, too, was not quite correct. It was considered lawful to seize and destroy enemy property *that would be used for war purposes*. Similarly, the property of an army's own citizens could be seized and destroyed if it would otherwise be captured by the enemy and *used for war purposes*. Lincoln was deliberately broadening the description of what armies could traditionally do within the frame of the law of war in order to make it sound like there was no meaningful constraint on the wartime seizure of property.

To conclude the point, Lincoln summed up the law of war as he wanted to characterize it:

> Civilized belligerents do all in their power to help themselves, or hurt the enemy, except a few things regarded as barbarous or cruel. Among the exceptions are the massacre of vanquished foes, and non-combatants, male and female.[97]

By asserting that even "civilized" armies could do anything except killing prisoners and non combatants, Lincoln was trying to imply that *any* property seizure of *any* kind must be acceptable military behavior under the customary law of war. This broader claim simply ignored the idea that there were legal limits to what a "civilized" army could do.

As if to acknowledge the weakness of his legal arguments, Lincoln then brushed aside the idea that the legality of the Emancipation Proclamation mattered at all. "But the proclamation, as law, either is valid, or is not valid," he wrote. "If it is not valid, it needs no retraction. If it is valid, it can not be retracted, any more than the dead can be brought to life."[98] The whole syllogism was astonishing in its rejection of legal logic. If the proclamation was an unconstitutional act beyond the power of the president, of course it ought to have been withdrawn. And whether the proclamation was lawful had nothing to do with the practical question of whether slavery could be resurrected.

Lincoln then tried to explain pragmatically why he thought emancipation was irreversible. The war had gone no worse since he announced the preliminary proclamation than before, he said weakly. And, he claimed, "some of the commanders of our armies . . . believe the emancipation policy, and the use of the colored troops, constitute the heaviest blow yet dealt to the rebellion; and that, at least one of those important successes could not have been achieved when it was, but for the aid of black soldiers."[99] The commander he had in mind was almost certainly Grant, and the important success was probably to the battle of Milliken's Bend, fought in June, at which freed African American soldiers had played a crucial role.*

A vague attribution of opinion to unnamed generals and claims of a single but-for victory fell well short of a compelling case for the military necessity of emancipation. Lincoln as much as admitted it: "I submit these opinions as being entitled to some weight against the objections, often urged, that emancipation, and arming the blacks, are unwise as military measures, and were not adopted, as such, in good faith."[100] The operative phrase was "some weight." No one who thought Lincoln was acting in bad faith when he emancipated the Confederate slaves as a military measure was going to be convinced by the president's public letter to Conkling.

Finally, almost as an afterthought, Lincoln addressed the situation of freed African Americans. He did so not in moral terms, but in

---

* At this point in the war, African American soldiers had also already fought bravely at Port Hudson and, more famously, at Fort Wagner, where the 54th Massachusetts Regiment suffered devastating casualties. But neither of these engagements could have been considered a military success overall.

terms of concrete self-interest, both for the former slaves and for the Union that depended on their help to win the war:

> [N]egroes, like other people, act upon motives. Why should they do any thing for us, if we will do nothing for them? If they stake their lives for us, they must be prompted by the strongest motive—even the promise of freedom. And the promise being made, must be kept.[101]

In Lincoln's rationalistic formulation, emancipation was essentially a trade: freedom for military service. For the bargain of mutual self-interest to succeed, African Americans needed to be able to rely on the Union's promise of freedom, made in the Emancipation Proclamation. Lincoln gave no hint that morality played any role in the obligation to keep the promise made by the Union. Rather, the promise of emancipation "must be kept," lest any weakening of Union resolve lead African Americans to abandon their side of the deal.

THE GETTYSBURG ADDRESS AND THE ROAD TO THE MORAL CONSTITUTION

Lincoln's open letter to Conkling shows that, as 1863 progressed, the president was pursuing two very different strategies with respect to justifying emancipation. One approach, addressed to the world at large, was moral: slavery was wrong and the Emancipation Proclamation could be depicted globally as ending it. (Notwithstanding the detail that the proclamation mostly applied where it would have no immediate effect.) The other approach, addressed domestically, was legal-pragmatic: the proclamation was necessary as a war measure, and legal because the Constitution gave the commander in chief the authority to do whatever was necessary to win the war.

Lincoln began to bring these two strands closer together in the Gettysburg Address, which he delivered on November 19, 1863. He did so subtly. His most famous speech never mentioned emancipation, and did not use the word "slavery." Yet the Gettysburg Address recast the Civil War as a war about freedom and equality, not a war to restore the union. More important still, it suggested that the Constitution that would follow the war would be something new—not a restoration of the old Constitution, but a "new birth of freedom" that would repair the wrongs of the original version.[102]

The address is so well-known that it can be difficult to glimpse the ways it reframed the conflict, and the Constitution. One way to see the changes wrought by the speech is to notice the avowedly biblical tone that Lincoln took, from the first words ("Four score and seven years") to the last ("shall not perish from the earth").[103] Garry Wills, writing in 1992, emphasized the classical Greek form of Lincoln's eulogy.[104] But the use of biblical language marked a much greater change for Lincoln, a nonreligious rationalist whose rhetoric had long been built on a combination of plain speech and pragmatic lawyer's vocabulary.

Lincoln's turn to biblical language and religious imagery began with the Gettysburg Address and culminated in his second inaugural address, which offered a full-blown theology of the Civil War, and of America itself. To explain the emergence of biblical, religious themes in Lincoln's most important public pronouncements, scholars have explored the challenges of Lincoln's personal life, the weight on him of the deaths suffered in the war, and the constantly present threat of his own death by assassination.[105]

Yet the most powerful explanation for Lincoln's biblical and religious turn is more obvious. Put simply, until the Emancipation Proclamation, Lincoln had never been *able* to present his political goals in moral terms. It would therefore have been inapposite for him to speak in terms of the Bible or religion, which Americans of Lincoln's time almost universally considered the sources of morality itself. That was because Lincoln's career had been devoted to the preservation of the compromise Constitution—a constitution that he himself acknowledged as a compromise with the immoral institution of slavery. The compromise Constitution required a politician who supported it to speak in the register of a law that was separate from morality, and a duty that ran to the Constitution, not to goodness or moral truth.

The Emancipation Proclamation fundamentally altered Lincoln's aims, and with it the register in which he could speak about them. Once slavery was to be purged from the nation, the Constitution that would emerge could be at one with morality, not in contradiction to it. Lincoln could therefore describe the aims of the war, of the Union, and of the Constitution in new, moralized terms. Once he chose to do that, the Bible provided the natural language through which he could express his meaning to an American, Christian audience.

The first sentence of the Gettysburg Address defined the United States as, from its birth, "a new nation, conceived in Liberty, and dedicated to the proposition that all men are created equal."[106] We are accustomed to noticing that the word "nation" differed strongly from the word "union," which Lincoln did not use in the address. The most significant feature of the first sentence, however, was Lincoln's claim that the United States was fundamentally devoted to liberty and equality. The Declaration of Independence used both words. But the Constitution denied both liberty and equality to people of African descent through its recognition and protection of slavery. If liberty and equality were true and universal goals for the nation, then slavery would have to go—and the Constitution would have to be replaced by something different.

Lincoln then explained that the Civil War was "testing whether that nation, or any nation so conceived and so dedicated, can long endure."[107] From his first inaugural address on, Lincoln had argued that the war was a test of whether the framers' republican constitutional government, born of compromise, could survive the Southern minority's demands for concessions. Now he was re-describing the nature of the challenge: the war, he was saying, was a test of whether a nation conceived in liberty and dedicated to equality could survive. In other words, the war was about whether slavery could continue to trump liberty and equality.

Read carefully, this was nothing short of a transformation of the meaning of the war. First self-consciously defined by Lincoln as a war for preservation of the union—not a war about the morality of slavery—it was now a war to end slavery. That was the effect of the Emancipation Proclamation: it provided the war with a moral purpose.

The "unfinished work" for which the soldiers at Gettysburg had died was thus not to restore the union, but to remake it without slavery. The "great task remaining before us" was to achieve the creation of a new order. So that "these dead shall not have died in vain," the nation needed "a new birth of freedom."[108] That meant a new Constitution, one that would be based on freedom in that it would exclude slavery.

The idea of "new birth" resonated with the essence of Christianity. New birth, all Americans understood, invoked the teaching of rebirth in Christ. That new birth conferred special freedom: what Protestants since Luther had called "Christian liberty." This was the true freedom in Christ, freedom from the law itself.[109]

Lincoln had not yet fully spelled out his analogy. But he was hinting that if the compromise Constitution was the Old Testament, then the new Constitution that would emerge would correspond to the New Testament. The Old Testament, not incidentally, sanctioned slavery. The new Constitution, corresponding to the New Testament, would stand for freedom—and would not allow slavery. The "government of the people, by the people, for the people" that must not "perish from the earth" would have to be a government somehow incorporating *all* the people.[110]

SLAVERY IN THE BALANCE

The overarching consequence of Lincoln's reformulation of the war as a moral war against slavery was that Lincoln now could not allow the war to end with the restoration of slavery. Yet by the summer of 1864, with an election looming, he also understood that he might not be able to stop that from happening. Despite his progress toward a moral reading of the Emancipation Proclamation—and hence of the war—it still remained possible for many observers to imagine the retraction and reversal of the Emancipation Proclamation.

Lincoln could easily lose his reelection campaign against Democratic candidate George McClellan, the general whom Lincoln had fired. The Union did not seem close to defeating the Confederacy. There was no political expectation that incumbency would help a president win. No president had even stood for reelection since Jackson. And if Lincoln lost to a Democrat, the most probable result would be a peace treaty recognizing the Confederacy. The Democratic platform called for peace. (It was drafted in part by Clement Vallandigham, who had returned without permission from his exile in the Confederacy.) A treaty ending the war might or might not restore the union by reuniting the states. But in any case, it would guarantee slavery, thus returning in some way to the antebellum compromise Constitution.

In the face of possible defeat, Lincoln chose to double down on his commitment to emancipation. A group of Confederate representatives had been sent to Niagara Falls to attempt to negotiate with the Lincoln administration, probably in the hopes of helping Democrats in the election by suggesting the South was willing to negotiate a peace under the right conditions. Refusing to acknowledge the Confederacy by sending any official representative of the administration to meet the delegation, Lincoln deputed Horace Greeley, the editor of the *New-York Tribune*. On July 18, 1864, he wrote a letter for Greeley to deliver at Niagara, addressed "To Whom It May Concern" in order to avoid giving the Confederacy any recognition.

The letter consisted of a single sentence. It stated that Lincoln was willing to consider "[a]ny proposition which embraces the restoration of peace, the integrity of the whole Union, and the abandonment of slavery."[111] The first two elements, peace and the restoration of the union, went without saying. The point of the letter was for Lincoln to make publicly clear, once and for all, that the emancipation of slaves was now an irreducible object of the war. The fact that he had to say so served as a reminder that a Democratic president might think otherwise.

Lincoln's first overt statement that the war could not end unless the South agreed to the end of slavery came in for immediate criticism from both Republicans and Democrats. Why, they wondered, would Lincoln give up the ability to use the restoration of slavery as a bargaining chip with the Confederacy?[112] The Republican National Committee met in New York and decided that it did not think Lincoln could be elected without retracting his insistence on the preservation of emancipation. The committee members sent Lincoln a private message suggesting that he should propose peace to Jefferson Davis with the "sole condition" that the union be re-formed—with no mention of slavery. Davis would say no, they reasoned, and Lincoln could no longer be blamed for blocking peace by insisting on abolition.

Lincoln wanted to respond to the critics. On August 17, 1864, he drafted what was framed as a public letter addressed to Charles D. Robinson, a Democratic newspaper editor. Robinson had challenged Lincoln to reconcile his insistence on preserving emancipation with the letter he had written to Horace Greeley in 1862 saying that if he "could save the Union without freeing any slave," he "would do it." Lincoln was now making emancipation a condition of peace. Thus, Robinson charged, he had reversed his earlier position.

In his draft letter to Robinson, Lincoln tried to claim, implausibly, that his views had not changed. He had written to Greeley in 1862 "in the utmost sincerity," he insisted, adding, "I am as true to the whole of it now, as when I first said it." Emancipation had been a war measure, he reasoned: "The way these measures were to help the cause, was not to be by magic, or miracles, but by inducing the colored people to come bodily over from the rebel side to ours."[113]

To support the claim that emancipation was a pragmatic war measure, Lincoln referred back to his letter to Conkling. But in doing so, he transformed the meaning of that letter. A year before, writing to Conkling, Lincoln had focused on pragmatic self-interest as the *sole* justification for emancipation. Emphasizing the mutual self-interest of the Union and African Americans, he had written that "the promise" of emancipation, "being made, must be kept." Now Lincoln revisited that sentence—and broadened the value of promise-keeping from self-interest to moral duty:

> I am sure you will not, on due reflection, say that the promise being made, must be *broken* at the first opportunity. I am sure you would not desire me to say, or to leave an inference, that I am ready, whenever convenient, to join in re-enslaving those who shall have served us in consideration of our promise. As a matter of morals, could such treachery by any possibility, escape the curses of Heaven, or of any good man?[114]

In this draft, Lincoln was making it explicit that reneging on emancipation would be not merely imprudent but fundamentally wrong. It would be "treachery"—and it would be wrong "as a matter of morals" to break the promise of freedom. He was not saying that slavery itself was immoral. He was suggesting that it would be immoral to promise freedom and then break the promise.

Lincoln went on in the draft letter to Robinson to emphasize pragmatism, arguing that announcing a retraction of the Emancipation Proclamation "would ruin the Union cause" because "[a]ll recruiting of colored men would instantly cease, and all colored men now in our service, would instantly desert us." He added a preelection partisan twist: "The party who could elect a President on a War & Slavery Restoration platform, would, of necessity, lose the colored force; and that force being lost, would be as powerless to save the Union as to do any other impossible thing." And in the last line of the draft letter, Lincoln wrote ambiguously: "If Jefferson Davis wishes, for himself, or for the benefit of his friends at the North, to know what I would do if he were to offer peace and re-union, saying nothing about slavery, let him try me."[115]

By bringing the morality of emancipation to the fore, even as he continued to provide pragmatic justifications for it, Lincoln was saying that the act of freeing slaves could not be reversed without committing a serious moral wrong. He was preparing to identify emancipation with moral duty. That would give the war a definite historical-moral meaning—even if Lincoln was voted out of office before he could win it.

Two days later, on August 19, 1864, Lincoln met with Frederick Douglass at the White House. The president and the greatest living abolitionist had first met a year before, when Douglass had simply walked into the White House and asked to see the president—a request to which Lincoln immediately acceded.[116] This time, Lincoln invited Douglass. The president read him the draft letter, presumably anticipating that Douglass would be pleased by the invocation of morality in connection with emancipation. Douglass understood that Lincoln was progressing toward a moral basis for emancipation. At the meeting, the president "showed a deeper moral conviction against slavery than I had ever seen before in anything spoken or written by him," Douglass later wrote. But Douglass thought that the sentence at the end of the letter inviting Jefferson Davis to "try me" might be read as a willingness to offer a "complete surrender of your antislavery policy."[117] Rather than encouraging Lincoln to send the letter, Douglass advised him to suppress it.

Lincoln never sent the letter to Robinson. Reflecting his worry that he would lose the election, he asked if Douglass would propose a plan to get word to slaves behind Southern lines that they should flee to the Union armies as soon as possible. Douglass believed that Lincoln's request stemmed from his concern that any slaves who had not actually been freed by coming under Union authority might be returned to slavery by a Democratic president.

On August 23, 1864, Lincoln wrote a secret memorandum that was to be opened only after the election—and that captured his thinking at what may have been the low point of his administration. "This morning," he wrote, "as for some days past, it seems exceedingly probable that this administration will not be reelected." If that happened, Lincoln wrote, "it will be my duty to so co-operate with the President elect, as to save the Union between the election and the inauguration; as he will have secured his election on such ground that he cannot possibly save it afterwards."[118]

The meaning of the document was somewhat obscure. Sealing it in an envelope, Lincoln had the members of his cabinet sign the outside without telling them what was inside. This act suggests that Lincoln was treating what is often called his "blind memorandum" as a kind of time capsule that he could reveal if necessary after November to prove that he formed the idea contained in it in August, before losing the election.

But what, exactly, was the idea? Eric Foner has argued that Lincoln was considering sacrificing emancipation in order to reach a peace deal with Jefferson Davis and save the union. The next day, August 24, Lincoln went so far as to draft a message to Davis offering peace "upon the restoration of the Union"—abandoning the demand for emancipation, just as the Republican National Committee had advised him to do.[119] The draft message to Davis would seem to suggest that the blind memorandum contemplated some such compromise.

In any case, Lincoln decided not to send the message to Davis. And because he won the election, his blind memorandum became a footnote to history, not a guide to future action. In his public conduct, therefore, Lincoln maintained the commitment to emancipation that he had made in his one-sentence "To Whom It May Concern" announcement. He never made a public statement that explicitly defended emancipation as a morally correct act, yet he accepted the moral interpretation of the Emancipation Proclamation that others put upon it. Perhaps the clearest statement was that of William Seward, who wrote to ambassador to the United Kingdom Charles Francis Adams that "the course of events has been such as to justify the assumption that, in point of fact, the war is a principal force in a revolution against African slavery."[120]

THE THIRTEENTH AMENDMENT

The reason Lincoln never explicitly adopted a moral defense of the Emancipation Proclamation on its own terms is, no doubt, that he recognized the logic of the view that it violated the Constitution. His efforts to justify the proclamation as a necessary war measure were directed precisely at justifying the constitutionality of an act that, he understood, broke all the norms of the compromise Constitution that had existed before the war. Had Lincoln publicly asserted that emancipation was right because slavery was wrong, regardless of its constitutionality, he would have admitted to violating the ideal of constitutional fidelity with which he had begun the war in the first place. He could not rest emancipation on solely moral grounds without repudiating the theory that he had a duty to defend the Constitution by all necessary means.

Yet by adopting emancipation and insisting on its irreversibility, Lincoln had effectively eliminated any possibility of return to the compromise Constitution that preceded the war. There could be no going back to what had been before. The compromise Constitution had been broken by the seceding states—and with emancipation, Lincoln had ensured that it would remain broken.

The only possible solution was a new Constitution, one that would not rest on the compromise of slavery. And if one rejected revolution, as a sitting president had to do, then there was just one way to make a new Constitution: through the adoption of a constitutional amendment that would outlaw slavery permanently. Under Article V of the Constitution, enacting such an amendment required passage by two-thirds of the House and the Senate and ratification by three-fourths of the states. If adopted, it would regularize Lincoln's Constitution-breaking act of emancipation. And unlike the Emancipation Proclamation, it would apply everywhere, not only in the seceding states but also in the slaveholding border states that were still in the Union.

A constitutional amendment to abolish slavery was first proposed in Congress as early as December 1863. In April 1864, the Senate, with the Confederate states unrepresented, passed an abolition amendment by the requisite two-thirds majority. But on June 15, 1864, the proposed amendment failed in the House of Representatives. The vote of 93 in favor and 65 against, almost entirely on party lines, fell short of a two-thirds majority.

With an eye on the election, Lincoln had previously delayed endorsing the proposal for a constitutional amendment on slavery. After the amendment failed in the House, he belatedly did so—but indirectly. The Republican National Convention that nominated Lincoln for president had adopted a platform that called for an abolition amendment. On June 27, 1864, after the Republican Party had officially nominated him, Lincoln wrote an acceptance letter endorsing the platform as a whole, without singling out abolition.

The Republican plank on slavery stated squarely that "Slavery was the cause, and now constitutes the strength of this rebellion." Because slavery was "hostile to the principles of Republican Government," the plank went on, "justice and the National safety demand its utter and complete extirpation from the soil of the Republic." This measured account of why slavery must be abolished included the idea that slavery was a source of strength for the Confederacy, thus hinting that its elimination was a genuine war aim—a measure to achieve "National safety." It also went further by declaring the incompatibility of slavery and republican government, and alluding to "justice."[121] This was not a full moral condemnation of slavery, but it came close: the only way slavery could be seen as "hostile" to republicanism was if republicanism insisted on the equality of all citizens.

The plank went out of its way to praise Lincoln for emancipation, even while echoing his publicly expressed view that the purpose had been to win the war: "[W]e uphold and maintain the acts and proclamations by which the Government, in its own defense, has aimed a deathblow at this gigantic evil," it read. Then the plank stated: "[W]e are in favor, furthermore, of such amendment to the Constitution, to be made by the people in conformity with its provisions, as shall terminate and forever prohibit the existence of slavery within the limits or the jurisdiction of the United States."[122]

The call for an abolition amendment was not the centerpiece of the Republican campaign to elect Lincoln in the fall of 1864—nor did it facilitate his victory. In the event, Lincoln lost the border states of Delaware and Kentucky, both of which still permitted slaveholding, as well as New Jersey, which bordered Delaware.* He won the election because the Democrat George McClellan was too extreme in his Southern sympathies, and because at long last, the Union began to win the war, starting with the fall of Atlanta in September.

His election secured, Lincoln made his first explicit public statement about an abolition amendment in the annual address that he sent

---

* Delaware would not ratify the Thirteenth Amendment until 1901.

to Congress in December 1864. He acknowledged that the House had failed to adopt the measure by a two-thirds majority, and that the composition of that body would not change until the new congressional session the following spring. Yet he politely asked the House to reconsider and pass the amendment now, "without questioning the wisdom or patriotism of those who stood in opposition." He pointed out that the results of the 1864 election showed "almost certainly" that the next Congress would pass the amendment by a two-thirds margin. Since the amendment was going to pass anyway, "may we not agree that the sooner the better?"[123]

To support his request, Lincoln argued that, by electing a substantial Republican majority in the House, the public had spoken in favor of abolition. In the election, he claimed, "the voice of the people now, for the first time, [was] heard upon the question." The popular will provided a reason for dissenters to change their votes:

> In a great national crisis, like ours, unanimity of action among those seeking a common end is very desirable— almost indispensable. And yet no approach to such unanimity is attainable, unless some deference shall be paid to the will of the majority, simply because it is the will of the majority. In this case the common end is the maintenance of the Union; and, among the means to secure that end, such will, through the election, is most clearly declared in favor of such constitutional amendment.[124]

This argument echoed the one Lincoln had made in his first inaugural address: that constitutional government could function only if the minority deferred to the majority. This was the "deference" due to "the will of the majority."

It was telling that Lincoln still justified abolition as a "means" to "the maintenance of the union"—not as a moral necessity in itself.

His caution reflected what had by now become a standard piece of his public discussion of slavery. When the state of Maryland was voting on a constitution that abolished slavery in October, Lincoln had sent a message stating, "I wish all men to be free . . . I wish to see, in process of disappearing, that only thing which ever could bring this nation to civil war."[125] By avoiding moral condemnation of slavery in favor of a union-oriented rationale for its abolition, Lincoln was no doubt trying to placate congressmen who had voted against the amendment the first time, and whose votes were now necessary for passage. Yet his reticence about declaring the moral wrongfulness of slavery also matched the public stance he had taken since announcing emancipation.

The story of how Lincoln and the Republicans got the House to pass what would become the Thirteenth Amendment at the end of January 1865 has been dramatically told in print by Doris Kearns Goodwin and memorialized in film by Steven Spielberg.[126] The moment-to-moment drama of this story is somewhat reduced if one keeps in mind what Lincoln had already told Congress in December: that the amendment was going to pass in March in any case, when the new Congress went into session.

The greater drama of the passage of the Thirteenth Amendment was its transformation of the prewar, compromise Constitution into a new Constitution that repudiated the very core of that compromise as it had existed from 1787 to 1861. No compensation was paid to slaveholders. The omission contradicted the original constitutional idea of the protection of property rights—but that did not matter, legally speaking, because an amendment to the Constitution could reverse, ignore, or violate other constitutional provisions. Lincoln, open to placating the South, and still recalling his long-term preference for compensated emancipation, actually proposed to his cabinet that Congress should offer $400 million in compensation to slaveholding states—both Confederate and border states—on the condition that the Confederacy surrender by April 1, 1865. The cabinet rejected Lincoln's idea unanimously, and he dropped it without further discussion.

Lincoln did not live to see the Thirteenth Amendment ratified. Twenty states had voted in favor of ratification by April 1865, including four states that were still part of the Confederacy, whose "ratification" came from provisional quasi-governments that Lincoln chose to treat as though they represented their states. In these states, which were effectively under military occupation, would-be voters had to take loyalty oaths renouncing secession. A tenth of eligible voters taking the oath was treated as a number sufficient to recognize the state government.[127] Lincoln believed that the total number of states to compute the three-quarters needed for ratification had to include the states of the Confederacy, whose secession he had never formally acknowledged.

But from the moment the amendment was sent to the states, it became inevitable that the new Constitution would no longer rest on a foundation of compromise with the immorality of slavery. The new Constitution would be a new birth of freedom: a moral Constitution.

THE THEOLOGY OF EMANCIPATION

Lincoln was inaugurated to his second term in office on March 4, 1865. The surrender of the Confederacy was a month away, and already understood to be imminent. The time had come to assign a lasting after-the-fact meaning to the war—and to the Constitution that was beginning to emerge from it.

In his second inaugural address, Lincoln fully embraced the view that the war had been about slavery. Southern slaves "constituted a peculiar and powerful interest," he said. And "[a]ll knew that this interest was, somehow, the cause of the war."[128]

The result of the war, Lincoln went on, had been his act of emancipation. Neither side, he said, "anticipated that the *cause* of the conflict"—

that is, slavery—"might cease with, or even before, the conflict itself should cease." Lincoln was saying that no one, himself included, had initially expected him to issue the Emancipation Proclamation. He had done so as a consequence of the war—a consequence that had been, he said, "fundamental and astounding."[129]

Once he had defined the war as a struggle over slavery, Lincoln could at long last offer a morally inflected account of why slavery was wrong. In a particularly famous passage of this extremely famous speech, he observed that both sides in the Civil War "read the same Bible, and pray to the same God; and each invokes His aid against the other." Then he commented pointedly: "It may seem strange that any men should dare to ask a just God's assistance in wringing their bread from the sweat of other men's faces."[130] This was, finally, a moral condemnation of slavery, and of the slave states for making slavery the basis for the war. In the eyes of God, Lincoln was suggesting, slavery could not be just.

No sooner had Lincoln condemned the morality of slavery than he mitigated the point: "[B]ut let us judge not that we be not judged."[131] The sentiment reflected Christian modesty and political expedience. Yet it also went further. The compromise Constitution that protected slavery had been the work of North and South alike. Lincoln knew he could not offer an unmitigated moral condemnation of slavery without impugning the North—and the Constitution.

Lincoln then turned to what can only be considered political theology, the use of distinctly religious ideas about God to explain political events and institutions. He offered nothing less than a theology of slavery. According to that theology, slavery was an offense against God; and the offense had been punished by a war that had devastated both North and South:

If we shall suppose that American slavery is one of those offences which, in the providence of God, must needs

come, but which, having continued through His appointed
time, He now wills to remove, and that He gives to both
North and South, this terrible war, as the woe due to those
by whom the offence came, shall we discern therein any
departure from those divine attributes which the believers
in a Living God always ascribe to Him?[132]

In Lincoln's formulation, slavery was America's original sin. It is
worth noticing that, like original sin itself, slavery was part of God's
providential plan, an evil which "must needs come." This was something close to an acknowledgment that the United States could not
have been built without slavery—and that the compromise over slavery had created and sustained the union.

In Christian theology, original sin could be redeemed by the blood
of the crucified Christ. In Lincoln's political theology, the sin of slavery
was paid for by the cost of the Civil War and the blood of its dead soldiers. The war might "continue until all the wealth piled by the bond-
man's two hundred and fifty years of unrequited toil shall be sunk, and
until every drop of blood drawn with the lash, shall be paid by another
drawn with the sword." Lincoln was imagining the wealth created by
slaves' work being used up in the war. If that occurred, then "as was
said three thousand years ago, so still it must be said 'the judgments of
the Lord, are true and righteous altogether.'"[133] If Christ's sacrifice to
redeem man from original sin was just in some divine sense, Lincoln
was saying, then the sacrifices of the war that redeemed the United
States from the sin of slavery were also just. Small wonder that Frederick Douglass told Lincoln after the speech that it had been "a sacred
effort."[134]

Paired with the "new birth of freedom" that Lincoln had proclaimed
in the Gettysburg Address, this theology of the Civil War recast the
breaking of the Constitution and its re-formation through the Thirteenth Amendment in a completely new, Christian moral light. In the

Protestant theology that was the common heritage of the great majority of nineteenth-century Americans, the Old Testament (or Hebrew Bible) was understood to focus on law—specifically the ritual law that governed the Israelites. That ritual law was part of the old covenant between God and his people. Christ had come to "fulfill" the law by displacing the ritual law and replacing it with the "moral law." Christianity thus heralded a new covenant, one available to all the peoples of the earth and encompassed in the text of the New Testament. "Christian liberty," in Protestant thought, was freedom from the old ritual law—a freedom found through the new covenant in Christ.

In Lincoln's proposed political theology, the old compromise Constitution took the place of the old covenant found in the Old Testament. Like the Judaism of the Old Testament, it came with original sin, and included no mechanism of salvation from it. The war had seen the breaking of the old covenant. Through the blood of the Civil War dead on both sides, the sin of slavery had been eliminated. A new covenant would emerge—in the form of the new Constitution. And like the moral law emphasized by Christianity, the new Constitution would be devoted to the moral truths of freedom and equality.

It is difficult to know whether Lincoln thought that God himself had brought about the extraordinary transformation that he was depicting in theological terms. Certainly belief in a personal, providential God would have represented a significant shift from everything we know about Lincoln's religious beliefs prior to assuming the presidency. Yet the crucial point is that it is not necessary to attribute any particular religious faith to Lincoln in order to understand his political theology of slavery, emancipation, and the new Constitution. All that is required is to recognize that, when he spoke of morality, Lincoln spoke of it in the same terms as his countrymen in the historical moment at which he lived. His political theology was, in the end, a moral accounting of the history of the United States: born in the immorality

of slavery and ultimately cleansed from that immorality by the cata-
clysm of the Civil War.

In that accounting, to be sure, Lincoln himself was the tool of salvation. Emancipation was the radically transformative act that ended
the compromise Constitution once and for all, and cleared the way for
the moral constitution to follow. The Thirteenth Amendment formal-
ized the new constitutional order by excluding slavery. The breaking
of the Constitution—by the war, by the suspension of civil liberties
that followed, and finally by emancipation—now took on the dimen-
sions of transcendent moral justice. All had been necessary, not so
much in the legal-constitutional sense of being required to win the
war, but in the cosmic sense of necessity that Lincoln now posited. It
was necessary for the Constitution to be broken so that the covenant
on which the United States was based could become moral.

Lincoln's grand and bold recasting of the meaning of his own and
the nation's constitutional trajectory marked the final step in his evolution as a constitutional thinker of the first order. He had begun, in his
Lyceum address in 1838, by embracing the received compromise Constitution as a binding legal agreement deserving "reverence" only insofar as it was based solely on "reason, cold, calculating, unimpassioned
reason." He had maintained that pragmatic, non-moral conception of
the Constitution through his election to the presidency, always insisting on the value of preserving the union, even at the cost of maintaining the constitutional guarantees that protected slavery.

In the wake of secession, Lincoln deemed that the compromise
Constitution had been broken by the South. That led him into the
delicate and complex position he took again and again over the next
several years: He himself broke the Constitution as he had previously
understood it while simultaneously insisting that his actions were justified by a necessity that inhered in the Constitution itself. Going to
war to coerce the wayward states to return broke the principle of the
consent of the governed; Lincoln justified it by the necessary nature

of majoritarian constitutional government. Suspending habeas corpus unilaterally broke the Constitution's commitment to civil liberty; Lincoln justified it by combining a literal reading of the suspension clause with the wildly expansive claim that he had to suppress free speech to save the union. Emancipation made Lincoln a dictator by what had been his own lights even after the war began; Lincoln justified it as a war measure that by necessity must be permitted to the commander in chief.

These claims made by Lincoln pressured, stressed, and ultimately broke his old idea of the Constitution as a kind of law based on cold reason. His powerful arguments from necessity, made over the course of the war, constantly raised and raised again the question of what made the constitutional union itself necessary in the deepest sense. Lincoln's political theology of the nation provided, at the very last, an answer. The Constitution and the nation could be re-formed so that their basis was no longer "unimpassioned reason" but moral truth achieved through the very essence of passion itself—the passion of the soldiers who had died, Christ-like, to atone for the sin of slavery. The new nation that would emerge would embody this morality, a morality of equality and justice. Its new Constitution would not be a compromise with injustice, but the embodiment of a higher, moral law.

Lincoln's political theology of the United States thus prefigured and required what came next: the moralizing of the Constitution through the adoption of constitutional amendments that would go beyond the abolition of slavery and guarantee equality and political participation for all. Lincoln hinted as much in his last public address, on April 11, 1865, when he spoke of extending the franchise "now" to some freed African Americans in Louisiana.[135] The Fourteenth Amendment, formulated in 1866 and ratified in 1868, overturned the *Dred Scott* decision and guaranteed to all Americans the "equal protection of the laws." The Fifteenth Amendment, proposed in 1869 and ratified in 1870, extended the right to vote to African American men, albeit not to women. Together, the three "Reconstruction amendments," as they are still called, amounted to the promise of a new, moral constitutional order, one that reconstructed the entire Constitution in the image Lincoln had created by emancipation.

As if to underscore the Christian imagination on which Lincoln had drawn, he himself became the literal martyr of the broken Constitution, the war, and the new moral Constitution he heralded. He was shot on April 14, 1865, less than a week after the Confederate surrender at Appomattox. By invoking the Latin adage "Sic semper tyrannis," his assassin, John Wilkes Booth, condemned Lincoln in language drawn straight from the critique of the president as a dictator who had broken the norms of the Constitution.

Lincoln died the next day. Every American schoolchild once was taught that at Lincoln's deathbed, Secretary of War Edwin Stanton said, "Now he belongs to the ages." Contemporary historical investigation indicates that Stanton probably said, "Now he belongs to the angels."[136] The confusion between secular and religious imagery and language is fitting, because Lincoln himself had consciously conflated the two in his great summing up of the ultimate meaning of the war, and of his role in it. The ages would indeed embrace the idea of Lincoln as a liberator, forgetting that he had to break the old Constitution to accomplish emancipation. Put in the terms of Lincoln's own political theology, the angels could easily be understood as the messengers who carried with them the truth of the new, moral Constitution that followed from breaking the original Constitution of slavery.

CONCLUSION

The Betrayal and Redemption of the Moral Constitution

BETRAYAL

Nothing could be neater than to end the story of Lincoln and the broken, compromise Constitution with the triumph of the moral Constitution that replaced it. The Thirteenth, Fourteenth, and Fifteenth amendments inaugurated a new era in U.S. constitutional history, one that continues to this day. The idea that the Constitution stands for a moral vision of liberty and equality has become so entrenched in our thinking that we can hardly conceive of the Constitution without it. One of the main reasons I wrote this book was to recover the reality of the compromise Constitution based on slavery—and to show how complicated, contradictory, and fraught it was for Lincoln and the nation to overcome that Constitution and remake it.

The only trouble with ending on the high note of the moral Constitution is that doing so might give the mistaken impression that Lincoln's moral vision for the Constitution was fully accomplished after his death. Nothing could be further from the truth. The moral Constitution was drafted and ratified. But within just a little bit more than a decade, that vision was betrayed. The reasons for the betrayal take us back to the old compromise Constitution that had in principle been repudiated. And the story of what happened next—at least, to the moral Constitution—turns out to be a harrowing, dramatic story of its own, one that deserves a separate book.

The betrayal I have in mind begins with the ultimate failure of the political and social experiment known as Reconstruction, which began shortly after Lincoln's death and ended, by most accounts, in 1877. There is an enormous body of historical literature about Reconstruction, and I will not even try to summarize it here. It is enough to say that, in its most radical form, as promoted and encouraged by committed northern Republicans, Reconstruction was intended to empower African Americans in the South, give them a proportionate share in political and economic life, and remake Southern society to achieve these goals. Reconstruction was at once a military occupation designed to enforce political reform and an active, noble effort by African Americans to embrace new rights to pursue equality and empowerment.

Many, probably most, Southern whites resisted Reconstruction from the start. That resistance was sometimes violent, as in the form of the insurgent paramilitary group known as the Ku Klux Klan. Southern whites eventually found ways to keep newly freed Black people disempowered economically, through sharecropping; socially, through segregation; and politically, through blocking or reversing enfranchisement.

Reconstruction also faced political challenges in Washington. Andrew Johnson, Lincoln's second vice president, was a Southern unionist from Tennessee, deeply antagonistic to the radical Republicans who were pushing Reconstruction in Congress. He vetoed the Civil Rights Act in 1865 and again in 1866. The law passed the second time over his veto—the first time a veto was overridden in the history of the United States. Johnson's impeachment in 1868 largely reflected congressional Republicans' firm belief that he was subverting the constitutional order by refusing to execute the Reconstruction laws they had passed.

Ulysses S. Grant, who became president in 1869, took Reconstruction more seriously, and opposed white Southern pushback. The Civil

Rights Act of 1871, also known as the KKK Act, the Force Act, or the Third Enforcement Act, authorized the use of federal troops to enforce equality and permitted the suspension of habeas corpus. Relying on the act, Grant deployed federal troops, declared martial law in nine South Carolina counties, and arrested thousands of suspected Klan members, some of whom were tried in federal court.

Gradually, however, Northern will to support Reconstruction faded, especially after the panic of 1873 and the subsequent economic depression. Republicans lost the House of Representatives in 1875. The disputed 1876 election provided an occasion to end the undertaking. Democrat Samuel Tilden of New York won almost 51 percent of the popular vote, and 184 electoral votes. Republican Rutherford B. Hayes of Ohio won just under 48 percent of the popular vote. In the first count of votes in the electoral college, Hayes had 165 electoral votes—but 20 more votes were contested. A special electoral commission was formed to decide what to do. What followed came to be called the Compromise of 1877. The commission awarded all 20 disputed votes to the Republican Hayes, giving him the election by a single electoral vote. In exchange for the presidency, Republicans in Congress agreed to stand down from the Reconstruction effort.[1] The very name "Compromise of 1877" ought to give the reader a sinking feeling, and an indication of what was happening: white Northerners were, once again, compromising with white Southerners over the subjugation of African Americans. In place of authorizing slavery, the way the antebellum constitutional compromises had done, the new postwar compromise effectively sold out African Americans' rights under the Reconstruction amendments. By ending Reconstruction, the North was implicitly agreeing to legalized segregation and the systematic disenfranchisement of African Americans. No wonder the Compromise of 1877 was also called the "Great Betrayal."

The Supreme Court treated this compromise as effectively permitted by the Constitution. In 1883, in a set of decisions known as the

Civil Rights Cases, the court held that Congress lacked the power to prohibit racial segregation by private actors. In 1896, the justices went further. In the notorious case of *Plessy v. Ferguson*, the court held that state-mandated racial segregation was constitutional, because separation was perfectly consistent with equality.

The separate-but-equal doctrine announced in the *Plessy* case may have been even worse than the holding in the *Dred Scott* case that African Americans could never be citizens. Chief Justice Taney's choice to interpret the Constitution as inherently racist was at least plausibly consistent with beliefs held by many of the founders. To interpret the Fourteenth Amendment as allowing state-mandated racial subordination betrayed the objectives of the Republicans who had drafted that amendment and forced the South to ratify it as a condition of being represented once more in Congress.

It is hard to overstate the degree to which these developments betrayed the moral Constitution. Together, the Compromise of 1877 and the Supreme Court decisions upholding systematic segregation and disenfranchisement relegated African Americans to a status that was in many places little better than slavery. If this was not a complete reversal of Lincoln's act of emancipation, it came remarkably close.

To understand why the betrayal happened, it is helpful to take seriously the warnings that Lincoln heard, and overrode, in the run-up to his decision to go to war. Skeptics like General Winfield Scott, his highest-ranking commander, told Lincoln that if he succeeded in coercing the seceding states to return to the Union, he would then face the nearly impossible challenge of forcing them to remain under the remit of federal law. Lincoln, for his part, insisted that constitutional government could survive in the long run only if the federal government had the capacity to coerce dissenting minority states.

On one level, the war would seem to have proved Lincoln right. After all, the Union did in fact ultimately coerce the Confederacy back to the Union. Yet on another level, Scott was right that the only way to elicit fealty from white Southerners after the war was by continued coercion. Once the Northern appetite to maintain that coercion faded, the only option remaining to Northern whites was to effect a compromise with Southern whites. The compromise entailed Northern whites agreeing to the subordination of African Americans—as they had done in earlier compromises in the past, only this time without the word "slavery" attached.

The postwar betrayal of the moral Constitution therefore grew out of conditions of racial subordination—just as the compromise Constitution had in the first place. National expansion was no longer the raison d'être of the union, since the United States had already expanded to exert control over the entirety of its territory between the Atlantic and the Pacific. The postwar compromise over race resulted simply from Northern exhaustion—and from the profound weakness of any truly racially egalitarian sentiment among Northern whites.

Here, too, Lincoln's actions and beliefs help provide an explanation. Lincoln himself never embraced the idea of Black racial equality, either publicly or privately. He assumed the continued social subordination of African Americans. In fact, it was precisely Lincoln's expectation that whites would never allow Blacks to live as equals in North America that fueled his longtime commitment to colonization schemes that would send freed African Americans out of the country forever. True, Lincoln stopped publicly advocating for colonization after he announced emancipation. But he had no concrete alternative ideas for how to achieve racial integration.

Lincoln's expectation of permanent or quasi-permanent Black social inequality therefore helps reveal why white Northerners were prepared to acquiesce in the re-subordination of Southern Blacks as soon as the energy of Reconstruction ran out. Northern whites had embraced the ideal of abolition over the course of the Civil War. Slavery, they agreed, was morally wrong. But they did not embrace the ideal of genuine racial equality, even if equality before the law was officially codified in the Constitution. They were thus perfectly willing to accept a new compromise, one that sold out the moral ideals of equality and restricted "liberty" to the principle that slavery was formally outlawed.

To make matters worse, the Supreme Court drew on antislavery traditions and achievements to adapt an entirely different moral vision of the Constitution. The Northern ideal of "free labor," originally conceived in opposition to the labor of slaves, evolved into a guarantee of freedom to labor as one wished—which meant the court lacked the authority to regulate labor contracts. The *Lochner* decision of 1905 cited the Fourteenth Amendment to strike down a New York state law that limited bakers to working ten hours a day and sixty hours a week for health reasons. According to the turn of the century court, the morality of the Constitution lay not in racial equality, but in economic liberty.

The betrayal of the Reconstruction amendments' guarantees of equality and political participation for African Americans lasted through two world wars and into the Cold War. Not until 1954 would the Supreme Court repudiate the separate-but-equal doctrine. Even after that, it would take the civil rights movement for African Americans to demand and ultimately achieve legal reforms that sought to restore equality and political participation—the Civil Rights Act of 1964 and the Voting Rights Act of 1965.

THE MORAL CONSTITUTION REDEEMED?

The redemption of the promise of the moral Constitution began slowly. Its most visible early signs came in litigation brought to the U.S. Supreme Court by the National Association for the Advancement of Colored People starting in the 1940s. Those cases, which made Thurgood Marshall famous, gradually and at first indirectly proposed the argument that the Fourteenth Amendment must be read to require genuine racial equality. In *Brown v. Board of Education*, Marshall brought this claim to the forefront. It took nearly two years and a change in chief justices for the court to announce that racial segregation was inherently unequal. But when the court in fact did so, unanimously reversing *Plessy v. Ferguson* in the spring of 1954, it marked a crucial watershed in the redemption of the promise of a moral Constitution devoted to equality.

The massive white Southern resistance that followed demonstrated that the courts alone could not redeem the moral Constitution. In the aftermath of the *Brown* decision, the modern civil rights movement was born. Its story—of bus boycotts, marches, and nonviolence in the face of continuing white Southern aggression—has become itself part of American constitutional discourse and legend. African Americans themselves took the lead in demanding the rights guaranteed them by the Constitution. Those rights were therefore not "given" by Northern white liberals, but grasped by the very people to whom they belonged.

Martin Luther King, Jr., emerged as the central figure in the public argument for the morality of the Constitution. His letter from the Birmingham jail is the closest thing to a modern addition to the constitutional canon—a state paper by a man who was not a state actor, but was actually imprisoned by the state. In the letter, King famously made the case that morality was superior to human law. "Thus it is," he wrote, "that I can urge men to obey the 1954 decision of the Supreme Court, for it is morally right; and I can urge them to disobey segregation ordinances, for they are morally wrong." Yet it is important to observe that King wrote on the assumption that the Constitution incorporated the morally correct value of equality. The rights due to African Americans were, he wrote, "constitutional and God given."[2]

King's insistence on morality led him to embrace and re-inscribe Lincoln's legacy as the maker of the moral Constitution. The iconic moment of King's career came in front of the Lincoln Memorial, where he delivered his "I Have a Dream" speech at the 1963 March on Washington. The Lincoln Memorial was itself designed as a secular temple in which Lincoln was enshrined as a god and the words of the Gettysburg Address and the second inaugural were inscribed on the walls as holy writ. Appearing before Lincoln, King embodied the fulfillment of a second stage of Lincoln's political theology.

This second episode fit as neatly into Protestant tradition as did Lincoln's own first attempt to offer a political theology of slavery, war, and emancipation. According to the beliefs of the Protestant Reformation, even after Christ's coming, the Church gradually fell into sin and error. The institutional Roman Catholic Church, according to the sixteenth-century reformers, had betrayed the teachings of the true Christ. The church then went into a period of "Babylonian captivity"— sinful exile from its deepest values and teachings.

The falling away of the church from the teachings of Christ corresponded remarkably with the betrayal of the moral Constitution in the decades between the end of Reconstruction and the rise of the civil rights movement. Lincoln's new birth of freedom had been betrayed. The solution to such a betrayal, according to Protestant reformers, was to go back to the core teachings of the Christian faith, recover their essence, and redeem the true meaning of the Bible. This was precisely what the civil rights movement proposed to do for the legacy of the moral Constitution. It must be redeemed by going back to its true meaning— and recovering Lincoln's legacy from the betrayal it had undergone.

It is one of the strange and fascinating confluences of history that the leader who did the most to bring about this American Reformation shared the name "Martin Luther" with the most important and influential figure in the Protestant Reformation.[3] King paralleled Lincoln in embodying individually the role of liberator. His "I've Been to the Mountaintop" speech made the comparison to the biblical Moses explicit. And King's assassination in April 1968, almost exactly 103 years after Lincoln's—and a day after he gave the most famous rendition of his mountaintop speech—cemented his place as the second saint and martyr of the moral Constitution.

The civil religion of the United States eventually came to incorporate King. Martin Luther King Day was intended to recognize the centrality of King's role in recalling the wayward country to the morality of the new birth of freedom. In a perfect world, King's objectives would have been wholly fulfilled, and the moral Constitution would today be treated as the guarantor of equality, liberty, and enfranchisement for all Americans.

But our fallen world is not the perfect world of the millennium. True, the ideal of the moral Constitution—embodying equality and liberty—has not been overtly abandoned in the United States by any major political movement in the half century since King's death. The moral Constitution has even won some notable victories. The marriage equality decision of 2015, *Obergefell v. Hodges*, represented a conjunction of equality and liberty. In the eyes of many Americans, the decision exemplified the continuing power of the moral Constitution to expand equality and freedom. King's legacy of the moral Constitution has not been formally betrayed in the way Lincoln's was.

Yet persistent inequality still exists in the United States, including inequality before the law, of the kind the moral Constitution prohibits. The reality is that the moral Constitution, like all constitutions, is not an end state but a promise of ongoing effort. Through the Constitution, we define our national project. But we never fully achieve it. Lincoln's legacy, then, is not the accomplishment of a genuinely moral Constitution. It is the breaking of the compromise Constitution—and the hope and promise of a moral Constitution that will always be in the process of being redeemed.

NOTES

Introduction

1. Quoted in Doris Kearns Goodwin, *Team of Rivals: The Political Genius of Abraham Lincoln* (New York: Simon & Schuster, 2005), 499.
2. Abraham Lincoln, "First Inaugural Address—Final Text," March 4, 1861, in *The Collected Works of Abraham Lincoln*, 9 vols., ed. Roy P. Basler (New Brunswick, N.J.: Rutgers University Press, 1953) (hereafter *CW*), 4:271.
3. Abraham Lincoln, "Gettysburg Address—Final Text," November 19, 1863, in *CW*, 7:23.
4. Abraham Lincoln, "Second Inaugural Address," March 4, 1865, in *CW*, 8:332.
5. See James Oakes, "The Great Divide," *The New York Review of Books*, May 23, 2019, 31. For an excellent review of broader trends in historical scholarship, see Michael E. Woods, "What Twenty-First-Century Historians Have Said About the Causes of Disunion: A Civil War Sesquicentennial Review of the Recent Literature," *Journal of American History* 99 (September 2012): 415–39.
6. Sometimes this hope was fueled by the idea that if Congress were to surround the Southern states with a "cordon" of freedom, then "slavery, like a scorpion, would sting itself to death." The words are those attributed to Thaddeus Stevens, Republican of Pennsylvania. See James Oakes, *The Scorpion's Sting: Antislavery and the Coming of the Civil War* (New York: W. W. Norton, 2014), 24.

1. The Compromise Constitution

1. Noah Feldman, *The Three Lives of James Madison: Genius, Partisan, President* (New York: Penguin Random House, 2017), 52.
2. Sven Beckert, *Empire of Cotton: A Global History* (New York: Vintage Books, 2014), 102–10.
3. Ibid., 103.
4. Ibid., 104.
5. Ibid., 106.
6. Ibid., 105–106.
7. Article 13, section 1, of the Indiana Constitution of 1851 said, "No negro or mulatto shall come into or settle in the State, after the adoption of this Constitution." The so-called Illinois Black Code or Black Law of 1853 was officially entitled "an act to prevent the immigration of free Negroes into this state."

8. Richard Campanella, *Lincoln in New Orleans: The 1828–1831 Flatboat Voyages and Their Place in History* (Lafayette: University of Louisiana at Lafayette Press, 2010), 59, 59n80.

9. Ibid., 61–62.

10. Ibid., 63–64.

11. Abraham Lincoln, "Speech at Chicago, Illinois," July 10, 1858, in *CW*, 2:492; Abraham Lincoln to Albert G. Hodges, April 4, 1864, in *CW*, 7:281; Douglas L. Wilson and Rodney O. Davis, ed., *Herndon's Informants: Letters, Interviews, and Statements about Abraham Lincoln* (Urbana: University of Illinois Press, 1998), 429. See also James Oakes, *The Radical and the Republican* (New York: W. W. Norton, 2007), 41–42.

12. On this aspect of the passage, see Joshua Wolf Schenk, *Lincoln's Melancholy* (Boston: Houghton Mifflin, 2006).

13. Abraham Lincoln to Mary Speed, September 27, 1841, in *CW*, 1:260.

14. Abraham Lincoln to Joshua F. Speed, August 24, 1855, in *CW*, 2:320.

15. Ibid.

16. Abraham Lincoln, "Autobiography Written for John L. Scripps," c. June 1860, in *CW*, 4:62. See also Campanella, *Lincoln in New Orleans*, 76–82.

17. Campanella, *Lincoln in New Orleans*, 210, citing William H. Herndon and Jesse William Weik, *Herndon's Lincoln: The True Story of a Great Life* (Chicago: Belford-Clarke, 1890), 1:76.

18. Lincoln, "Autobiography Written for John L. Scripps," in *CW*, 4:64; Campanella, *Lincoln in New Orleans*, 211–12.

19. Abraham Lincoln to Jesse W. Fell, enclosing autobiography, December 20, 1859, in *CW*, 3:512.

20. Scott D. Dyar, "Stillman's Run: Militia's Foulest Hour," *Military History* (2006), 38–44, 72.

21. See Noah Brooks, "Personal Reminiscences of Lincoln," *The Century Magazine*, 1878, reprinted in Francis Parkman, ed., *A Library of American Literature: From the Earliest Settlement to the Present Time*, vol. VIII (New York: Charles L. Webster & Co., 1892), 483; Francis F. Browne, *The Every-Day Life of Abraham Lincoln* (Lincoln: University of Nebraska Press, 1995 [1886]), 107; see also Christopher W. Anderson, "Native Americans and the Origin of Abraham Lincoln's Views on Race," *Journal of the Abraham Lincoln Association*, 37, no. 1 (Winter 2016), 11, 21. For the likelihood that Lincoln was referring to Stillman's Run, not a later battle at Kellogg's Grove, see The Lincoln Log: A Daily Chronology of the Life of Abraham Lincoln, entry for May 15, 1832, www.thelincolnlog.org/.

22. Abraham Lincoln, "Speech in the U.S. House of Representatives on the Presidential Question," July 27, 1848, in *CW*, 1:509–10.

23. Don E. Fehrenbacher and Virginia Fehrenbacher, eds., *Recollected Words of Abraham Lincoln* (Stanford, Calif.: Stanford University Press, 1996), 363.

24. Wilson and Davis, *Herndon's Informants*, 18–19.

25. Abraham Lincoln, "Communication to the People of Sangamo County," March 9, 1832, in *CW*, 1:8–9.

26. "New York Ratifying Convention. Remarks (Francis Childs's Version), [20 June 1788]," Founders Online, National Archives, founders.archives.gov/documents /Hamilton/01-05-02-0012-0005. Original source: *The Papers of Alexander Hamilton*, vol. 5, *June 1788–November 1789*, ed. Harold C. Syrett (New York: Columbia University Press, 1962), 16–26.

27. Sean Wilentz, *The Rise of American Democracy* (New York: W. W. Norton, 2005), 225–27.

28. Ibid., 230.
29. John Quincy Adams, diary entry, March 3, 1820, in *John Quincy Adams and the Politics of Slavery: Selections from the Diary*, ed. David Waldstreicher and Mathew Mason eds. (New York: Oxford University Press, 2017), 77. See also the transcript at classroom.monticello.org/view/74055/. Adams was serving as Monroe's secretary of state, and he supported the Missouri Compromise. Yet after a long conversation with John C. Calhoun in the aftermath of the deal, he noted his feeling "that the bargain between Freedom and Slavery contained in the Constitution of the United States, is morally and politically vicious."
30. That said, the lower courts upheld the law. The Supreme Court justice James Iredell, riding circuit, wrote an important opinion explaining that the First Amendment did nothing more than prohibit prior restraints—effectively, advance censorship—and had no application to punishment of speech after the fact. See James Iredell, Charge to the Grand Jury, in case of *Fries*, 9 Fed. Cas. 829, no. 5, 126 C.CD.Pa. 1799. For Madison's rejoinder, see Feldman, *Three Lives of James Madison*, 429–30.
31. The idea that the union was not of intrinsic value, but existed to serve the greater goal of liberty, could be traced back to the framers. Madison and other early nationalists, such as Hamilton, had sought to reform the Articles of Confederation so that the states would be able to remain united and act together effectively. Disunion, they believed, would threaten their "liberty"—by which they primarily meant their independence. If the states could not maintain the union, they would become vulnerable to takeover by Britain or other neighboring imperial powers. During the constitutional convention of 1787, the delegates repeatedly told one another that if they failed, the union would likely fail as well. When they managed to reach consensus, the preamble to the Constitution they drafted began with a clear statement of its aim: to form a more perfect union. "More perfect" was not a grammatical error. By "perfect," the framers meant a union that was complete, the technical, legal sense of the term. The union as it existed under the Articles of Confederation was not complete. The union under the Constitution was to be more complete—more perfect—than what had come before.

 Once the Constitution was in place, and the United States no longer seemed likely to lose its independence, the justification for union gradually shifted. It remained customary to say that the union protected Americans' liberty. But "liberty" no longer referred mainly to independence from foreign powers. Increasingly, the liberty protected by the union was a more abstract ideal of free citizens participating in republican government. Writing during the War of 1812, which he strongly opposed, the Virginia congressman John Randolph of Roanoke told a correspondent that the union was to be valued only insofar as it was a "means of securing the safety, liberty, and welfare" of the republic. The union was "not itself an end to which these should be sacrificed." Randolph's ideas presaged those of Calhoun. See John Randolph to Josiah Quincy, January 29, 1814, in *Life of Josiah Quincy of Massachusetts*, ed. Edmund Quincy (Boston: Fields, Osgood, 1867), 349.
32. Daniel Webster, "The Reply to Hayne," 1830, in *The Great Speeches and Orations of Daniel Webster* (Boston: Little, Brown, 1891), 269.
33. "South Carolina Ordinance of Nullification, November 24, 1832," Avalon Project, avalon.law.yale.edu/19th_century/ordnull.asp.
34. Russell McClintock, *Lincoln and the Decision for War: The Northern Response to Secession* (Chapel Hill: University of North Carolina Press, 2008), 126–27.

35. Andrew Jackson, "Respecting the Nullifying Laws of South Carolina: Proclamation," December 10, 1832, in *The Statutes at Large and Treaties of the United States of America*, ed. George Minot and George P. Sanger (Boston: Little, Brown, 1859), 11:772.

36. Ibid.

37. Ibid., 774.

38. Ibid., 776.

39. Ibid., 778–79.

40. Ibid., 780.

41. Ibid., 781.

42. Ibid., 780.

43. On the Jackson-as-Caesar trope, see Edwin A. Miles, "The Whig Party and the Menace of Caesar," *Tennessee Historical Quarterly* 27, no. 4 (1968): 361–79. See also Jon Meacham, *American Lion: Andrew Jackson in the White House* (New York: Random House, 2008), 278.

44. William W. Freehling, *Becoming Lincoln* (Charlottesville: University of Virginia Press, 2018), 46.

45. Quoted in Eric Foner, *The Fiery Trial: Abraham Lincoln and American Slavery* (New York: W. W. Norton, 2011), 33–34.

46. Dan Stone and Abraham Lincoln, "Protest in Illinois Legislature on Slavery," March 3, 1837, in *CW*, 1:75.

47. American Anti-Slavery Society, *The Constitution of the American Anti-Slavery Society* (New York: American Anti-Slavery Society, 1838), 3.

48. See William M. Wiecek, *The Sources of Antislavery Constitutionalism in America, 1760–1848* (Ithaca, N.Y.: Cornell University Press, 1977), 169.

49. William Lloyd Garrison, "On the Constitution and the Union," *The Liberator*, December 29, 1832.

50. American Anti-Slavery Society, *Declaration of Sentiments* (New York: American Anti-Slavery Society, 1833), 2. See also Wiecek, *Sources of Antislavery Constitutionalism in America*, 170.

51. Stone and Lincoln, "Protest in Illinois Legislature on Slavery," in *CW*, 1:75n2.

52. Ibid., 1:75.

53. Ibid., 1:75n2.

54. Ibid., 1:75.

55. Ibid., 1:75n2.

56. Martin Van Buren, "Inaugural Address," March 4, 1837, https://millercenter.org/the-presidency/presidential-speeches/march-4-1837-inaugural-address.

57. Ibid.

58. Abraham Lincoln, "Address Before the Young Men's Lyceum of Springfield, Illinois," January 27, 1838, in *CW*, 1:108.

59. Foner, *Fiery Trial*, 27–29.

60. Lincoln, "Address Before the Young Men's Lyceum," in *CW*, 1:109.

61. Ibid., 1:111, 114.

62. Ibid., 1:115.

63. William Jay, *A View of the Action of the Federal Government in Behalf of Slavery* (New York: American Anti-Slavery Society, 1839), 21.

64. "Speech by Charles Lenox Remond Delivered at Marlboro Chapel, Boston, Massachusetts, May 29, 1844," in *Black Abolitionist Papers*, vol. 3, *The United States, 1830–1846*, ed. C. Peter Ripley (Chapel Hill: University of North Carolina Press, 1991), 442.

65. Ibid.

66. Ibid., 443–44.

67. *The Constitution a Pro-Slavery Compact; or, Extracts from the Madison Papers, &c.*, ed. Wendell Phillips (New York: American Anti-Slavery Society, 1845), v–vi, viii–ix.

68. William Lloyd Garrison, "Repeal of the Union," *The Liberator*, May 6, 1842, 71.

69. Matthew Mason, "Federalists, Abolitionists, and the Problem of Influence," *American 19th Century History* 10, no. 1 (February 2009): 6.

70. Quoted in Henry Mayer, *All on Fire: William Lloyd Garrison and the Abolition of Slavery* (New York: W. W. Norton, 1998), 444–45.

71. See, for example, comments of Dr. Hudson at the Cazenovia Anti-Slavery Convention, *National Anti-Slavery Standard*, March 18, 1847: "The history of this country proves the understanding of the Northern, Southern, Eastern, and Western states, that the Constitution was a slaveholding bargain . . . [N]ot until quite recently has any one understood the Constitution to be anything else but a slaveholding bargain."

72. Angelina Grimké, *Letters to Catherine [sic] E. Beecher in Reply to an Essay on Slavery and Abolitionism Addressed to A. E. Grimké* (Boston: Isaac Knapp, 1838), 9–10.

73. Angelina Grimké, *An Appeal to Women of the Nominally Free States* (Boston: Isaac Knapp, 1838), 8.

74. Thomas Cole, January 27, 1838, speech reported in "Annual Meeting of the Mass. A.S. Society," *The Liberator*, February 23, 1838, 30. Cole is described as "a colored citizen of Boston."

75. Ibid.

76. Ibid.

77. *Documentary History of the Ratification of the Constitution: Ratification of the Constitution by the States*, vol. 10, *Virginia* (Madison: State Historical Society of Wisconsin, 1990), 1338–39. See also "Slave Trade and Slaveholders' Rights," Founders Online, founders.archives.gov/documents/Madison/01-11-02-0091.

78. Madison slyly recounted the charge to the other Virginians at the ratifying convention. See *Documentary History of the Ratification of the Constitution*, 1339. On the original episode in Philadelphia, see Feldman, *Three Lives of James Madison*, 161–62.

79. See David Blight, *Frederick Douglass: Prophet of Freedom* (New York: Simon & Schuster, 2018), 191. On Gerrit Smith, see John Stauffer, *The Black Hearts of Men: Radical Abolitionists and the Transformation of Race* (Cambridge, Mass.: Harvard University Press, 2002), passim.

80. Lysander Spooner, *The Unconstitutionality of Slavery* (Boston: Bela Marsh, 1845), 20, reprinted in *The Collected Works of Lysander Spooner*, vol. 4, ed. Charles Shively (Weston, Mass.: M&S Press, 1971). For another tract in a similar vein, see Joel Tiffany, *A Treatise on the Unconstitutionality of American Slavery: Together with the Powers and Duties of the Federal Government in Relation to That Subject* (Cleveland: J. Calyer, 1849).

81. Spooner, *Unconstitutionality of Slavery*, 57.

82. See, for a range of digitized sources, Colored Conventions Project, "About the Colored Conventions," coloredconventions.org/about-conventions/, and University of Delaware: Colored Conventions Project, udspace.udel.edu/handle/19716/16733.

83. *Minutes of the State Convention of the Colored Citizens of Ohio Convened at Columbus Jan. 15th, 16th, 17th, and 18th, 1851* (Columbus: E. Glover 1851), 8.

84. Ibid., 9.
85. Ibid., 10.
86. Ibid.
87. Ibid.
88. Ibid.
89. Ibid., 11.
90. Ibid.
91. Frederick Douglass, "Oath to Support the Constitution," *The North Star*, April 5, 1850, 2. See also Blight, *Frederick Douglass*, 215.
92. Frederick Douglass, "Change of Opinion Announced," *The North Star*, May 15, 1861.
93. "Speech by Charles Lenox Remond Delivered at Marlboro Chapel," in *Black Abolitionist Papers*, 443.
94. Speech of Robert Purvis, *National Anti-Slavery Standard*, May 23, 1857. See also similar remarks by Purvis reported in the *National Slavery Standard*, December 26, 1857.
95. "Mr. Robert Purvis (Colored) Assails Washington," *Village Record*, October 30, 1860.
96. Howard Holman Bell, "A Survey of the Negro Convention Movement" (unpublished PhD diss., Northwestern University, 1953), 178–83; Shawn C. Comminey, "National Black Conventions and the Quest for African American Freedom and Progress, 1847–1867," *International Social Science Review* 91, no. 1 (2015): 1–18. On the feuds between Purvis and Douglass, see Ivy Melissa Klenetsky, "Robert Purvis, Black Abolitionist and Radical Feminist: The Career of An Egalitarian Elitist" (unpublished PhD diss., New York University, 2009), 163–72.
97. Lincoln, "Autobiography Written for John L. Scripps," in *CW*, 4:65.
98. Abraham Lincoln to Williamson Durley, October 3, 1845, in *CW*, 1:347.
99. Ibid., 1:348.
100. Ibid.

2. The Breaking Constitution

1. Lincoln, "Autobiography Written for John L. Scripps," in *CW*, 4:66.
2. Abraham Lincoln, "'Spot' Resolutions in the United States House of Representatives," December 22, 1847, in *CW*, 1:421.
3. Abraham Lincoln, "Speech in the United States House of Representatives: The War with Mexico," January 12, 1848, in *CW*, 1:432.
4. Ibid., 1:437.
5. Ibid., 1:438.
6. Ibid.
7. Ibid., 1:439.
8. Ibid.
9. Ibid., 1:442n9.
10. Ibid., 1:439.
11. Abraham Lincoln, "Speech in the U.S. House of Representatives on the Presidential Question," July 27, 1848, in *CW*, 1:505.
12. Ibid.
13. Ibid.
14. Abraham Lincoln, "Eulogy on Henry Clay," July 6, 1852, in *CW*, 2:129.
15. Ibid., 2:132.

16. Daniel Webster, Speech in the Senate, "The Constitution and the Union," March 7, 1850, www.senate.gov/artandhistory/history/resources/pdf/Webster 7th.pdf.

17. Ibid.

18. William H. Seward, Speech in the Senate, "Freedom in the New Territories," March 11, 1850, www.senate.gov/artandhistory/history/resources/pdf /SewardNewTerritories.pdf.

19. Abraham Lincoln, "Address before the Wisconsin State Agricultural Society, Milwaukee, Wisconsin," September 30, 1859, in *CW*, 3:471–82.

20. Arvarh E. Strickland, "The Illinois Background of Lincoln's Attitude Toward Slavery and the Negro," *Journal of the Illinois State Historical Society* 56, no. 3 (Autumn 1963): 474–94.

21. Abraham Lincoln, "Speech at Peoria, Illinois," October 16, 1854, in *CW*, 2:253–54.

22. Ibid., 2:255.

23. Ibid., 2:268.

24. Ibid.

25. Ibid., 2:269.

26. Ibid.

27. Ibid.

28. Ibid., 2:270.

29. Ibid., 2:272.

30. Ibid.

31. For contrasting views on the "lost speech," see Freehling, *Becoming Lincoln*, 186–88; Oakes, "The Great Divide," 32, 32n4; Elwill Crissey, *Lincoln's Lost Speech: The Pivot of His Career* (New York: Hawthorn Books, 1967). Freehling argues that the only words that matter were "SOUTHERN DISUNIONISTS, We won't go out of the Union, and you SHAN'T." In his view, this line captures the notion that Lincoln's aim was "saving the Union's majority rule from minority blackmail"—not any antislavery sentiment. Freehling, *Becoming Lincoln*, 187–88. Oakes, following Crissey, thinks a September 1896 reconstruction of the speech by Henry C. Whitney in *McClure's* magazine may be "plausible." In that version, Lincoln said he would "draw a cordon, so to speak, around the slave States, and the hateful institution, like a reptile poisoning itself, will perish by its own infamy." The reconstructed speech was much more an attack on the institution of slavery than otherwise may be found anywhere in Lincoln's writings.

32. Abraham Lincoln to Joshua F. Speed, August 24, 1855, in *CW*, 2:320.

33. Ibid.

34. Ibid., 2:322–23.

35. Ibid., 2:323.

36. Ibid.

37. Herndon and Weik, *Herndon's Lincoln*, 1:384.

38. Abraham Lincoln, "Speech at a Republican Banquet, Chicago, Illinois," December 10, 1856, in *CW*, 2:385.

39. On Taney's acts of manumission and provision, see Timothy S. Huebner, "Roger B. Taney and the Slavery Issue: Looking beyond—and before—*Dred Scott*," *Journal of American History* 97, no. 1 (June 2010): 17, 20. Huebner points out that Taney freed his slaves at a young age, did not sell them or profit from their sale, and did not purchase slaves subsequently.

40. James F. Simon, *Lincoln and Chief Justice Taney: Slavery, Secession, and the President's War Powers* (New York: Simon & Schuster, 2006), 16, 90.

41. *Dred Scott v. Sandford*, 60 U.S. 393, 410 (1857).
42. Ibid., 447.
43. Abraham Lincoln, "Speech at Springfield, Illinois," June 26, 1857, in *CW*, 2:401.
44. Ibid., 2:400–401.
45. Ibid., 2:401.
46. Ibid.
47. Ibid., 2:405–406.
48. Mark 3:25. See also Matthew 12:25. Sam Houston had used similar wording in a speech in 1850, saying, "For a Nation divided against itself cannot stand."
49. Abraham Lincoln, "'A House Divided': Speech at Springfield, Illinois," June 16, 1858, in *CW*, 2:461.
50. Ibid., 2:461–62.
51. Ibid., 2:467.
52. See, for example, the following quote from "Free-Soilism," *Washington Union*, November 17, 1857, 2, cited (unfavorably!) by Douglas in a Senate speech that was in turn quoted by Lincoln in the first Lincoln-Douglas debate:
    The constitution declares that the citizens of each State shall be entitled to all the privileges and immunities of citizens in the several States. Every citizen of one State coming to another has, therefore, a right to the protection of his person, and that property which is recognized as such by the Constitution of the United States, any law of a state to the contrary notwithstanding.
53. Abraham Lincoln, "Speech at Bloomington, Illinois," September 12, 1854, in *CW*, 2:230–31.
54. Lincoln, "'A House Divided,'" in *CW*, 2:467.
55. Abraham Lincoln, "First Debate with Stephen A. Douglas at Ottawa, Illinois," August 21, 1858, in *CW*, 3:16.
56. Abraham Lincoln, "Second Debate with Stephen A. Douglas at Freeport, Illinois," August 27, 1858, in *CW*, 3:41.
57. Abraham Lincoln, "Third Debate with Stephen A. Douglas at Jonesboro, Illinois," September 15, 1858, in *CW*, 3:131–32.
58. Lincoln, "Second Debate with Stephen A. Douglas," in *CW*, 3:42.
59. Ibid.
60. Abraham Lincoln, "Sixth Debate with Stephen A. Douglas at Quincy, Illinois," October 13, 1858, in *CW*, 3:255.
61. Ibid.
62. Stephen Douglas, ibid., 3:268.
63. Abraham Lincoln, "Seventh and Last Debate with Stephen A. Douglas at Alton, Illinois," October 15, 1858, in *CW*, 3:300.
64. Ibid., 3:303.
65. Ibid., 3:307–308.
66. Ibid., 3:315.
67. Abraham Lincoln, "Address at Cooper Institute, New York City," February 27, 1860, in *CW*, 3:530.
68. Ibid., 3:527.
69. Ibid., 3:535.
70. Ibid., 3:537.
71. Ibid., 3:538.
72. Ibid.
73. Ibid., 3:541.
74. Ibid., 3:547.

75. Ibid., 3:550.

76. Ibid.

77. Ibid.

78. See Matthew Karp, "The Mass Politics of Antislavery," *Catalyst* 3 (Summer 2019), 131–78; Matthew Karp, "The People's Revolution of 1856: Radical Populism, National Politics, and the Emergence of the Republican Party," *Journal of the Civil War Era* 9 (December 2019): 524–45.

79. James Oakes, *The Crooked Path to Abolition: Abraham Lincoln and the Antislavery Constitution* (New York: W. W. Norton, 2021), xxvii, xxiv (describing the change in author's views), 182–85 (arguing that secessionists' reading of Lincoln was based on a "real threat").

80. The most influential work here remains Eric Foner, *Free Soil, Free Labor, and Free Men: The Ideology of the Republican Party before the Civil War*, rev. ed. (New York: Oxford University Press, 1995), 11–72. For other economics-oriented explanations of Republicanism, see John Ashworth, *Slavery, Capitalism, and Politics in the Antebellum Republic*, vol. 2, *The Coming of the Civil War, 1850–1861* (Cambridge: Cambridge University Press, 2007), 173–303; Marc Egnal, *Clash of Extremes: The Economic Origins of the Civil War* (New York: Hill and Wang, 2009), 101–49, 205–57. See also Karp, "Mass Politics," n. 9.

81. Oakes, *The Scorpion's Sting*; compare Oakes, *The Crooked Path*, 184.

82. Lincoln, "Address at Cooper Institute," in *CW*, 3:550.

3. The Choice of War

1. "Congressional Serial Set," *Journal of the Congress of the Confederate States of America, 1861–1865* 1 (February 1904): 7–12, memory.loc.gov/cgi-bin/query/r?ammem/hlaw:@field(DOCID+@lit(cc0015)).

2. Jefferson Davis, "Jefferson Davis' First Inaugural Address, February 18, 1861," in *The Papers of Jefferson Davis* (Baton Rouge: Louisiana State University Press, 1971), 7:45–51, jeffersondavis.rice.edu/archives/documents/jefferson-davis-first-inaugural-address.

3. Constitution of the Confederate States, Preamble.

4. Alexander Hamilton Stephens, "Speech Delivered on the 21st of March, 1861, in Savannah, Known as 'The Corner Stone Speech,' Reported in the *Savannah Republican*," in *Alexander H. Stephens, in Public and Private: With Letters and Speeches, Before, During, and Since the War*, ed. Henry Cleveland (Philadelphia: National Publishing Company, 1886), 717–29.

5. Constitution of the Confederate States, art. I, § 9(4); art. IV, § 2(1); art. IV § 3(3).

6. Lincoln, "First Inaugural Address," in *CW*, 4:271.

7. Ibid., 4:263.

8. Georgia's declaration on the causes of secession even named Lincoln: "The party of Lincoln, called the Republican party, under its present name and organization, is of recent origin. It is admitted to be an anti-slavery party . . . By antislavery it is made a power in the state."

9. Lincoln, "First Inaugural Address," in *CW*, 4:270.

10. Ibid., 4:263.

11. Ibid., 4:263–64.

12. The passage is sometimes quoted as using the word "hypocritical," but that is an error. The draft text clearly says "hypercritical." See Harold Holzer, *Lincoln President-Elect: Abraham Lincoln and the Great Secession Winter 1860–1861* (New York: Simon & Schuster, 2008), 466.

13. Lincoln, "First Inaugural Address," in *CW*, 4:263–64.

14. "Confederate States of America—Declaration of the Immediate Causes Which Induce and Justify the Secession of South Carolina from the Federal Union," The Avalon Project, avalon.law.yale.edu/19th_century/csa_scarsec.asp.

15. Ibid.

16. Lincoln, "First Inaugural Address," in *CW*, 4:265.

17. Ibid.

18. Ibid., 4:264–65.

19. Ibid., 4:265.

20. The seceding states had mostly preferred not to say they were making a revolution. Davis, in his inaugural address, insisted that because state constitutions and bills of rights "recognize in the people the power to resume the authority delegated for the purposes of government," it was an "abuse of language" to call secession a revolution. But the argument was available to the Confederacy nonetheless. Stephens, Davis's vice president, argued explicitly in March that the creation of the Confederacy was "one of the greatest revolutions in the annals of the world," albeit a peaceful one "accomplished without the loss of a single drop of blood." Stephens, "Speech Delivered on the 21st of March, 1861, in Savannah, Known as 'The Corner Stone Speech.'"

21. Lincoln, "First Inaugural Address," in *CW*, 4:265.

22. James Buchanan, State of the Union address, December 3, 1860, Teaching American History, teachingamericanhistory.org/library/document/1860-state-of-the-union-address.

23. Ibid.

24. Ibid.

25. Ibid.

26. James Madison, "Debates in the Federal Convention of 1787," Teaching American History, teachingamericanhistory.org/resources/convention/debates/0531-2/.

27. James Buchanan, State of the Union address.

28. Ibid.

29. Lincoln, "First Inaugural Address," in *CW*, 4:263.

30. Ibid.

31. Ibid., 4:266.

32. Ibid.

33. Ibid., 4:271.

34. See Winfield Scott to James Buchanan, December 15, 1860, forwarded by Abraham Lincoln to Francis P. Blair, Sr., December 21, 1860, in *CW*, 4:158.

35. Ibid.

36. McClintock, *Lincoln and the Decision for War*, 194.

37. Winfield Scott to William Seward, March 3, 1861, in *The Works of James Buchanan: Comprising His Speeches, State Papers, and Private Correspondence*, ed. John Bassett Moore (Philadelphia: J. B. Lippincott, 1910), 11:300.

38. Ibid., 11:301.

39. McClintock, *Lincoln and the Decision for War*, 194.

40. Joseph Holt, "Letter to Lincoln with remarks by General Scott, March 5, 1861," in *Lincoln Papers*, Library of Congress, ww.loc.gov/resource/mal.0779200/?sp=1&st=text.

41. McClintock, *Lincoln and the Decision for War*, 121, 230.

42. General Winfield Scott, "General Scott's Memorandum for the Secretary of War," quoted in Samuel Wylie Crawford, *The History of the Fall of Fort Sumpter* [*sic*] (New York: F. P. Harper, 1896), 363.

43. Holt, "Letter to Lincoln with remarks by General Scott, March 5, 1861." See also Abraham Lincoln to Winfield Scott, March 9, 1861, in *CW*, 4:279.

44. Robert Anderson to S. Cooper, March 2, 1861; see McClintock, *Lincoln and the Decision for War*, 202n31.

45. Edward Bates, diary entry, March 9, 1861, in *The Diary of Edward Bates: 1859–1866*, ed. Howard K. Beale (New York: De Capo Press, 1971), 177, cited in McClintock, *Lincoln and the Decision for War*, 202n33.

46. "Important Statement by the Ex-Governor of Kentucky," *Mississippi Valley Historical Review* 28, no. 1 (June 1941): 7–71; McClintock, *Lincoln and the Decision for War*, 196.

47. McClintock, *Lincoln and the Decision for War*, 197.

48. Ibid., 214.

49. Ibid., 214n64.

50. Ibid., 215.

51. Ibid., 232–33.

52. Ibid., 233.

53. Ibid.; Glenna R. Schroeder-Lein, *Lincoln and Medicine* (Carbondale: Southern Illinois University Press, 2012), 18.

54. McClintock, *Lincoln and the Decision for War*, 237.

55. Abraham Lincoln to Robert S. Chew, April 6, 1861, in *CW*, 4:323.

56. Abraham Lincoln, "Reply to a Committee from the Virginia Convention," [April 13, 1861], in *CW*, 4:330–31.

57. Abraham Lincoln, "Proclamation Calling Militia and Convening Congress," April 15, 1861, in *CW*, 4:331–32.

58. Ibid.

59. Ibid., 4:332.

60. Jeremiah S. Black, "Power of the President in Executing the Laws," in *Official Opinions of the Attorneys General of the United States Advising the President and Heads of Departments in Relation to Their Official Duties* (Washington, D.C.: R. Farnham, 1869), 9:518.

61. Ibid., 9:522.

62. Ibid., 9:523.

63. John Witt, *Lincoln's Code: The Laws of War in American History* (New York: Free Press, 2013).

64. Lincoln, "Proclamation Calling Militia and Convening Congress," in *CW*, 4:332.

65. Ibid.

66. Abraham Lincoln, "Address to the New Jersey Senate at Trenton, New Jersey," February 21, 1861, in *CW*, 4:236. On the context for the speech, see Ted Widmer, *Lincoln on the Verge: Thirteen Days to Washington* (New York: Simon & Schuster, 2020), 364-72.

67. Lincoln, "First Inaugural Address," in *CW*, 4:267.

68. Ibid.

69. Ibid., 4:267–68.

70. *Journal of the Congress of the Confederate States of America, 1861–1865*, U.S. Serial Set, nos. 4610–16 (1904–1905) 1:873, 1:877.

71. Lincoln, "First Inaugural Address," in *CW*, 4:268.

72. Ibid.

73. Thomas Hobbes, *Leviathan*, Richard Tuck ed. (Cambridge: Cambridge University Press, 1996), 127. The context for Hobbes's statement was a forceful rejection of the separation of powers, which Hobbes blamed for the English Civil War.

74. Feldman, *Three Lives of James Madison*, 144–50.

75. Lincoln, "Proclamation Calling Militia and Convening Congress," in *CW*, 4:332.

76. Ibid.

77. Ibid.

78. James M. McPherson, *Battle Cry of Freedom: The Civil War Era* (New York: Oxford University Press, 2003), 279.

79. Abraham Lincoln, "Message to Congress in Special Session," July 4, 1861, in *CW*, 4:430–32.

80. Ibid., 4:439.

81. Ibid.

82. Ibid.

83. Ibid., 4:440.

84. Anna Ella Carroll, *The Great American Battle, or, The Contest between Christianity and Political Romanism* (New York: Miller, Orton & Mulligan, 1856).

85. Sarah Ellen Blackwell, *A Military Genius: Life of Anna Ella Carroll of Maryland* (Washington, D.C.: Judd & Detweiler, 1891).

86. Anna Ella Carroll, "Reply to the Speech of Hon. J.C. Breckinridge, delivered in the United States Senate, July 16th, 1861, September 9, 1861," in Sarah Ellen Blackwell, *Life and Writings of Anna Ella Carroll*, vol. 2, *Civil War Papers in Aid of the Administration, and Closing Years of a Noble Life* (Washington, D.C.: Judd & Detweiler, 1895), 33.

87. Ibid.

88. Lincoln, "Message to Congress in Special Session," *CW*, 4:440.

89. Ibid.

90. Ibid., 4:439–40.

91. Ibid., 4:440.

92. Seward Memorandum, April 1, 1861, in *CW*, 4:317n1. See also McClintock, *Lincoln and the Decision for War*, 236.

4. Political Prisoners

1. Abraham Lincoln to Winfield Scott, April 25, 1861, in *CW*, 4:344.

2. Ibid.

3. Ibid.

4. Francis Carpenter, "A Day with Governor Seward at Auburn, July 1870," *Seward Papers*, University of Rochester, Reel 196; William H. Seward Papers in Library of Congress, folder 6634. See also Brian McGinty, *Lincoln and the Court* (Cambridge, Mass.: Harvard University Press, 2008), 70, 325n15.

5. Abraham Lincoln to Winfield Scott, July 2, 1861, in *CW*, 4:419.

6. Benjamin Franklin Butler, *Private and Official Correspondence of Gen. Benjamin F. Butler: During the Period of Civil War* (Norwood, Mass.: Plimpton Press, 1917), 1:81.

7. Ibid., 1:84.

8. *Ex parte Merryman*, 17 F. Cas. 144 (C.C.D. Md. 1861).

9. George Cadwalader to Roger Taney, May 26, 1861, in *The War of the Rebellion: A Compilation of the Official Records of the Union and Confederate Armies*, series 2 (Washington, D.C.: Government Printing Office, 1880–1901), 1:576.

10. Brian McGinty, *The Body of John Merryman: Abraham Lincoln and the Suspension of Habeas Corpus* (Cambridge, Mass.: Harvard University Press, 2011), 28.

11. *The American Annual Cyclopædia and Register of Important Events of the Year 1861* (New York: D. Appleton, 1862), 356.

12. Quoted in McGinty, *The Body of John Merryman*, 30.

13. Quoted in Simon, *Lincoln and Chief Justice Taney*, 189. See also George William Brown, *Baltimore and the 19th of April 1861: A Study of the War* (Baltimore: Johns Hopkins University Press, 1887), 90.

14. McGinty, *Lincoln and the Court*, 76-77.

15. Samuel Tyler, *Memoir of Roger Brooke Taney* (Baltimore: J. Murphy & Co., 1872), 427.

16. "The Merryman Case.; Decision of Chief Justice Taney," *The New York Times*, June 4, 1861, www.nytimes.com/1861/06/04/archives/the-merryman -case-decision-of-chief-justice-taney.html.

17. *Ex parte Merryman*, 17 F. Cas. at 148.

18. "The Merryman Case," *The New York Times*.

19. Ibid.

20. Ibid.

21. Ibid.

22. Ibid.

23. Ibid.

24. Ibid.

25. Ibid.

26. Ibid.

27. Ibid.

28. Ibid.

29. Ibid.

30. Ibid.

31. Ibid.

32. Ibid.

33. Ibid.

34. Ibid.

35. Abraham Lincoln, "Memorandum: Military Arrests," [c. May 17, 1861], in *CW*, 4:372.

36. McGinty, *Body of John Merryman*, 105, 215n20.

37. Ibid., 105, 215n21.

38. Abraham Lincoln to Edward Bates, May 30, 1861, in *CW*, 4:390.

39. Johnson in fact published his views in the *National Intelligencer* on June 20. See Frank Moore, *The Record of the Rebellion* (New York: Putnam, 1861), 2:185. See also McGinty, *Body of John Merryman*, 107.

40. Lincoln, "Message to Congress in Special Session," in *CW*, 4:429.

41. Ibid., 4:429, 4:441n48. See also McGinty, *Body of John Merryman*, 99.

42. Lincoln, "Message to Congress in Special Session," in *CW*, 4:429.

43. Ibid., 4:429-30.

44. Ibid., 4:441n50. See also McGinty, *Body of John Merryman*, 99.

45. Lincoln, "Message to Congress in Special Session," in *CW*, 4:430.

46. Ibid.

47. Ibid.

48. Ibid.

49. Ibid., 4:430-31.

50. Anna Ella Carroll, "The War Powers of the General Government," in Blackwell, *Life of Anna Carroll*, 47. Carroll says she wrote the essay in the fall of 1861 and that it was in circulation in Washington, D.C., by December 1861.

51. Ibid., 78.

52. Ibid., 78–79.

53. Quoted in McGinty, *Body of John Merryman*, 117.

54. Edward Bates, the attorney general, had finally published a lengthy opinion on July 5 purporting to refute Taney's opinion. But the attorney general's opinion rested on a highly doubtful distinction. It purported to find a difference between a general suspension of the writ of habeas corpus, which it acknowledged that only Congress could do, and a refusal to certain individuals of the privilege of being released pursuant to the writ, which the attorney general insisted was within the president's power. The argument was insufficient to convince skeptical congressmen (or almost any lawyer since).

55. Quoted in McGinty, *Body of John Merryman*, 119.

56. See David B. Sachsman, ed., *A Press Divided: Newspaper Coverage of the Civil War* (New York: Routledge, 2014), 238–40.

57. Ibid.

58. F. K. Howard, *Fourteen Months in American Bastiles* (London: H. F. Mackintosh, 1863), 9.

59. On Carmichael, see Simon, *Lincoln and Chief Justice Taney*, 234–36.

60. Mark E. Neely, Jr., *The Fate of Liberty: Abraham Lincoln and Civil Liberties* (Oxford: Oxford University Press, 1992), 75. See also William C. Harris, *Lincoln and the Border States* (Lawrence: University Press of Kansas, 2014), 71–75.

61. Jonathan W. White, *Abraham Lincoln and Treason in the Civil War: The Trials of John Merryman* (Baton Rouge: Louisiana State University Press, 2011), 65–67.

62. "Important Order from Secretary Stanton," *The New York Times*, February 15, 1862, 5. See also William A. Blair, *With Malice Toward Some: Treason and Loyalty in the Civil War Era* (Chapel Hill: University of North Carolina Press, 2014), 55.

63. Abraham Lincoln, "Executive Order No. 1—Relating to Political Prisoners," The American Presidency Project, www.presidency.ucsb.edu/node/202458.

64. Abraham Lincoln, "Proclamation Suspending the Writ of Habeas Corpus," September 24, 1862, in *CW*, 5:437.

65. Ibid., 5:436.

66. Ibid., 5:437.

67. Harold Holzer, *Lincoln and the Power of the Press: The War for Public Opinion* (New York: Simon & Schuster, 2015), 337, 339, 343, 346.

68. *The American Annual Cyclopædia and Register of Important Events of the Year 1861*, 328–29; Holzer, *Lincoln and the Power of the Press*, 352–54.

69. Holzer, *Lincoln and the Power of the Press*, 345–46.

70. Robert S. Harper, *Lincoln and the Press* (New York: McGraw-Hill, 1951), 115.

71. *The American Annual Cyclopædia and Register of Important Events of the Year 1861*, 328.

72. Ibid., 328–29.

73. Holzer, *Lincoln and the Power of the Press*, 339–40, 625n15, 625n17.

74. Ibid., 338–39. Holzer lists W. W. Glenn, Francis Key Howard, Arunah Arbell, and Daniel Deckart; James McMaster was another.

75. Harper, *Lincoln and the Press*, 116; John T. McGreevy, *Catholicism and American Freedom: A History* (New York: W. W. Norton, 2004), 68.

76. "Political Prisoners," *The New York Times*, September 24, 1861, 1.

77. Holzer, *Lincoln and the Power of the Press*, 358.

78. Bruce Ragsdale, "The Sedition Act Trials," Federal Judicial Center, 2015, www.fjc.gov/sites/default/files/trials/seditionacts.pdf.

79. Holzer, *Lincoln and the Power of the Press*, 356.

80. Ibid., 357.

81. Si Sheppard, *The Partisan Press: A History of Media Bias in the United States* (Jefferson, N.C.: McFarland, 2007), 159–60.

82. Holzer, *Lincoln and the Power of the Press*, 422.

83. Sheppard, *Partisan Press*, 159–60.

84. Ibid., 159.

85. Dennis A. Mahony, *The Prisoner of the State* (New York: Carleton, 1863), 6.

86. *The American Annual Cyclopædia and Register of Important Events of the Year 1862* (New York: D. Appleton, 1863), 480.

87. Holzer, *Lincoln and the Power of the Press*, 373, 631n121.

88. Ibid., 366–67.

89. Ibid., 357.

90. Ibid., 336.

91. Abraham Lincoln, "Proclamation Suspending Writ of Habeas Corpus," July 5, 1864, in *CW*, 7:425.

92. David W. Bulla, *Lincoln's Censor: Milo Hascall and Freedom of the Press in Civil War Indiana* (West Lafayette, Ind.: Purdue University Press, 2009); Edwin M. Stanton to Major General A. E. Burnside, June 1, 1863, in "War of the Rebellion: Official Record of the Civil War," ehistory, The Ohio State University, ehistory.osu.edu/books/official-records/118/0724.

93. *The American Annual Cyclopædia and Register of Important Events of the Year 1864* (New York: D. Appleton, 1865), 423. At the same time, Burnside also closed the *Jonesboro Gazette*. See Holzer, *Lincoln and the Power of the Press*, 425.

94. *Chicago Times*, September 24, 1862; see Harper, *Lincoln and the Press*, 259.

95. *Chicago Tribune*, June 4, 1863. See also Harper, *Lincoln and the Press*, 257.

96. *The American Annual Cyclopædia and Register of Important Events of the Year 1863* (New York: D. Appleton, 1864), 424.

97. Quoted in Craig D. Tenney, "To Suppress or Not to Suppress: Abraham Lincoln and the Chicago Times," *Civil War History* 27, no. 3 (1981): 255.

98. Bulla, *Lincoln's Censor*, 192, 192n54; Jeffrey A. Smith, *War and Press Freedom: The Problem of Prerogative Power* (Oxford: Oxford University Press, 1999), 116.

99. *The American Annual Cyclopædia and Register of Important Events of the Year 1863*, 424.

100. Ibid., 424.

101. Tenney, "To Suppress or Not to Suppress," 248, 256–57. See also Bulla, *Lincoln's Censor*, 192; Smith, *War and Press Freedom*, 116.

102. Stanton to Burnside, June 1, 1863.

103. Tenney, "To Suppress or Not to Suppress," 253.

104. Abraham Lincoln, "Proclamation Suspending Writ of Habeas Corpus," September 15, 1863 in *CW*, 6:451.

105. Ibid.

106. Ibid.

107. See, e.g., White, *Abraham Lincoln and Treason*, 76–77; see also James A. Dueholm, "Lincoln's Suspension of the Writ of Habeas Corpus: An Historical and Constitutional Analysis," *Journal of the Abraham Lincoln Association* 29, no. 2 (Summer 2008), 47–66, http://hdl.handle.net/2027/spo.2629860.0029.205 (citing John G. Nicolay and John Hay, *Abraham Lincoln* [New York: Century, 1904], 8:40).

108. Ibid.
109. Abraham Lincoln, "Proclamation 113—Declaring Martial Law and a Further Suspension of the Writ of Habeas Corpus in Kentucky, July 5, 1864," The American Presidency Project, www.presidency.ucsb.edu/documents/proclamation-113 -declaring-martial-law-and-further-suspension-the-writ-habeas-corpus.
110. Holzer, *Lincoln and the Power of the Press*, 490.
111. *The American Annual Cyclopædia and Register of Important Events of the Year 1864*, 389–94.
112. Holzer, *Lincoln and the Power of the Press*, 495–96.
113. *The American Annual Cyclopædia and Register of Important Events of the Year 1864*, 393–94.
114. Carl Schmitt, *Political Theology: Four Chapters on the Concept of Sovereignty* (Chicago: University of Chicago Press, 1985), 5. The famous first sentence of the book reads, "Sovereign is he who decides on the exception."
115. Carl Schmitt, *Dictatorship: From the Origin of the Modern Concept of Sovereignty to Proletarian Class Struggle* (London: Polity Press, 2014), 118.
116. Ibid., 119.
117. Clinton Rossiter, *Constitutional Dictatorship: Crisis Government in the Modern Democracies* (1948; repr. New Brunswick, N.J.: Transaction Publishers, 2002), 224.
118. Ibid., 230.
119. Ibid., 237.
120. The low estimate is that of Mark Neely, the modern historian who has done the most to explore the numbers. The high estimate appeared in *The American Annual Cyclopædia and Register of Important Events of the Year 1865* (New York: D. Appleton, 1866), 414, which in turn cited the Provost Marshal's office in Washington in reporting 38,000 prisoners arrested "without the benefit of the writ of habeas corpus" from June 1861 to January 1, 1866. As Neely notes, the *Cyclopædia* yearbook entry details how this number includes those housed at the Old Capital Prison, whose records reported "sixty-five hundred prisoners of war, forty-five hundred real and fancied offenders against the State, and twenty-five hundred deserters and bounty jumpers." Neely settles on his lower-bound estimate by relying on research by James Ford Rhodes, an important turn-of-the-twentieth-century Civil War historian. Rhodes, upon seeing the 38,000 number reported by Princeton historian Alexander Johnston, reportedly was in disbelief and called Colonel F. C. Ainsworth, head of the Record and Pensions Office of the War Department, to make a search of the files. The colonel's clerk uncovered records for some 13,535 civilian prisoners recorded by the commissary general of prisoners from February 1862 through the end of the war. It was this number that Rhodes put in his *History of the United States from the Compromise of 1850* (London: Macmillan, 1893, in three volumes), and this number "has been accepted by most historians ever since." Ultimately, Rhodes could not find any authority for the original number reported in the *Cyclopædia* yearbook upon which Johnston had relied and called it "really nothing but a guess." See Mark E. Neely, Jr., "The Lincoln Administration and Arbitrary Arrests: A Reconsideration," *Journal of the Abraham Lincoln Association* 5 (1983): 6–7.
    Neely notes that "no careful work" has been done on the numbers. He also points out that those historians who have attempted it have mostly done so in setting out to defend Lincoln. See Neely, *The Fate of Liberty*, 113. John A. Marshall's *American Bastille*, written in 1869, the leading anti-Lincoln work on

detentions in the era, suggested that "FORTS, PENITENTIARIES, JAILS, BARRACKS, and PRISON CAMPS . . . contained, during the short period of FOUR YEARS, as variously estimated, from TEN to TWENTY THOUSAND men, besides women and children, FREE citizens of FREE STATES." John A. Marshall, *American Bastille: A History of the Illegal Arrests and Imprisonment of American Citizens During the Late Civil War*, 22nd ed. (Philadelphia: Thomas W. Hartley, 1876), 753.

121. General Orders, No. 38 (Department of the Ohio), April 13, 1863, available at https://www.americanhistorycentral.com/entries/general-orders-no-38-depart ment-of-the-ohio.

122. *Ex parte Vallandigham*, 68 U.S. 243 (1863).

123. Abraham Lincoln to Erastus Corning and Others, June 12, 1863, in *CW*, 6:262.

124. Ibid., 6:260.

125. Ibid., 6:263.

126. Ibid.

127. Ibid., 6:264.

128. Ibid.

129. Ibid.

130. Ibid., 6:266.

131. Ibid., 6:266–67.

132. Ibid., 6:265.

133. Ibid.

134. Ibid., 6:265–66.

135. Ibid., 6:267.

136. Ibid.

137. The classic article is Werner Jaeger, "Aristotle's Use of Medicine as Model of Method in His Ethics," *Journal of Hellenic Studies* 77 (1957): 54–61.

138. Lincoln to Corning and Others, June 12, 1863, in *CW*, 6:267.

5. Emancipation and Morals

1. Witt, *Lincoln's Code*, 198.

2. *War of the Rebellion*, 3:467.

3. Lincoln to Frémont, September 3, 1861, in *CW*, 5:506.

4. John C. Frémont to Abraham Lincoln, September 8, 1861, in *CW*, 5:507n3.

5. Abraham Lincoln to Orville Browning, September 22, 1861, in *CW*, 5:531.

6. Ibid.

7. Oakes, *The Crooked Path*, 145, and more generally 143–54, calls this decision "the critical first step toward a policy of military emancipation." As Lincoln's letter to Browning suggests, the jump from non-return to eventual emancipation was by no means legally or logically necessary or inevitable.

8. Lincoln to Orville Browning, September 22, 1861, in *CW*, 5:531–32.

9. Ibid., 5:532.

10. Ibid.

11. Witt, *Lincoln's Code*, 70–71, 75–77, 198, 203–16.

12. Ibid., 204.

13. Carroll, "War Powers of the General Government," 64.

14. Ibid., 66.

15. Ibid., 67.

16. Thaddeus Stevens, January 22, 1862. "'Subduing the Rebellion,' January 22,

1862, in Congress," in *The Selected Papers of Thaddeus Stevens*, vol. 1, *April 1865– August 1868*, ed. Beverly Wilson Palmer and Holly Byers Ochoa (Pittsburgh: University of Pittsburgh Press, 1997), 246.

17. Frederick Douglass, "The Reasons for Our Troubles: Speech on the War Delivered in National Hall, Philadelphia, January 14, 1862," *Douglass' Monthly*, February 1862, rbscp.lib.rochester.edu/4381.

18. Seward Memorandum, April 1, 1861, in *CW*, 4:317n1. See also McClintock, *Lincoln and the Decision for War*, 236.

19. Foner, *Fiery Trial*, 189–95.

20. Ibid.

21. Abraham Lincoln, "Annual Message to Congress," December 3, 1861, in *CW*, 5:47–48.

22. First Confiscation Act, 12 Stat. 319 (1861).

23. See Abraham Lincoln, "Message to Congress," March 6 1862, in *CW*, 5:144–45.

24. "Landmark Legislation: The District of Columbia Compensated Emancipation Act," U.S. Senate, www.senate.gov/artandhistory/history/common /generic/DCEmancipationAct.htm; Daniel R. Goodloe, "Daniel Goodloe Tells the Story of Compensated Emancipation," *Evening Star*, December 8, 1894. (Goodloe chaired the compensated emancipation commission set up in D.C. after the law was passed.)

25. "An Act to secure Freedom to all Persons within the Territories of the United States," June 19, 1862, Thirty-Seventh Congress, session II, chap. 110–12, 116, 119 (Washington, D.C.: Library of Congress), www.loc.gov/law/help /statutes-at-large/37th-congress/session-2/c37s2ch111.pdf.

26. Foner, *Fiery Trial*, 204, reports that the 1860 census recorded fifteen slaves in Nebraska and twenty-nine in Utah. New Mexico abolished slavery in December 1861.

27. David Williams, *I Freed Myself: African American Self-Emancipation in the Civil War Era* (New York: Cambridge University Press, 2014).

28. For an account of how Lincoln allowed individual military commanders to adopt different policies, see Foner, *Fiery Trial*, 171–81; 206–15. Foner writes that by the summer of 1862, "a general rule was becoming more and more necessary." Ibid., 209.

29. Second Confiscation Act, 12 Stat. 589 (1862).

30. Foner, *Fiery Trial*, 215–16.

31. Frank A. Flower, *Edwin McMasters Stanton: The Autocrat of Rebellion, Emancipation, and Reconstruction* (New York: W. W. Wilson, 1905), 184–85.

32. Orville Browning, *The Diary of Orville Hickman Browning*, ed. Theodore Calvin Pease and James G. Randall (Springfield: Illinois State Historical Library, 1927), 1:558.

33. Foner, *Fiery Trial*, 213.

34. "Civil War: Confiscation Acts," The Lehrman Institute, www.mrlincoln andfreedom.org/civil-war/congressional-action-inaction/confiscation-acts.

35. Abraham Lincoln, "To the Senate and House of Representatives," July 17, 1862, in *CW*, 5:329.

36. Ibid.

37. Ibid.

38. Ibid., 5:330.

39. Ibid., 5:331.

40. Ibid., 5:531n3.

41. Foner, *Fiery Trial*, 217, 217n28; Gideon Welles, *Diary of Gideon Welles* (Boston: Houghton Mifflin, 1911), 1:70; Benjamin P. Thomas and Harold M. Hyman, *Stanton: The Life and Times of Lincoln's Secretary of War* (New York: Alfred A. Knopf, 1962), 175.

42. Fehrenbacher and Fehrenbacher, *Recollected Words of Abraham Lincoln*, 470.

43. Abraham Lincoln, "Emancipation Proclamation—First Draft," July 22, 1862, in *CW*, 5:336.

44. Ibid.

45. Ibid., 5:336-37.

46. Foner, *Fiery Trial*, 385n32; Francis Bicknell Carpenter, *Six Months at the White House with Abraham Lincoln: The Story of a Picture* (New York: Hurd and Houghton, 1866), 20-23.

47. Foner, *Fiery Trial*, 219.

48. Ibid.

49. Ibid., 223.

50. Kate Masur, "The African American Delegation to Abraham Lincoln: A Reappraisal," *Civil War History* 56, no. 2 (2010): 117, 126, 129-31.

51. Ibid.

52. Abraham Lincoln, "Address on Colonization to a Deputation of Negroes," August 14, 1862, in *CW*, 5:371.

53. Ibid., 5:371-72.

54. Ibid., 5:372.

55. Ibid.

56. Ibid.

57. Frederick Douglass, "The President and His Speeches," *Douglass' Monthly*, September 1862, 705-707.

58. Ibid., 705-707; Foner, *Fiery Trial*, 225, 225n48.

59. Douglass, "The President and His Speeches," 705-707.

60. Horace Greeley, "The Prayer of Twenty Millions," *New-York Tribune*, August 20, 1862.

61. Abraham Lincoln to Horace Greeley, August 22, 1862, in *CW*, 5:388.

62. Ibid.

63. Ibid., 5:389.

64. Abraham Lincoln, "Preliminary Emancipation Proclamation," September 22, 1862, in *CW*, 5:433-34.

65. Ibid., 5:434.

66. Ibid., 5:434-35.

67. Ibid., 5:434.

68. Emer de Vattel, the writer on the law of nations most cited by the founding generation in the United States, writing in the mid-eighteenth century, maintained that movable property could be seized by an occupying army but that real property in land could not be seized. He also maintained that property seized by an enemy must be returned to its original owners after the war if and when it was no longer in possession of the enemy. See Emer de Vattel, *The Law of Nations; or, Principles of the Law of Nature, Applied to the Conduct and Affairs of Nations and Sovereigns*, trans. Thomas Nugent (1758; repr. Indianapolis: Liberty Fund, 2008), 593-613.

69. Emer de Vattel cites Roman law to say that slaves can be recovered after the war. See de Vattel, *The Law of Nations*, 605-606.

70. Lincoln, "Preliminary Emancipation Proclamation," in *CW*, 5:436.

71. *Cincinnati Enquirer,* January 4, 1863. See also Michael Burlingame, *Abraham Lincoln: A Life* (Baltimore: Johns Hopkins University Press, 2008), 2:471, 2:471n483.

72. Benjamin Robbins Curtis, *Executive Power* (Boston: Little, Brown, 1862).

73. Abraham Lincoln, "Reply to Emancipation Memorial Presented by Chicago Christians of All Denominations," September 13, 1862, in *CW,* 5:421.

74. Curtis, *Executive Power,* 15–16.

75. Ibid., 16.

76. Ibid., 21.

77. Ibid., 23.

78. Charles P. Kirkland, *A Letter to the Honorable Benjamin R. Curtis: Late Judge of the Supreme Court of the United States, in Review of his Recently Published Pamphlet on the "Emancipation Proclamation" of the President* (New York: A. D. F. Randolph, 1863).

79. Ibid., 30. See also Benjamin Robbins Curtis, "Pamphlet 17: Executive Power," in *Union Pamphlets of the Civil War 1861–1865* (Cambridge, Mass.: Harvard University Press, 2013), 1:470.

80. Curtis, "Pamphlet 17," 1:473.

81. T. J. Barnett to Samuel L. M. Barlow, October 6, 1862, Huntington Library collection, Box 40, Folder 4. See also Foner, *Fiery Trial,* 231, 231n60 (note that the "September 15" letter in n. 60 is actually dated September 25). On T. J. Barnett, see Iver Bernstein, *The New York City Draft Riots: Their Significance for American Society and Politics in the Age of the Civil War* (New York: Oxford University Press, 1990), 12.

82. Frederick Douglass, "Emancipation Proclaimed," *Douglass' Monthly,* October 1862.

83. Ibid.

84. Abraham Lincoln, "Emancipation Proclamation," January 1, 1863, in *CW,* 6:29.

85. Ibid., 6:30.

86. Karl Marx, "Comments on the North American Events," *Die Presse,* October 12, 1862, in *Karl Marx, Frederick Engels: Collected Works* (New York: International Publishers, 1975), 19:248.

87. David Armitage, *The Declaration of Independence: A Global History* (Cambridge, Mass.: Harvard University Press, 2007).

88. Lincoln, "Emancipation Proclamation," in *CW,* 6:29.

89. Ibid., 6:29.

90. Ibid., 6:30.

91. Ibid., 6:29–30.

92. Abraham Lincoln to James W. Conkling, August 26, 1863, in *CW,* 6:408.

93. Ibid.

94. Ibid.

95. Ibid.

96. Ibid.

97. Ibid.

98. Ibid.

99. Ibid., 6:408–409.

100. Ibid., 6:409.

101. Ibid.

102. Lincoln, "Gettysburg Address—Final Text," in *CW,* 7:23.

103. Ibid.

104. Garry Wills, *Lincoln at Gettysburg: The Words That Remade America* (New York: Simon & Schuster, 1992).

105. There is a vast literature on the topic of Lincoln and religion. For a sampling, including the idea of a "heightened" interest after Willie's death, see Mark E. Neely Jr., "Religion," in *The Abraham Lincoln Encyclopedia* (New York: McGraw-Hill, 1982), 261.
106. Lincoln, "Gettysburg Address—Final Text," in *CW*, 7:23.
107. Ibid.
108. Ibid.
109. Noah Feldman, "The Intellectual Origins of the Establishment Clause," *NYU Law Review* 77, no. 2 (May 2002).
110. Lincoln, "Gettysburg Address—Final Text," in *CW*, 7:23.
111. Abraham Lincoln to "Whom It May Concern," July 18, 1864, in *CW*, 7:451.
112. Foner, *Fiery Trial*, 304–305.
113. Abraham Lincoln to Charles D. Robinson, August 17, 1864, in *CW*, 7:499–500.
114. Ibid., 7:500.
115. Ibid., 7:500–501.
116. Frederick Douglass, *The Life and Times of Frederick Douglass* (Boston: De Wolfe & Fiske Co., 1892), 421.
117. Foner, *Fiery Trial*, 306–307, 306n39.
118. Abraham Lincoln, "Memorandum Concerning His Probable Failure of Reelection," August 23, 1864, in *CW*, 7:514.
119. Abraham Lincoln to Henry J. Raymond, August 24, 1864, in *CW*, 7:517; Foner, *Fiery Trial*, 306–307.
120. William Seward to Charles Francis Adams, December 5, 1864, in *Papers Relating to Foreign Affairs, Accompanying the Annual Message of the President*, vol. 6, Government Printing Office, 1865, 368.
121. Abraham Lincoln, Reply to Committee Notifying Lincoln of His Renomination," June 9, 1864, in *CW*, 7:381.
122. Ibid., 7:381–82.
123. Abraham Lincoln, "Annual Message to Congress," December 6, 1864, in *CW*, 8:149.
124. Ibid.
125. Abraham Lincoln to Henry W. Hoffman, October 10, 1864, in *CW*, 8:41.
126. Goodwin, *Team of Rivals*, 204–205; *Lincoln*, directed by Steven Spielberg (2012, Dreamworks Pictures).
127. John Harrison, "The Lawfulness of the Reconstruction Amendments," *University of Chicago Law Review* 68 (2001): 384–89.
128. Lincoln, "Second Inaugural Address," in *CW*, 8:332.
129. Ibid., 8:333.
130. Ibid.
131. Ibid.
132. Ibid.
133. Ibid.
134. Douglass, *Life and Times of Frederick Douglass*, 365–66; Oakes, *The Radical and the Republican*, 242.
135. Abraham Lincoln, "Last Public Address," April 11, 1865, in *CW*, 8:403. Lincoln said that he would "prefer" that the franchise be "conferred on the very intelligent, and on those who serve our cause as soldiers." This fell short of full enfranchisement of course. This was consistent with Lincoln's gradualism, which still had not left him.
136. Adam Gopnik, "Angels and Ages: Lincoln's Language and His Legacy," *New Yorker*, May 28, 2007.

Conclusion: The Betrayal and Redemption of the Moral Constitution

1. When Reconstruction ended is an open topic among historians. Jesse Kass, Reply by James Oakes, "When Did Reconstruction End?," *The New York Review of Books*, March 12, 2020, www.nybooks.com/articles/2020/03/12/when-did -reconstruction-end/.

2. Martin Luther King, Jr., "Letter from a Birmingham Jail," April 16, 1963, *Christianity and Crisis* 23 (27 May 1963): 89–91.

3. King was named Michael King, Jr., after his birth in 1929. In 1934, his father traveled to Germany for a meeting of the Baptist World Alliance. On his return, Michael Sr. took the name Martin Luther King and renamed his son. Hence, the name Martin Luther King cannot be described as a "coincidence."

ACKNOWLEDGMENTS

For exemplary research assistance, I am grateful to Samarth Desai, Nate Orbach, Mohamed Light, David Shea, April Xiaoyi Xu, Mikaela Gilbert-Lurie, Hassaan Shahawy, and Katie Schuff. Shannon Whalen-Lipko worked tirelessly on many aspects of the book, even as she simultaneously and skillfully managed every other part of my professional life. I benefited enormously from close readings and insightful comments by Jill Goldenziel, Michael Alexander, and Peter Baugher. Alex Star, who has taught me so much about writing and thinking in the last two decades, edited the book with characteristic brilliance and generosity. I would like to express my gratitude to Andrew Wylie for his peerless representation. The ideas in the book were enriched by the faculty workshop at the Harvard Law School and by countless conversations with my friends at the Society of Fellows. I would like to thank Julia Allison for many things, among them pointing out to me that the depth of my respect for Lois Silver, master teacher, called out for recognition. In dedicating this book to Mrs. Silver's memory, I honor her extraordinary dedication to her students and to her institution, the Maimonides School. Much of the writing and footnoting of this book took place at home under Covid conditions. I am especially grateful to the staff of the Langdell Library who helped me immensely with online sources. I ask the indulgence of scholars for those instances in which online sources have had to be used and cited in place of paper sources that were inaccessible to me.

INDEX

abolition, 269; Cole on compromise Constitution and eventual, 66–67; in Kentucky, 20; Lincoln, A., on, 54–55, 59, 118, 123, 269, 270; *see also* gradual abolition

abolitionists: American Anti-Slavery Society and, 54–55, 62, 64–65; Constitution and, 61–69; Constitution condemnation by, 8, 55; Constitution meaning according to Black, 69–75; Republican Party sentiment on, 257; *see also specific abolitionists*

"Act to secure Freedom to All Persons within the Territories of the United States, An," of Lincoln, A., 259–60

Adams, John Quincy, 255; Clay as secretary of state of, 35; Federalist administration of, 39; Missouri Compromise and, 331n29; on original Constitution slavery compromise, 43; on presidential slavery emancipation powers, 255, 285–86, 286n

African Americans, 292; colonization of, 25, 76, 258, 271–74, 278; on Constitution, 62; Day on votes of, 70–71; Douglas, H., on voting immorality of, 70; Fifteenth Amendment right to vote, 317–18; Langston on vote of, 72–73; Lincoln, A., Civil War blame, 273–74;

Lincoln, A., Mississippi trip attack by, 25; in military, 215, 261, 293, 297 and n; Militia Act of 1862 on state enlistment of, 215, 261; Taney on, 106–107, 109; on union, 62–63

amendments, to Constitution: *Brown v. Board of Education* and, 12, 325; First Amendment, 45, 222–23, 331n30; Fifth Amendment, 124, 258; Tenth Amendment, 198–99; Thirteenth Amendment, 307–12; Fourteenth Amendment, 317, 324–25; Fifteenth Amendment, 317–18; Lincoln, A., and Stone on slavery and, 56–58; Reconstruction and, 12, 86n

American Anti-Slavery Society: abolitionists' establishment of, 54–55, 62, 64–65; on Constitution's proslavery position, 63–64; Declaration of Sentiments for, 55; union dissolution policy, 62

American Colonization Society, 25, 76

American Cyclopedia, The: on newspaper closings, 229; on newspaper editors' arrests, 219–21, 344n120

American system: of economy development, 36; Jackson veto of, 36

Anderson, Robert, 151, 153–55

Anti-Nebraska Convention, Lincoln, A., speech at, 100

Arkansas, secession of, 172–73